DAILY
HOPE FOR
Hurting
HEARTS

A Devotional by
GREG LAURIE

DAILY
HOPE FOR
Hurting
HEARTS

A Devotional by

GREG LAURIE

KERYGMA™
PUBLISHING

ALLEN
DAVID
BOOKS

DAILY HOPE FOR *Hurting* HEARTS

Unless otherwise indicated, all Scripture quotations are taken from: *The Holy Bible,* New King James Version © 1984 by Thomas Nelson, Inc.

Scripture quotations marked (NIV) are from *The Holy Bible,* New International Version®, NIV®. Copyright © 1973, 1978, 1984 by International Bible Society. Used by permission of Zondervan Publishing House.

Scripture quotations marked (TLB) are taken from *The Living Bible,* Copyright © 1971 by Tyndale House Publishers, Wheaton, Illinois.

Scriptures marked (AMPLIFIED) are taken from the *Amplified® Bible,* Copyright © 1954, 1958, 1962, 1964, 1965, 1987 by The Lockman Foundation. Used by permission (www.Lockman.org).

Scripture quotations marked (NASB) are taken from the *New American Standard Bible®,* Copyright © 1960, 1962, 1963, 1968, 1971, 1972, 1973, 1975, 1977, 1995 by The Lockman Foundation. Used by permission (www.Lockman.org).

Scripture quotations marked (NLT) are taken from *The New Living Translation,* Copyright © 1996, 2004 by Tyndale Charitable Trust. Used by permission of Tyndale House Publishers. All rights reserved.

Scripture quotations marked (THE MESSAGE) are taken from *The Message,* by Eugene Peterson. Copyright © 1993, 1994, 1995, 1996, 2000, 2001, 2002. Used by permission of NavPress Publishing Group. All rights reserved.

Scripture quotations marked (PHILLIPS) are from *The New Testament in Modern English,* Revised Edition © 1958, 1960, 1972 by J. B. Phillips.

Printed in the United States of America

ISBN 0-9762400-0-9

Published by: Kerygma Publishing—Allen David Books
Coordination: FM Management, Ltd.
Cover & Interior design: Highgate Cross+Cathey
Editor: Highgate Cross+Cathey
Interior design: Highgate Cross+Cathey
Production: Highgate Cross+Cathey

Monday

"Lazarus is dead, and for your sake I am glad I was not there, that you may believe." (John 11:14-15)

Have you ever had a crisis overwhelm you—maybe even to the point where you didn't think you could survive the experience? Have you ever found yourself facing a set of circumstances so crushing, so utterly devastating, that you couldn't imagine how you could ever get through? Have you ever wondered why God allowed a tragedy in your life or in the life of someone close to you?

Perhaps you have found yourself saying, in so many words, *"Lord, where were You?"*

In John 11, the Bible gives us a true life account of two sisters who had to wrestle with all of those questions. It's the story of an unexpected death, and how it brought a great trial of faith and shattered the happiness of a close-knit little family. But it is also the story of how Jesus responds to such situations—and how God can gain glory through it all.

In our lives here on earth, we will experience pain, grief, sickness, and the death of loved ones. I know that may be a depressing point, but it's true, and we might just as well come to grips with it and stop running from it. It might be the death of a spouse, an infant, a teenager, a sibling, or someone who might be close to us in age. And suddenly we are made aware of our own mortality.

That was the case with Mary, Martha, and Lazarus. They were a tight, loving little family, and then suddenly one of them was at the point of death. But ironically, it was through this experience that they learned even more about the power and love of Jesus Christ.

Jesus said to His grieving friend, Martha, "Did I not say to you that if you would believe you would see the glory of God?" (John 11:40).

It's not easy to believe in the goodness and glory of God when your heart is breaking. But when you do, when you rest your full faith and confidence in God—even when nothing else on earth seems to make sense— you will never, never be the loser…in this life, or the next.

Tuesday

Moreover we know that to those who love God, who are called according to his plan, everything that happens fits into a pattern for good. (Romans 8:28, PHILLIPS)

I survived a crazy childhood, growing up in an alcoholic home, with my mom being married and divorced seven times. But I came to Christ in high school, at the age of seventeen, and turned my life over to the Lord.

The stats all say that if you come from a divorced home, you will most likely end up divorced yourself. But by God's grace and against all odds, my wife and I are closing in on our thirty-fifth wedding anNIversary. So all in all, in spite of the heartbreaks in those early days, it's been a pretty happy story. *Lost Boy*, the film that tells my life story, closes with our family walking down the street together, and it's almost as though you could write the words on the screen: "And they lived happily ever after" at the end of the story.

I had been showing this film in various churches in different parts of the country, and I would speak afterwards, telling the story of Joseph, how he faced many adverse circumstances in his life, and how God brought good results out of evil circumstances. Not that bad is good, but God can bring good *out of* bad, and bring glory to His great name through it all.

And then came that morning in July 2008 when we got the terrible, incomprehensible news that our thirty-three-year-old son Christopher had been killed in a car crash on the freeway.

Good out of bad? The best results out of the worst circumstances? Was the message of "Lost Boy" still true, or was it all a sham?

Even in the depths of our grieving, we had to say, yes, the message of that movie hadn't changed. The chronicle of God's grace and faithfulness that we told in *Lost Boy* is as true as ever. We found ourselves in the midst of a life chapter we would have never, never chosen, but God will still bring good out of bad…bring glory to Himself.

Wednesday

He has made everything beautiful in its time. He has also set eternity in the hearts of men… (Ecclesiastes 3:11, NIV)

When my granddaughter Stella was very little, she made good use of the word "more" when she really liked something. Her favorite food was quesadillas. No matter what time of the day—breakfast, lunch, or dinner—she wanted quesadillas. Only she called it a "dilla."

"Stella, what would you like to eat?"

"Dilla."

And usually when I would give her one, she would then say, "More."

It was the same when I read her a Bible story before bedtime. As soon as I finished the story, she said, "More." So I read her another story, and at the end she said, "More." So I did another. "More." And another. "More." And on and on it would go.

Quesadillas and stories about Jesus are good things, and to this day, we're always happy to supply Stella with all she wants—of both. Sometimes, however, this desire for "more" can create problems for us—especially if we're craving more of the wrong things. (Like ice cream or Krispy Kreme doughnuts.)

Deep down inside, we're all like little Stella saying, "More." We always want a little bit more out of life—the newest, the latest, the freshest, the coolest. We want more. That's the way God has wired us. But here's the problem: As much as we see, taste, and experience life, it always seems like it just isn't quite enough.

Do you know why that is? As we read in today's opening verse, God has placed a seed of eternity deep in our innermost being (see Ecclesiastes 3:11). In our heart of hearts, there is a recognition that this world will not be able to deliver on its promises. No matter what this world gives us, we find ourselves wanting more. More life. More hope. More joy. More peace. More satisfaction and, ultimately, more of the presence of God Himself.

In heaven, those desires will be fulfilled in a way beyond what we can imagine. But until that day when we cross over to the other side, He willingly gives us more and more and more of Himself. And that's the closest thing we have to heaven on earth.

Thursday

You then, my son, be strong in the grace that is in Christ Jesus...
Endure hardship with us like a good soldier of Christ Jesus.
(2 Timothy 2:1, 3, NIV)

It's absolutely true that when you trust Christ as Savior, God removes a whole set of problems you used to have—including the nagging guilt and that empty sense of aimlessness in life that used to haunt you.

But we also need to understand something else. There will be a whole new set of problems that will take the place of your old problems. Because the day that you put your trust in Jesus Christ, you enter into a battle—spiritual warfare with the devil and his demons—that will last for the rest of your life. Some are surprised to find that the Christian life is not a playground, but a battleground. And that is why the apostle Paul said, "Endure hardship with us like a good soldier of Jesus Christ."

Some have believed in what we might describe as a watered-down gospel. This is a gospel that promises forgiveness, but rarely tells you of the need to repent of your sin. It's a gospel that promises peace and plenty, but never warns of persecution. It's a gospel that says God wants you to be healthy and wealthy, and never have any problems to speak of. It's a gospel that says you can so wrap yourself in God's favor that there will always be a parking space available for you at the mall.

My friend, that is not the gospel of the New Testament. What am I saying here? That God wants you to be sick, poor, and miserable? That He doesn't want you to be happy? No, that's not my point. I believe that happiness will come as you really follow the Lord. But it is a byproduct—a fringe benefit—of belonging to God in Christ.

The essence of the Christian life is knowing God and walking with Him. It's about sticking with Him when the sky is blue and also when it's filled with clouds or choked with smoke. It's about walking with the Lord through thick and thin, and pressing on through every heartache and trial that happens to come our way.

Friday

Every desirable and beneficial gift comes out of heaven. The gifts are rivers of light cascading down from the Father of Light.
(*James 1:17,* THE MESSAGE*)*

We need to hold everything God has given us loosely. We like to say, "*My* life, *my* marriage, *my* kids, *my* career, *my* 401k…" and on it goes.

But wait. *Everything* you have has come to you as a gift from God.

Maybe you drive your new set of wheels through the carwash and admire the way it sparkles and gleams after you wipe it down. Don't forget…that was given to you—it's a good gift from the Father. Or you drive up into the driveway of your home. Don't take it for granted! God has graced you and privileged you to live there.

You get up in the morning and feel like a million bucks, or finish a game of tennis and grab a nice long shower…don't forget. Your health and strength are a gift from God.

"Oh," you say, "but I'm very careful to eat only organic stuff and I have a regular exercise routine." Good for you. But remember, God gave you your health. God has given you your life. God has given you your wife or husband and blessed you with children. He has given you everything. Hold it loosely. He may leave it in your hands for years; then again, He might take it tomorrow. That's up to Him to decide. But it all belongs to Him, and we would do well to praise Him every day for what He has given us.

The truth is, everybody suffers. Calamity comes into every life—the righteous and the unrighteous, the godly and the ungodly. The good news is that the Lord can use suffering in the lives of His sons and daughters…to strengthen us spiritually…to make us more Christ-like…to use us to minister to and comfort others…and to prepare us for future tasks that are completely off our personal charts.

What comfort we have in Christ! What an indescribable hope! He is worthy of our complete trust and confidence, no matter what we might be enduring at the moment. He has thousands of years of experience helping, comforting, and saving those who reach up to Him in faith.

Weekend

And the believers were filled with joy and with the Holy Spirit.
(Acts 13:52, NLT)

Imagine that you bought a new car, drove it around town for a few days, and really liked the way it performed for you. But suddenly it started sputtering, and not running as well as it had in the beginning. Finally, it just chugged to a stop and wouldn't go any further.

"What's the problem here?" you ask. "I just bought this car. I don't even have a couple of hundred of miles on it yet."

You have that stalled-out new car towed back to the dealer, demanding an explanation. "Hmm," he says, slipping the key into the ignition and trying to start it a couple of times. "Umm...sir... do you see this little light on your fuel gauge? Some people call that an idiot light. It means you're out of gas. You need to fill your car up with gas every now and then."

"Oh," you say. "I never thought of that."

"Yes sir. You see, you've got to keep refilling your car over and over if you want to keep going."

The same is true in life. You're cruising along, enjoying life and the scenery, experiencing peace and success in your family, your marriage, your business, and your ministry. Suddenly, however, problem after problem starts cropping up, and life suddenly doesn't seem to be working very well.

Maybe you need a refill. Maybe you need to say, *"Lord give me the power of Your Holy Spirit to be a better husband. Give me the power of the Holy Spirit to be a better father, a better grandmother, a better witness, a better student, a better employee—to be a better whatever You have called me to be."*

We may ask and receive the filling of the Holy Spirit in the morning, but by the time late afternoon comes along, we have allowed that filling to drain out of us.

The apostle Paul wrote: "May the God of hope fill you with all joy and peace as you trust in him, so that you may overflow with hope by the power of the Holy Spirit" (Romans 15:13, NIV). God wants us to come to Him again and again for refilling and refueling. The fact is, we have a never-ending need, and He has an inexhaustible supply.

Monday

Jesus loved Martha and her sister and Lazarus. Yet when he heard Lazarus was sick, he stayed where he was two more days. (John 11:5-6, NIV)

D on't rush past those words. Let them sink in. *God loves you.* Truly. Deeply. Eternally. God will never allow anything to happen in your life as His child that is not motivated by His everlasting love for you. In Jeremiah 31:3, God says, "I have loved you with an everlasting love; Therefore with lovingkindness I have drawn you."

Mary and Martha knew this. In fact, they were sure of it. They knew Jesus loved each member of their family. We can see that in John 11 in the way they appealed to Jesus in this crisis. They didn't say, "Lord, the one that is devoted to You is sick." Or even, "The one that loves You is sick." But rather they said, "The one that You love is sick."

That's a good thing to remember when we make our appeal to God. Never appeal on the basis of your own devotion, faithfulness, or love.

"Lord, Your great servant is calling upon You now."

No. Because I'm not a great servant.

"Lord, the one who loves You so passionately is asking for help now."

No. Because my love is fickle and inconsistent.

The truth is, we're too often distracted, unfaithful, and loveless. No, our approach ought to be, *"Lord, the one that You love is in need. Please help."*

He has declared His love for us over and over again. Notice, they didn't even tell Him what to do. They didn't say, "Drop whatever You're doing, rush home to us, and do something now." They just said, in effect, "We wanted to let You know, because we believe You will know exactly what to do."

The word John used to describe the love of Jesus for Lazarus is the Greek word *agape*. It isn't "brother love," it is God's supernatural, beyond-all-boundaries, all-consuming love.

God's love for us may be demonstrated in ways we won't always understand. In this story, though we know Jesus had the power to heal, we read that He delayed His response. He could have come sooner, but He didn't. Why would He do that?

Because Jesus wanted to do more than they were expecting.

And we have been telling the story of what He eventually did for that little family for the last 2,000 years.

Tuesday

"Lord," Martha said to Jesus, "if you had been here, my brother would not have died." (John 11:21, NIV)

Martha was never one to hold her tongue. You always knew where you stood with this lady! "Lord," she said, "if You had been here, my brother would not have died." To paraphrase it, *"Where were You anyway, Jesus?"*

Maybe you've said something similar during or after some crisis in your life.

"Lord, where were You when my parents divorced?"

"Lord, where were You when we got that diagnosis of cancer?"

"Lord, where were You when our marriage fell apart?"

"Lord, where were You when I lost my job?"

"Lord, where were You when my child got in trouble?"

"Lord, where were You when my loved one died?"

Please notice that Jesus didn't reprove Martha for what she said. It's not wrong to tell God exactly how you feel. I think we sometimes get the idea that it's irreverent or sinful to express our real fears or the doubts of our heart, even to God.

When we read the Psalms, however, we learn that there were many times when David and the other psalmists really "let down their hair" with God. They cried out to Him, and emptied the contents of their hearts in His presence.

I have done this many times. In my pain, I will cry out to God. Sometimes the reality that my son is gone hits my heart like a sledge hammer, and I say, "Oh, God. I can't believe this! I can't handle this pain!" But then I will preach to myself and I'll say, "Now Greg, listen to me. Your son is alive—more alive than he has ever been before. He's in the presence of the Lord, and you *are* going to see him again in just a few years." And I will remind myself of the promises of God.

My prayers, however, are wide open and honest. I pour out my heart before God, describing my pain to Him. But I also remind myself of God's truth. And this is what prayer is.

God wants us to cry out to Him.

He invites us to pour out our hearts before Him.

David writes: "Trust in him at all times, O people; pour out your hearts to him, for God is our refuge." (Psalm 62:8, NIV)

Wednesday

"Naked I came from my mother's womb, and naked shall I return there. The Lord gave, and the Lord has taken away; blessed be the name of the Lord." (Job 1:21)

Think about the way Job responded to devastating circumstances. Talk about having your life fall apart! Job lost *seven sons and three daughters* in one unimaginable day. And that was in addition to losing all his possessions and his health! But what did Job do? The Bible says he did not charge God foolishly. Instead, he cried out to the Lord.

In fairness, Job did go on to question God in the days to come, saying, "Lord, why?" There's nothing wrong with asking God why, as long as you don't get the idea that He somehow owes you an answer. Frankly, God doesn't owe you or me an explanation.

Concerning our recent tragedy, I too have asked "why?". Why did this happen? Why couldn't it have been me instead of Christopher? Why did the Lord take him? I have many such questions roiling in my heart.

Not long after Christopher's passing, Pastor Chuck Smith made this statement to me: "Never trade what you don't know for what you do know." Those words stopped me in my tracks a little. I asked myself, "Well, what do I know for sure?"

I know that God loves me.

I know that God loved and loves my son.

I know that God loves my family that remains with me.

I know that Christopher is well and alive in the best place he could ever be.

I know that God can make good things come out of bad.

I know that we'll all be together again—not so very long from now—on the Other Side.

I KNOW those things. I'm as sure as I can be. So I'm making the choice to stand on what I know instead of what I don't know.

So if you were to ask me, "Greg, why did this happen?" my answer is, "I don't know. And I don't know that I will ever know. I just know that I need God more than I have ever needed Him in my life."

Thursday

"But he who received the seed on stony places, this is he who hears the word and immediately receives it with joy; yet he has no root in himself, but endures only for a while. For when tribulation or persecution arises because of the word, immediately he stumbles." (Matthew 13:20-21)

Jesus spoke of people who hear the Word of God, but it never quite takes root. These people appear to be converted, and even motivated. They seem to be living on an emotional high, and even try to bring others to Christ. Yet they are a picture of soil embedded with rocks. The good seed of God's Word breaks ground and shoots up, but no fruit ever appears. No real change ever results. Theirs was not a true encounter with God.

Why did they fall away? It's possible they built their faith on the wrong foundation. Maybe they responded to the gospel because a friend of theirs did. But conversion is not a group effort; you have to make your own commitment to Jesus. Another possibility may be that unbelief set in, causing them to begin doubting God at their first emotional low. Or they gave up at the first sign of persecution for the gospel's sake.

If you are a true follower of Jesus, there will be hardships—times of trial, and seasons when you don't feel God is near you. And there will be times when people give you a hard time for no other reason than the fact that you say you're a Christian. In fact, you would have more cause to worry about your faith in Christ if everybody approved of you and patted you on the back!

Here's the bottom line: *You can't build your faith on life's circumstances, or count on the events in your life to make perfect sense.* You can't build it on a friend's approval or a pastor's example. You can't even build it on a church. We need to build our faith on Christ alone. He is our Rock and our Foundation, and no matter what else happens in life, He will never fail you.

Friday

"As for Mephibosheth," said the king, "he shall eat at my table like one of the king's sons."…So Mephibosheth dwelt in Jerusalem, for he ate continually at the king's table. And he was lame in both his feet.
(2 Samuel 9:11, 13)

The Bible tells us that when David sought out Jonathan's son to show him kindness, Mephibosheth was living in a miserable little backwater town called Lo-debar. When the prophet Amos spoke of this place, he said, "And just as stupid is this bragging about your conquest of Lo-debar…" (see Amos 6:13). The name really means "the place of no pasture." Take it from me; you wouldn't want to own real estate in Lo-debar. It was a dry, parched, crummy place to live. In my mind's eye, I picture a place with boarded up houses and stores, mongrel dogs wandering around, and tumbleweeds rolling down the streets.

But where were we when Jesus Christ found us? Right there! We were living in Lo-debar, a miserable, arid, dried-up place. And just like David sought out Mephibosheth, Jesus Christ sought us. It's worth noting that it wasn't Mephibosheth who looked for David; it was David who looked for Mephibosheth. That might not seem significant, but it really is. David wanted to have a relationship with him. We read in 2 Samuel 9:5, "Then King David sent and brought him out of the house of Machir the son of Ammiel, from Lo Debar." David was persistent. He would not give up on Mephibosheth.

This is a reminder to us that we need to reach out to our friends, our neighbors, and even our enemies who don't know Christ. They don't realize it, but they are living in Lo-debar. No matter how big a home they might have or how many possessions, they are living in a scorched, desolate place—"without hope and without God in the world" (see Ephesians 2:12). So we need to ask God to place an urgency in our hearts to speak to others about our hope in Christ. We all know people who need someone to reach out to them. That's exactly what David did. And that's what we need to do, too.

Weekend

To everything there is a season...A time to weep, and a time to laugh; a time to mourn, and a time to dance. (Ecclesiastes 3:1, 4)

Sorrows come into all of our lives. And while none of us enjoy them, they're as much a reality of life on planet earth as mosquitoes, rainy days, and the flu virus. You will experience heartache, as Cathe and I have, as well as disappointments, letdowns, and heartbreaks.

That's not pessimism or gloomy talk; it's simply the fabric of life on a fallen planet.

You also will lose loved ones. It's inevitable that the older you grow, the more you will lose. There might even come a day when you will recognize that you actually have more friends who have gone to heaven than you have on earth, and that it probably won't be long until you join them.

But there also will be times of laughter and occasions of great joy and celebration. One of the lessons I've learned from life is to enjoy the good times. Don't take them for granted. Savor the sweet moments, because you can be sure some bitter times will come down the road. But thank God that any and every "bad moment" will first have to go through Him, because He continues to be in control of all circumstances that surround our lives.

God can use suffering in your life, and He will. If you allow Him to teach you, He can use the dark and difficult days to shape you, refine you, deepen you, and to make you into a more compassionate man or woman. And sometimes God even uses suffering to bring you to your spiritual senses—especially if you've wandered away from Him.

If your heart is filled with sorrow and heartache right now, then I want you to know that Jesus Christ can bring you comfort. The apostle Peter tells us, "So, humble yourselves under God's strong hand, and in his own good time he will lift you up. You can throw the whole weight of your anxieties upon him, for you are his personal concern" (1 Peter 5:6-7, PHILLIPS).

Cast your cares upon Him, and He will give you strength in your time of need.

Monday

The secret things belong to the Lord our God, but those things which are revealed belong to us and to our children forever…
(Deuteronomy 29:29)

The old hymn states, *"I need Thee every hour."* For me, that is literally true. I do need Him every hour, and I need Him desperately. In fact, I need Him every sixty seconds. In times of deep sorrow I will sometimes call out my son's name, "Christopher!" Then immediately I will say, "Jesus!" I have never been so conscious of my utter dependence upon the Lord, just to make it through my days. And that is a fact that is both heartbreaking and wonderful.

And what about the days ahead? In his insightful commentary on the book of Job, Chuck Swindoll writes:

> "God never promised He would inform us about His plan ahead of time. He just promised He has one. Ultimately it is for our good and His glory. He knows and we don't. That is we shrug and say, 'I don't know.' But I do know this: The death of His Son was not in vain. Christ died for you. And if you believe in Him He will forgive your sins and you will go to live with Him forever. You will have heaven and all the blessings of it. I know that. It is a tough journey getting there. Full of confusion and struggles, shrugs, and followed by a lot of 'I don't knows.' But when the heavens open and we are there, there will be no more shrugs, and we will be able to say, 'Now I know.'"[1]

If God explained to us everything we wanted to know, it still wouldn't satisfy our hearts. His answers would only raise more and more questions. In the end, we don't need His answers as much as we need *Him*. His presence. His peace. Philippians 4:7 tells us about His peace that surpasses, or transcends, understanding. One translation calls it a "peace which is far more wonderful than the human mind can understand."[2]

So there are innumerable things we could ask God as to why this happened or that happened. But the bottom line is simply this: Our lives are in His hands, and we must trust Him.

Tuesday

He will wipe every tear from their eyes. There will be no more death or mourning or crying or pain, for the old order of things has passed away. (Revelation 21:4, NIV)

Jesus is God, with all the attributes of Deity. But He is also the Son of Man, who feels our pains and our sorrows. Isaiah 53 reminds us, "He was despised and rejected—a man of sorrows, acquainted with deepest grief." The passage goes on to say, "Yet it was our weaknesses he carried; it was our sorrows that weighed him down" (Isaiah 53:3, 4 NLT).

He not only carried your sin, He carried your *sorrow*. We're told in Psalm 56:8 (TLB), "You have seen me tossing and turning through the night. You have collected all my tears and preserved them in your bottle! You have recorded every one in your book."

On a tour of Israel a number of years ago, my sons Christopher, Jonathan, and I were exploring the old city of Jerusalem. At one point in our ramblings, we stopped at an antiquities store, and I noticed a number of little bottles in various sizes and shapes. I asked the shopkeeper, "Sir, what are these bottles for?"

"Oh," he said, "those are Roman tear bottles."

"What were they used for?" I asked.

"Well, the Romans believed that when a loved one dies, you need to keep your tears in a bottle. So they would store the tears in these little containers."

I have a tear bottle now. But it's not one on earth. It's in heaven. And I'm not the one who has to collect my own tears, because God has already said He would do that.

So why does God keep our tears in a bottle? Because He sees and cares about every one of them. He takes note of our every tear. He hears our every sigh. And the Bible says that a day is coming when God will wipe away all of the tears accumulated over all of our years from our eyes.

Wednesday

Jesus said to her, "I am the resurrection and the life. He who believes in Me, though he may die, he shall live. And whoever lives and believes in Me shall never die. Do you believe this?" (John 11:25-26)

Jesus was saying to His grieving friend, "Martha, listen to Me. Death is not the end! You're acting as though it's over with. It's *not* over with." And at this point, I think He was speaking of something greater and more profound than the resurrection of Lazarus, which He would accomplish within that very hour. After all, raising Lazarus from the dead—exciting and joyful as that may have been—was only a temporary proposition. Lazarus would just have to die again in a few years!

I think the bigger message was this: "Death is not the end. This is temporary. One day I will get rid of death altogether, and whoever believes in Me will live forever."

Jesus wept at the death of His friend and the sorrow of Lazarus's two grieving sisters. But the death of His friend also brought Him anger.

Verse 33 tells us: "Therefore, when Jesus saw her weeping, and the Jews who came with her weeping, He groaned in the spirit and was troubled."

The Greek word used for "troubled" here could be translated *angry*. Why was Jesus angry? Was He angry with Mary and Martha for not believing? I don't think so. I think Jesus was angry at death itself, because this was never God's plan. God's plan was to have us live forever. God's plan was that these bodies would never age or wear out or experience sickness or limitations.

So He was angry over that, and He wept. But these weren't tears of "frustration." God is never frustrated. Jesus was angry and then did something about it that had been planned from eternity past. He gave up His life on a Roman cross, dying for the sins of the world, and then rising again from the dead. And the Bible says He has become the "firstfruits" of those that sleep, which means He went before us.[3]

And because He went before us into death and came out victorious on the other side, those of us who now live and face death can be confident and unafraid.

Thursday

Jesus called out in a loud voice, "Lazarus, come out!" The dead man came out… (John 11:43, NIV)

Raising Lazarus from the dead was a great miracle…one of the greatest in the New Testament. And to this very day, God will work just that way at certain times and in certain places; He will step into your life and dramatically, miraculously, change your circumstances. You will go to the doctor, and hear him say, "I'm really sorry. There's nothing we can do for you. You'd better just get your affairs in order, because you only have a short time to live." But you cry out to the Lord to do that which only He can do, and He does a miracle and heals you. He steps into your adverse circumstances and intervenes.

What do we do in a situation like that? We glorify the Lord. And sometimes that's the way He gains glory, by completely removing the difficulty from us.

But that's not the only way He is glorified. Sometimes God is glorified *through* the adversity.

The apostle Paul had one particular physical condition afflicting him that had him so distressed, so troubled, that he cried out to God for relief.

> I was given a physical handicap—one of Satan's angels—
> to harass me…Three times I begged the Lord for it to
> leave me, but his reply has been, "My grace is enough for
> you: for where there is weakness, my power is shown the
> more completely." Therefore, I have cheerfully made up
> my mind to be proud of my weaknesses, because they
> mean a deeper experience of the power of Christ. I can
> even enjoy weaknesses, suffering, privations, persecutions
> and difficulties for Christ's sake. For my very weakness
> makes me strong in him.
> (2 Corinthians 12:7-10, PHILLIPS)

In effect, Paul concluded: "All right, if God says I am to endure this, then that's what I'll do. If it's all for Christ's good, and part of His good plan, then I'll be content with whatever He chooses to give me."

Suffering can strengthen us, if we let it. It can make us more like the Lord. When a Christian suffers and gives glory to God through it all, it reassures the rest of us that there will never be a valley so deep that God won't get us through it.

Friday

So we don't look at the troubles we can see now; rather, we fix our gaze on things that cannot be seen. For the things we see now will soon be gone, but the things we cannot see will last forever.
(*2 Corinthians 4:18, NLT*)

Do you remember that expression the astronauts used to use when everything in the flight was moving along perfectly? They would say, "All systems are go."

Sometimes it's like that in our lives as believers. All systems are go. Everything seems to be working out, with no real problems to speak of. And then, without warning, some unexpected trial or sorrow comes crashing into our lives, like a meteor falling out of space. Just that quickly, the bottom seems to drop out of life, and we feel devastated.

That's something many of us have faced. Others of us feel discouraged because *nothing* seems to be happening. At one point in your life, it may have seemed as though God was preparing you for something. Doors were opening, and He was doing great things in your life. Then it was as though everything went into freeze frame. Now you find yourself waiting…and waiting and waiting. And as you wait you pray, "Lord, I thought You were coming back soon. I thought time was short, and that the urgency was real. But here I am, available and ready, and You don't seem to be calling on me."

Surely Moses could have felt that way. I'm sure that in his youth, when he saw that Egyptian mistreating the Hebrew, it seemed like a good idea to strike the man down. But then he found out it was the worst thing he could have done. He spent the next forty years on the backside of the desert, just tending sheep and figuring his life was over. And then—unexpectedly—God re-commissioned him at the burning bush, and his life began anew.

If you find yourself going through a time of testing and trials, recognize that God has a purpose in it. All that He has allowed into your life today will prepare you and train you for what He sees in your life tomorrow.

Weekend

There was a believer in Joppa named Tabitha (which in Greek is Dorcas). She was always doing kind things for others and helping the poor. About this time she became ill and died. Her body was washed for burial and laid in an upstairs room. But the believers had heard that Peter was nearby at Lydda, so they sent two men to beg him, "Please come as soon as possible!"

So Peter returned with them; and as soon as he arrived, they took him to the upstairs room. The room was filled with widows who were weeping and showing him the coats and other clothes Dorcas had made for them. (Acts 9:36-39, NLT)

Sometimes I'm a little amused when I read obituaries in the newspaper or hear what's said at some peoples' funerals. Whoever the deceased was, he or she was the greatest person who ever lived. There was never a person more compassionate, loving, or caring. This is because when someone dies, we want to say the best about him or her.

But what if we told the truth at funerals? What if someone stood up and said, "This guy was a jerk, right? He squandered his life. How many people did he rip off—including those of us right here in this room? Let's face it, he was selfish. He didn't care about others. All he cared about was himself. And quite frankly, I'm kind of glad he's gone, aren't you?"

Of course we would never say that. Instead, we might even stretch the truth about how wonderful a person he was.

If someone were to sum up your life, what would they say you lived for? What would they remember you for? That will be your legacy. Wouldn't you like it to be honestly said of you, "This person loved God. She cared about the things of God. He really cared about other people. This person really lived for the Lord"?

The ultimate waste is to throw your life away, to squander it. Yet so many people do. One day, you will breathe your last breath. One day, you will make your last statement. One day, you will eat your last meal. What will you be remembered for?

Live a life that matters. Live a life that makes a difference. Live a life for Him and you will never regret it.

Monday

"These things I have spoken to you, that in Me you may have peace. In the world you will have tribulation; but be of good cheer, I have overcome the world." (John 16:33)

We may wish we could dodge all the unpleasantness of life on a broken planet, but none of us gets a pass on suffering. Some will suffer more than others. Some will face more calamity and heartache. We know that. But we will all experience tragedy in this life, and most of us will know what it means to have a loved one die unexpectedly.

When you see something like that happen in the life of another believer, when you see a Christian suffering through one of these heartbreaking seasons of life and glorifying God through it all, it gives you hope. You say to yourself, "She made it through, so I can, too. He's giving God glory through the worst of it, so I do that as well."

God can be glorified through the suffering of a Christian, and He can use it to display His power to a lost world. Unbelievers could look at some of our lives and say, "You Christians talk about your faith, but your lives are pretty good, all things considered."

But what do they say when they see us go through a time of setbacks, injustice, or suffering, and still maintain a sweet spirit and a strong faith? Some of these people outside of the faith might very well say, "How do they do that? Could this faith of theirs be genuine? Could there really be something to it?" The trials and hardships give the believer a platform from which they can give witness to their faith in Christ. Why? Because they are actually living it out in the real world.

Think of Corrie ten Boom, who lost her father and sister in a Nazi concentration camp, but miraculously survived herself. She spent the rest of her life telling people that there is no pit so deep that God is not deeper still. And she was able to forgive those who had perpetrated these evils on her family and friends.

You just have to pay attention to a woman like that, because she faced such horrendous circumstances in her life and honored God through it all.

Tuesday

They are being tested by many troubles, and they are very poor. But they are also filled with abundant joy, which has overflowed in rich generosity. (2 Corinthians 8:2, NLT)

Falsely accused and arrested on trumped up charges in the city of Philippi, missionaries Paul and Silas were severely beaten and placed in stocks in the city dungeon. Somewhere around midnight, and even though their backs had been ripped open with a Roman whip, they began to sing praises to God.

Suddenly an earthquake rocked that prison, breaking the prisoners' chains and throwing open every prison door. That fact wasn't lost on the jailer, who was about to kill himself. Why? Because if he lost any prisoners, he would be executed anyway.

> That's when Paul shouted from the inner dungeon, " Don't harm yourself. We are all here."
>
> The jailer called for lights, rushed in and fell trembling before Paul and Silas. Then he brought them out and asked, "Sirs, what must I do to be saved?"
>
> They replied, "Believe in the Lord Jesus and you will be saved—you and your household." Then they spoke the word of the Lord to him and to all the others in his house… Then immediately he and all his family were baptized. The jailer…was filled with joy because he had come to believe in God—he and his whole family. (Acts 16, vv. 28-32, 33, 34, NIV)

Why did that hardened Roman jailer believe in God? Because he had seen something with his own eyes that didn't make any earthly sense. He saw two men who had been savagely beaten for no good reason praise and worship their God right through the middle of a dark night in a dungeon.

And his response was, "What must I do to be saved? I've been listening to you guys. I've been watching you. And I want what you have." Paul and Silas had earned the right to preach the gospel in that dark place, and God was glorified through the way they responded to their suffering.

Wednesday

Cast your cares on the Lord and he will sustain you. (Psalm 55:22, NIV)

In my email to my son before his fatal accident, I concluded by saying, "Better things are coming."

Was I wrong?

I don't think so. No, they weren't the "better things" I would have chosen for Christopher, or for his family. I would have chosen long life for him, and the privilege of seeing his children and grandchildren grow up and serve the Lord.

Paul speaks of those "better things" in Philippians 1:23, when he wrote: "For I am hard-pressed between the two, having a desire to depart and be with Christ, which is far better." Speaking of "better," he uses a superlative form of that word, which means *far, far, far* better.

The best is yet to come when we meet the Lord in heaven. Saying goodbye to Christopher has certainly not been "better" for me, for my wife, or for his wife. But it *is* better, beyond all argument, for him.

So where is the Lord in our moments of tragedy, heartbreak, and anxiety? Where was He at the time of Christopher's accident, on that July day, a little after nine o'clock in the morning?

He was with me.

He was with Christopher.

And He is still with both of us. In the same way, He will be with you in your good days and your bad days. He will be with you at the birth of a baby and the death of a loved one, who seems to be departing this life much, much too soon.

As the book of Hebrews assures us:

> God has said, "I will never, never fail you nor forsake you." That is why we can say without any doubt or fear, "The Lord is my Helper, and I am not afraid…
> (Hebrews 13:5-6, TLB)

David said, "Even though I walk through the valley of the shadow of death, I will fear no evil, for You are with me." And that is the great hope of every believer. We will never, never be alone. God will be with us through everything we face, and the best is yet to come when we meet Him in glory.

Thursday

"Call to Me, and I will answer you, and show you great and mighty things, which you do not know." (Jeremiah 33:3)

What a remarkable verse. What a magnificent invitation! God spoke these words originally to the prophet Jeremiah when he was imprisoned by an evil king who hated his messages from the Lord. So there he was, imprisoned, and with uncertain future, and God said, "Call Me. Pray to Me. I will answer you. I'll show you things beyond what you could have ever dreamed."

And He says the same thing to each of us! But He won't show us those "great and mighty things" unless we do call.

In Luke 18:1, Jesus said, in effect, "Men always ought to pray and not lose heart." If you ever needed an answer for why you ought to pray, that's the best one right there. *Jesus told you to.* Beyond the simple blessing of obedience, however, those of us who pray will experience the joy and satisfaction of answered prayers—such as the salvation of a loved, a divine healing, or God's special provision in our lives.

Prayer is God's appointed way for us to obtain things. James 4:2 says, "You do not have because you do not ask." There are potential answered prayers waiting for you…answers that you won't receive unless you ask for them.

Maybe you have wondered, *Why is it that I never seem to know what the will of God is for my life?* Again, you do not have, because you do not ask. *Why is it that I never have the opportunity to lead people to Christ?* You do not have because you do not ask. *Why am I always just scraping by and never seem to have enough?* You do not have because you do not ask. *Why do I have this affliction or problem that won't go away?* You do not have because you do not ask.

Let me be clear here: I am *not* suggesting that if you pray, you will never be sick again, never have an unpaid bill, or never wonder what God's will is for your life. But I am saying there are many times when God will indeed heal you, provide for you, and reveal His will to you. He's just waiting for you to ask.

Friday

Love endures long and is patient and kind.
(1 Corinthians 13:4, AMPLIFIED*)*

Can you imagine the world we would live in if people operated by the principle that says, "Don't look out for your own needs and interests, but for the needs of others?" Yet we live in a culture that tells us to forget about others and to look out for "Number One." What a terrible, dead-end philosophy that is!

One thing we should bear in mind about God's love is that it is patient. And as part of the body of Christ, our love should be patient as well.

The verse that begins today's devotional says, "Loves endures long." Another way to translate that phrase is, "Love is *long-tempered.*" This common New Testament term is used almost exclusively in speaking of being patient with *people*, rather than being patient with circumstances or events. Love's patience is the ability to be inconvenienced again and again.

The last words of Stephen, the first martyr of the church, were those of patient forgiveness: "Lord, do not charge them with this sin" (Acts 7:60). As he was dying, he prayed for his murderers rather than for himself. This is the same kind of love Jesus spoke of that turns the other cheek. It's the kind of love that has as its primary concern not its own welfare, but the welfare of others.

And love is kind. Just as patience will take anything from others, kindness will give anything to others. To be kind means to be useful, serving, and gracious. It is active goodwill. Love not only feels generous; it *is* generous. Love not only desires the welfare of others; love *works for it.*

If, however, you wait for this emotion to come and settle over you like the morning dew, you may be waiting a long, long time. Remember, love is active. Love is kind. So just *be* kind, even if you don't feel kind. Step out with kind, loving actions, and your feelings will follow along behind.

So carve out the time…write the check…carry another's load… invest yourself in really listening…and lend a hand whether you feel competent or not. And most of all, be quick to forgive…as the Lord is quick to forgive you.

Weekend

"But forget all that—it is nothing compared to what I'm going to do! For I am about to do something new. See, I have already begun! Do you not see it? I will make a pathway through the wilderness, and create rivers for them in the dry wasteland!" (Isaiah 43:18-19, NLT)

You remember how God fed the Israelites with manna. Every morning they would wake up, step out of their tents, and there would be the manna just waiting for them. But this "bread from heaven" had one limiting characteristic: It wouldn't keep overnight.

Bottom line: *God didn't want His people to live off yesterday's manna.* The Lord wanted them to be dependent on Him on a regular basis and gather it fresh each day.

In the same way, you can't live off the provision or experiences of last week, last year, or twenty years ago. God wants to do something fresh and new in your life today and tomorrow. No, you can't live off experiences, but you can *learn* from them.

Saul of Tarsus went out of his way to hunt down Christians. But he came to realize that he wasn't serving God but the devil. Then he was transformed and went on to become the apostle Paul. He could say, *"I press toward the goal for the prize of the upward call of God in Christ Jesus. (Philippians 3:14)*

In other words, "From now on, from this day forward, I press on, I reach forward." I wish this would be true in the lives of more believers. What a difference it would make in this world around us if we had that kind of ambition, that kind of drive to serve God as we used to serve ourselves.

Beginning today, let's recommit ourselves to the study of the Word of God, to prayer, and to winning at least one person to Christ in the next twelve months.

As Christians, we have unprecedented opportunities for our lives to make a difference. There is so much to do, so much growth that needs to take place in our lives, and so much more to accomplish. It's time to step into the future. To step into what God is doing *today.*

Monday

"For where your treasure is, there your heart will be also."
(Luke 12:34, NIV)

In thirty-five years of pastoral ministry I have talked about heaven countless times, given innumerable messages on life after death, and counseled scores of people who lost loved ones.

I thought I knew a little bit about this subject. But when an unexpected, sudden death happens in your own family, it's a whole new experience. My desire to be in heaven is greater now than ever before, and heaven is more real to me now than at any time I can remember.

Why? Because I have an investment there now.

The Bible tells us that when a believer dies, he or she immediately enters God's presence. There is great glory in that place, fullness of joy at God's right hand, and pleasures forevermore.

That doesn't mean you stop missing your loved one. But it does mean that you know you will see that person again. People will often say, "I'm so sorry you lost your son." I know what they mean, and I appreciate it. But the truth is, I haven't "lost" my son because I know where he is, and I will join him one day. And all believers will join their loved ones one day soon.

I saw a headline in a newspaper after my son's accident. It said: "Christopher Laurie dead." But that's not true. He's not dead. He is more alive than he has ever been before, because Jesus said, "I am the resurrection and the life and he that believeth in Me, though he were dead, yet shall he live" (John 11:25-26 KJV).

When you are a believer in Christ, you know you will never die.

No, I'm not in major denial here. I understand that this body ceases to function and begins to decay. But the *real* you—your soul, your spirit—goes on to one of two places, heaven or hell. And I know that God holds my son safely in His arms at this very moment. The Bible says, "There is a time to mourn," but I do not mourn as a person who has no hope. The Bible says we have hope as believers, no matter what the temporary circumstances of our lives might be. We all need to be reminded that life is short, death is inevitable, and eternity is real.

Tuesday

Teach us to number our days and recognize how few they are; help us to spend them as we should... Teach us to realize the brevity of life, so that we may grow in wisdom... You have made my life no longer than the width of my hand. My entire lifetime is just a moment to you; at best, each of us is but a breath. (Psalms 90:12; 39:5, NLT)

When you've had an encounter with death—a near-death experience of your own or the sudden passing of a loved one—it inevitably leads to a few essential questions. *What is life all about, anyway? Why am I alive...and what am I really living for?*

In other words, what gets you out of bed in the morning? What gets your blood pumping? Is it an alarm clock or a calling that gets you up each and every day? Every one of us needs some motivating passion, some ideal, something that gives our lives purpose that drives us on. Unfortunately some people don't know what they're living for.

Many people are merely marking time, instead of enjoying their lives. Their favorite day of the week is "someday." Someday my ship will come in. Someday my prince (or princess) will come. Someday it's all going to get better. Someday my life will change. A recent study revealed that ninety-four percent of the people surveyed were simply *enduring* the present, while "waiting for something better to happen."

But here's what people don't plan on. They don't plan on death. And they never envision it to coming around the corner unexpectedly. When you're young you tell yourself, "I don't have to even think about that for another fifty or sixty years." And that may true. But death knocks at every door. The Bible says that each of us has an appointment with death: "Just as man is destined to die once, and after that to face judgment..." (Hebrews 9:27, NIV).

That appointment may come later than you expected. On the other hand, it may come much, much sooner. Statisticians tell us that 3 people die every second, 180 every minute, and 11,000 every hour. That means that every day 250,000 people enter into eternity.

What's the bottom line? Live every day as though you may never have another one. Live ready to step into God's presence at any moment.

Wednesday

"For to me, to live is Christ and to die is gain." (Philippians 1:21, NIV)

The apostle Paul wrote those words from a dungeon in Rome, facing imminent execution, and Christians through the centuries have repeated them. But not everyone will love those words. Some will think a person who says, "To live is Christ" is nuts. They'll think, "This is a guy who's got his head in the clouds." Or maybe, "This is a woman who's so heavenly minded she's no earthly good."

But that's not true. Far from it! Those who think of the next world do the most for this one. My concern is for people who are so earthly minded they're no heavenly good!

The apostle Paul loved life. And the simple fact is, no one loves life more than the Christian. We can enjoy it because we know it comes to us from the hand of a loving God. That beautiful sunset… that's the signature of my Father who happens to be the Creator of all. That wonderful meal…the joy of love and marriage…the comfort of family and friends…the satisfaction of a hard day's work. All of these are beautiful gifts from the hand of our Father.

But as blessed as we may be in this life, there is more…more than what we are experiencing on this earth. All the great things we do experience in the here-and-now are just hints of heaven, of something better that will come for the man or the woman who has put faith in Jesus Christ.

C. S. Lewis made this statement: "All the things that ever deeply possessed your soul have been hints of heaven. Tantalizing glimpses, promises never quite fulfilled, echoes that died away just as they caught your ear." He went on to say, "If I find in myself a desire which no experience in this world can satisfy, the most probable explanation is I was made for another world."[4]

There is another place, another time, another life. And life on earth, be it 9 years or 90 years, is a nanosecond compared to eternity. Even so, it is here on this earth where we will decide where we will spend eternity. Trusting in Jesus Christ as Savior and Lord is the only key that will open the doors of heaven to us after we leave this life.

Thursday

This hope we have as an anchor of the soul, both sure and steadfast, and which enters the Presence behind the veil. (Hebrews 6:19)

I've been known to grow very impatient waiting for fruit to ripen, especially bananas. Overripe, mushy bananas are worthless—except for making banana bread. I like bananas when they're not quite green, but barely yellow. Sometimes in my impatience, however, I will eat a green banana. Then I will have a stomachache for an hour because I couldn't wait for it to ripen.

God is doing a work in us, waiting for the fruit to ripen. As Romans 5:5 tells us, "Now hope does not disappoint, because the love of God has been poured out in our hearts by the Holy Spirit who was given to us." As we come through troubles and sorrows in life, not only do we ripen spiritually, but we also develop hope.

What hope does this world have? Is it in some politician who's supposed to come and solve all our problems? Is it in the White House? Congress? The Tea Party? Government programs? I hope not. Even the best-intentioned leaders can't resolve the basic conflicts inside us. God offers us a hope far greater than anything humankind can offer. It's a hope that becomes the very anchor of our soul, as Scripture describes in Hebrews 6:18-19 (NLT): "Therefore, we who have fled to [Jesus] for refuge can have great confidence as we hold to the hope that lies before us. This hope is a strong and trustworthy anchor for our souls. It leads us through the curtain into God's inner sanctuary."

I love that old hymn, "The Solid Rock," which says, "My hope is built on nothing less than Jesus' blood and righteousness; I dare not trust the sweetest frame, but wholly lean on Jesus' name. On Christ the solid rock I stand. All other ground is sinking sand, all other ground is sinking sand."

Those are good words. Our hope is not in this changing world. We have free access to God, and that is where we need to anchor ourselves. That is where we draw our strength in times of trouble.

Friday

We can rejoice, too, when we run into problems and trials, for we know that they help us develop endurance. And endurance develops strength of character, and character strengthens our confident hope of salvation. And this hope will not lead to disappointment. For we know how dearly God loves us, because he has given us the Holy Spirit to fill our hearts with his love. (Romans 5:3-5, NLT)

The fact that God has chosen us, forgiven us, and given us free access into His presence means that our existence isn't some "cosmic accident," and that our lives are guided by neither chance nor luck, neither fate nor karma. It means we are guided by His providence.

There is, therefore, real meaning and purpose when I go through tribulation. *It's not for nothing.* Before we met Christ, we might have thought of hardships or difficulties as random effects of nature, and something merely to be endured. But now we can know that God is in control of all circumstances that surround our lives as believers.

As Paul said, "We can rejoice, too, when we run into problems and trials, *for we know that they help us develop endurance* (Romans 5:3 NLT). Paul wasn't simply gritting his teeth and enduring these experiences; he was glorying in them. This doesn't mean Paul was a masochist. Rather, he was saying, "I glory in it, because tribulation produces something I need." He made a choice. When he was going through hardship, he decided that he wasn't going to become bitter; he was going to become better.

Hardships and tribulation come into all of our lives. The Bible is clear on that point. So when those difficult days do come, you have a choice. You can get mad at God and turn your back on Him. Or you can embrace that difficulty and attempt to learn what God seeks to teach you, so you will become better instead of bitter. It's a choice. Hardships will come, but how you respond to them is entirely up to you.

Weekend

"Be careful that you do not forget the LORD your God... Otherwise, when you eat and are satisfied, when you build fine houses and settle down, and when your herds and flocks grow large and your silver and gold increase and all you have is multiplied, then your heart will become proud and you will forget the LORD your God, who brought you out of Egypt, out of the land of slavery." (Deuteronomy 8:11-14, NIV)

As they were (at long last) poised to enter the Promised Land, God warned the Israelites that the real danger to their lives had just begun.

Prior to this point, Israel had wandered in a desolate wilderness for forty years, completely dependent upon God for everything. Every day they would step outside of their little tents, and there would be manna waiting for them, just like the morning paper. God gave them fresh water to drink, a cloud to guide and shade them by day, and a pillar of fire to light their camp by night.

Yes, wilderness living came with plenty of hardships. But those very difficulties compelled them to look to the Lord every day, depending on Him for everything.

But then He brought them to the brink of the Promised Land, and they could look across the Jordan and see lush green hills, rippling fields of wheat, flowing rivers, and trees loaded with fruit. They could hardly wait to get in! But God said, "Be careful! Watch out, or you'll get fat and sassy and forget all about Me. Then your troubles will really begin."

We've all experienced it; when our lives are hit with uncertainty, danger, or pain, we fall to our knees and cry out to God. God can use adversity to bring us closer to Him—which is actually where we will experience the greatest blessings of life.

C. S. Lewis writes: "God whispers to us in our pleasures, He speaks in our conscience, but He shouts in our pains: It is His megaphone to rouse a deaf world."[5]

The psalmist said, "Before I was afflicted I went astray, but now I obey Your word... It was good for me to be afflicted, so that I might learn Your decrees" (Psalm 119:67, 71, NIV).

Monday

For to me, living means opportunities for Christ, and dying—well, that's better yet! But if living will give me more opportunities to win people to Christ, then I really don't know which is better, to live or die! Sometimes I want to live, and at other times I don't, for I long to go and be with Christ. How much happier for me than being here! But the fact is that I can be of more help to you by staying! (Philippians 1:21-24, TLB)

Paul says, "For me to live is Christ." If you were to fill in that blank, what would you say? For me to live is...what?

Some might say, "For me to live is to just live." In other words, they just take it a day at a time. Life for them is mere existence. They don't have any philosophy to speak of, and don't like to contemplate the meaning of life. They just live for the moment, seeking to satisfy their desires, whatever they might be. This type of person is very uncomfortable with any discussion about life and its meaning.

Others would take it a step further and say, "For me to live is *pleasure*. For me to live is parties...to have this or that experience." I know that particular train of thought all too well. Before I was a Christian, I experimented with drugs, partied, and did all that stuff. And I knew the answer to my hunger for "more" in life was not in those things.

It was sort of like being at an amusement park. You wait for two hours for a ride that lasts a minute and a half. And that's the way it is with life before you come to Christ: you wait and wait to have your little pleasure. But the "fun" or excitement of that pleasure is short-lived at best, and usually has a lot of guilt attached to it.

Others might be more noble and say... "Ah yes, for me to live is to acquire knowledge. I have multiple degrees. I have studied, and I'm an intelligent person." That's all well and good. But if your pursuit of knowledge fails to take God into account, you *will* end up empty—in this life and the next.

Tuesday

What shall I choose? I do not know! I am torn between the two: I desire to depart and be with Christ, which is better by far."
(Philippians 1:22-23, NIV)

The word the apostle Paul uses for "depart" in this passage could be translated in several different ways. One definition means "to strike the tent." In other words, to break camp. To be honest with you, my favorite part of the whole tent-camping experience is when we're getting ready to break camp and leave! I can hardly wait to get home and get into that hot shower. In this passage, Paul is saying, "I'm ready to break camp, leave this place, and move on, and let me tell you friends...*I can't wait.*"

That word "depart" could also be used to describe a prisoner being released from shackles. Ironically, when Paul made this statement he was actually chained up in a dungeon in Rome. His chains were made of iron, but perhaps you're dealing with chains of a different sort: an addiction to drugs, alcohol, or pornography. Whatever it is, Paul is saying that there's coming a day when you will be released from these shackles.

There is one additional way "depart" could be translated. The word was also used to describe untying a boat from its moorings, prior to setting sail.

We understandably feel great sadness when a loved one leaves us, and sometimes we feel sorry for that person. But stop and think about it. Think about the port they have left, and the port they're heading for. If you stood on the wharf and said goodbye to someone sailing off in a leaky, rusty old freighter bound for Outer Siberia, well, that would be pretty sad. But if you went down to the dock and saw that they were boarding a beautiful new cruise ship destined for Tahiti, you might be more inclined to feel sorry for yourself instead! After all, you would be the one left standing on the shore, and your loved one would be on his or her way to great adventure and a beautiful destination.

And heaven, in the presence of Jesus Christ, is exactly as Paul describes it: "better by far"— infinitely better than life on earth.

Wednesday

They will never again be hungry or thirsty; they will never be scorched by the heat of the sun. For the Lamb on the throne will be their Shepherd. He will lead them to springs of life-giving water.
(Revelation 7:16-17, NLT)

Why is heaven better than earth? It's better because we're moving from a tent to a mansion. The Bible compares heaven to a city, a garden, and a paradise, and we can attempt to wrap our minds around these images. But then again, the majesty and beauty of heaven will always be difficult for a finite mind to grasp. The general idea, however, is that one day we will leave a broken-down shack with a leaky roof for a mansion far better than anything we could ever find on earth. There will be no more devil, no more temptation to sin, and we will be reunited with loved ones in the presence of Jesus Christ.

Here's the way the writer of the book of Hebrews describes it:

> You have come to Mount Zion, to the city of the living God, the heavenly Jerusalem, and to countless thousands of angels in a joyful gathering. You have come to the assembly of God's firstborn children, whose names are written in heaven. You have come to God himself, who is the judge over all things. You have come to the spirits of the righteous ones in heaven who have now been made perfect. You have come to Jesus, the one who mediates the new covenant between God and people…
> (Hebrews 12:22-24, NLT)

It sounds like a place where I'd like to be!

The reality of heaven is immediate after we leave this life. We will exhale our last lungful of earthly air and take the next breath of celestial air on the other side. Paul said, "I want to depart and be with Christ." Notice he didn't say, "I want to depart and go into a waiting room somewhere." Or, "…depart and go into a state of suspended animation or soul sleep." No. He said, "Depart and *be with Christ*." The Bible tells us that to be absent from the body is to be present with the Lord (see 2 Corinthians 5:6).

There is no better place to be in all of time and eternity.

Thursday

When Jesus heard it, He said to them, "Those who are well have no need of a physician, but those who are sick. I did not come to call the righteous, but sinners, to repentance." (Mark 2:17)

It's worth noting that every person Jesus had conversations or contact with was in a different situation, and He dealt with each one differently. This is because He recognized that even though we all share many of the same problems and basic needs, every man, woman, and child is a unique individual, with unique needs.

He didn't deal with Nicodemus out on the rooftop that night (the only time He ever mentioned the phrase "born again") in the same way He spoke to the Samaritan woman at the well—or to Zacchaeus in the tree, or to the woman taken in adultery. In His encounters with people, Jesus was like a physician, treating each person with his or her unique needs as an individual.

But everyone's underlying need for salvation from sin is the same. He basically said, "I want to let you know that I didn't come to bring the righteous to repentance, but I came to bring sinners, because those who are whole don't need a physician."

I think the hard thing about being a doctor must be seeing people, for the most part, only when they're sick! They usually don't have their patients stop by and say, "Hey, Doc, I'm feeling good and I just wanted to tell you that. Want to go to lunch?" You don't usually call your doctor when you're feeling at the top of your game. You call when you're feeling sick, and your doctor will have you come in to his or her office, examine you, and apply the specific remedy to the area of need. For some of us who don't enjoy going to the doctor, we have to be *really* sick.

Jesus is the Great Physician. He came to heal the brokenhearted, preach deliverance to the captives, give sight to the blind and freedom to the oppressed. He has already determined your precise areas of need, whatever they may be, and He will minister to you as an individual.

Friday

For he raised us from the dead along with Christ, and we are seated with him in the heavenly realms because we are united with Christ Jesus.
(Ephesians 2:6, NLT)

A Christian is someone who lives in two dimensions. The apostle Paul explained it this way: "Since you have been raised to new life with Christ, set your sights on the realities of heaven, where Christ sits in the place of honor at God's right hand. Think about the things of heaven, not the things of earth." (Colossians 3:1-2, NLT).

These verses are saying that believers truly do live in a spiritual dimension—where we walk in the Spirit, and know God in the Spirit. Yet as human beings, we also live and move in physical bodies here on earth. Our challenge as Christians, then, is to transfer what we have in the spiritual realm into the day-to-day ebb and flow of events in the earthly realm.

When I travel to another country and pass through its borders, I still maintain my U.S. citizenship. When I went to Israel a few years ago, although I had my passport that indicated I am an American, I had to live in their culture. As a result, there were a few things I needed to adapt to. When I needed currency, for example, I took funds from my bank in the U.S. and converted them into shekels to use in the Israel. Of course, I didn't know what the exchange rate was, so on my first day there, I may have tipped someone fifty dollars to carry my bags to my room. (He was really nice to me the rest of the day.)

As Christians, we have riches, treasures, *real assets*, waiting for us in heaven. When the Bible speaks of "the heavenlies," however, we need to recognize that it's not only talking about something waiting for us in heaven after we die. Rather, it talking about the supernatural realm. So before we can effectively walk as believers, much less engage in spiritual battle, we need to learn about the supernatural resources God has given to us. We also need to understand that they are treasures God wants us to start tapping into in the here-and-now, as well as in the bye-and-bye. They are provisions available to any believer who is walking with God.

Weekend

"If the world hates you, you know that it hated Me before it hated you."
(John 15:18)

Jesus became very popular during His earthly ministry. He spoke
in a way that people could understand. Reaching out to hurting
people and down-and-outers, He became known as a friend of
sinners. All that really irritated the religious authorities. Clearly, He
was a threat to their legalistic system of works. For that reason, He
became public enemy number one. Jesus Christ, the Son of God, was
a wanted man.

In the same way, there are people today who hate Jesus Christ
and everything He stands for. They despise His teachings. They can
become outraged at the respectful mention of His name. And if you
follow Jesus Christ and His teachings and stand up for what you
believe, then they will hate you, too. In fact, Jesus said we should
remember that if the world hates us, it hated Him first. He chose us
out of the world, and therefore the world hates us. We can expect to
be persecuted (see John 15:18-20).

We are representatives of Christ. And if you think people
hate Christians in general, then try being a pastor! Because I'm a
representative of God, some people will take all their anger out on
me. "Why does God do this?" they demand. "Why doesn't God do
that?" Actually, I accept the fact that I'm a representative of God.
I'm not ashamed of it. But some people will hate us for it.

It isn't easy being rejected or scorned by others, is it? Most of us
like to be liked. We have no desire to offend people unnecessarily,
and we try to live our life in a kind and gracious way. But because
we are representatives of Christ—and simply for that reason
alone—we *will* upset and even anger people. Why? Because they
know we stand for biblical values and biblical truth. It's like being a
light in a dark place; if your eyes have grown used to the darkness,
the light is uncomfortable—even hateful.

I must hasten to add that the Bible offers no consolation for
Christians who are hated for being jerks or hard to get along with.
But if you are hated simply because you love and follow Jesus, you
have real cause to celebrate. (See Matthew 5:10-12.)

Monday

We don't yet see things clearly. We're squinting in a fog, peering through a mist. But it won't be long before the weather clears and the sun shines bright! We'll see it all then, see it all as clearly as God sees us, knowing him directly just as he knows us!" (1 Corinthians 13:12, THE MESSAGE*)*

We all have legitimate questions. Why did this happen? Why didn't that happen? And of course, I have mine, too. But the truth is, even if we had some of the most troubling questions in our hearts answered, we wouldn't be satisfied. The answers would only raise more questions! The Bible doesn't promise us a peace that necessarily gives understanding, but it promises a peace that *passes* human understanding (Philippians 4:7).

I received a letter from Warren Wiersbe, a great author and Bible teacher, after my son went to heaven. He said: "As God's children we live on promises, not on explanations. And you know as well as I do the promises of God." He went on to say, "When we arrive in heaven we will hear the explanations, accept them, and we will say, 'May God be glorified.'"

In my time of grieving, I found myself with many questions, and I didn't seem to have many answers. Nevertheless, here's what I know for sure: I know my son, Christopher Laurie, is with the Lord. And I know one day all of my questions will be answered. In our opening Scripture we read: "We don't yet see things clearly. We're squinting in a fog, peering through a mist." The old King James version says, "For now we see through a glass, darkly."

It reminds me of a car with tinted windows. Someone drives by and you're straining to look through the glass. You're saying, "Who's in there?" That's how it is for us sometimes. We try to look at heaven. We try to figure out the big questions of life. But it's hard to make it out. Maybe we see a little silhouette, but we're not even sure about that.

But one day the view will be clear to the farthest horizons, and we will see as clearly as God sees us now. Until that time, "We walk by faith, not by sight" (2 Corinthians 5:7).

Tuesday

But we are citizens of heaven, where the Lord Jesus Christ lives. And we are eagerly waiting for him to return as our Savior.
(Philippians 3:20, NLT)

An old chorus begins, "This world is not my home, I'm just a passin' through…." That is literally true. The Bible says that when you put your faith in Jesus Christ, you become a citizen of heaven, because that is your real home.

That is why we find ourselves with a deep-down longing for something this earth can never deliver. And that is also why we will always be a bit out of tune with this world and all it celebrates. Have you noticed? Sometimes the world will parade its toys and its so-called pleasures before you, and you'll find yourself saying deep down in your spirit, "That just leaves me cold. That's not what I desire. That's not what I want at all." As followers of Jesus, we've tasted much, much better things than these!

C. S. Lewis described this longing with these words: "There have been times when I think we do not desire heaven, but more often than not I find myself wondering whether in our heart of hearts, we have ever desired anything else." He went on to say, "It is the secret signature of each soul, the incommunicable and unappeasable want. It is the inconsolable longing."[6]

I liken it to a homing instinct that God has placed inside some of his creatures. We all know that some animals have a mysterious ability to migrate or travel great distances to very specific locations. It's like a natural GPS system that God has placed inside of them.

One of these days we'll be going home, too—home to a place we've never been. Heaven is more real to me than it has ever been, because of those who are already there. My son Christopher is there, as is my mom, and the father who adopted me. Friends I have known through the years are on the other side now, and many familiar faces from our church.

Don't get me wrong: There is much wonder, beauty, joy, and fulfillment in this life God has given us on earth. But what makes all these things even better is the sure knowledge that the best is yet to come.

Wednesday

*Three of Job's friends heard of all the trouble that had fallen on him.
Each traveled from his own country…and went together to Job to
keep him company and comfort him… Then they sat with him on the
ground. Seven days and nights they sat there without saying a word.
(Job 2:11, 13, THE MESSAGE)*

I used to surf with my sons. When you're out there in the ocean waiting for a wave and see a really big one coming, you have to make a choice. You have to decide what you will do with that wave. If you don't take action to ride the wave, it can pick you up and slam you down into what we used to call the soup, or the whitewater. And when you're in that turbulent, angry water, you can quickly lose perspective, even losing the sense of "which way's up?"

The other way to handle a mega wave is to catch it, and ride it as best you can.

Grief can be like those ocean waves. Sometimes you will encounter a grieving person who has managed to ride the swells for awhile, and he's keeping his head above water. Then at other times, you will see him when he's been caught in the wave, crushed by its force, and seemingly lost all perspective.

So when you ask a grieving person "how are you?" he or she may find that difficult to answer. Maybe it would be better to simply say, "I'm praying for you," "I'm sorry," or "I love you."

Sometimes a person may want to talk about their grief. At other times, it's the last thing they want to do. If you want to say something to a grieving person, pray that the Lord will give you the right words. And if you don't know what the right words are, just give that person a hug and don't speak at all.

Yes, Proverbs 25:11 does say, "A word fitly spoken is like apples of gold in settings of silver." But by the same token, a word *unfitly* spoken can be very difficult to bear.

In the long run, your presence means more than your words.

Thursday

For God in all his fullness was pleased to live in Christ, and by him God reconciled everything to himself. He made peace with everything in heaven and on earth by means of Christ's blood on the cross. (Colossians 1:19–20, NLT)

Many of the blessings the Bible promises are still in our future. The hope of heaven and our new, wonderful resurrection bodies is still ahead. But the peace of God? That is our present possession. That's something that belongs to us here and now. From the first moment that we place our faith in Christ, we can begin to experience the peace of God.

Philippians 4:7 promises, "The peace of God, which surpasses all understanding, will guard your hearts and minds through Christ Jesus." I know this peace in my life, and if you belong to Jesus, I'm sure you know it as well. I can think back to the day when I put my faith in Christ at age seventeen. One of the first things I remember is a sense of peace filling my heart. It was as though someone had slipped a heavy backpack from my shoulders. It wasn't until later that I read that the Bible promises peace.

Many people think that peace is simply an absence of conflict or anxiety. If you could imagine it on a dial, they think if they could get the needle out of the negative red zone and up to "normal," they would be experiencing peace. But biblical peace is much more than that. It is a strong, elevating, positive good in our lives. It isn't just an absence of anxiety; it is the presence of something wonderful beyond our comprehension.

Peace has been given to us as a gift from God, because we have been justified by faith. It's not describing a feeling; it's describing *a fact*. It doesn't come from what we are, but from what He has done.

It's a cause *and* effect in our lives. The cause: being justified by faith in Christ. The effect: peace beyond any human explanation. But you can't have the effect without the cause! In other words, you can't have the peace *of* God until you first have peace *with* God.

If we are fighting with God and continually resisting His plan and purpose for our lives, then we will not experience His peace.

Friday

Casting down arguments and every high thing that exalts itself against the knowledge of God, bringing every thought into captivity to the obedience of Christ. (2 Corinthians 10:5)

We all live in the same world, and sometimes we see and hear things we wish we had never seen or heard. This can happen when it isn't our choice at all—it's just a part of walking daily through a broken world that's in rebellion against God. You'll be exposed to things that you don't want to be exposed to at times.

In your free time, however, you get to control what you view or listen to or read. When it comes to movies, TV, radio, downloaded music, books or magazines, you have control over these things.

At this writing, my computer has six gigabytes of memory. By the time this book is published, that probably won't seem like very much. But right now, it seems like a lot to me. I have every Bible program I can get my hands on loaded onto the hard drive. That way, I can access them when I'm traveling, so I can still study and prepare for my messages.

But I only have so much space on my hard drive. Even if I have six gigs, I will eventually fill it up. When I try to load a new program, a little message will pop up on my screen that tells me I have no more memory available. If I want to load a new program, then I'll have to throw something out. Otherwise, I need to get a new hard drive.

Wouldn't it be great if, when the devil comes with his temptations, a little sign would appear that says, "Memory full. Heart and mind are filled to capacity with the things of God."

I like how the apostle said it in the book of Philippians:

"Fix your thoughts on what is true and good and right. Think about things that are pure and lovely, and dwell on the fine, good things in others. Think about all you can praise God for and be glad about" (Philippians 4:8, TLB).

After all, the best defense is a good offense. So instead of being open and vulnerable to the attacks of the devil through our imaginations, let's fill our minds with thoughts of God, thoughts of heaven, and meditation on His life-changing Word.

Weekend

For God did not give us a spirit of timidity (of cowardice, of craven and cringing and fawning fear), but [He has given us a spirit] of power and of love and of calm and well-balanced mind and discipline and self-control. (2 Timothy 1:7, AMPLIFIED)

Sometimes when we hear that a person is "spiritual," we think of him or her as being out of touch, not living in the real world, or (how shall I say it?) *weird.* But nothing could be further from the truth, because the truly spiritual man or woman will be a very practical person as well.

A Spirit-filled believer will live a life that honors and glorifies God. Ephesians 5 tells us, "Be filled with the Spirit. Speak to one another with psalms, hymns and spiritual songs. Sing and make music in your heart to the Lord" (vv. 18-19, NIV).

When we think about being filled with the Spirit, we might imagine some wild emotional experience. And though being filled with the Spirit can and sometimes will include emotions, it won't necessarily always be that way.

What exactly did the apostle Paul mean when he used the term "filled." One translation of the word pictures a steady wind filling the sails of a ship. So the idea is that the wind of God wants to fill the sails of your ship as you are moving along the sea of life. In another place in Scripture, the same word is translated *permeated,* picturing the truth that God wants to soak and saturate everything that we say or think or do.

To be filled with the Spirit means that the Holy Spirit is a part of all that you're involved in. He's a part of your prayer life. He's a part of your worship life. He's a part of your business life. He's a part of your vacation. He's a part of everything you that touches your life in any way. That is what it is to be a Spirit-filled and Spirit-led believer.

Is this some big one-time experience, never to be repeated? No, because the original language implies this is something you should be receiving over and over and over again.

Be *continually* filled with the Spirit.

Monday

Our dying bodies make us groan and sigh, but it's not that we want to die and have no bodies at all. We want to slip into our new bodies so that these dying bodies will be swallowed up by everlasting life. God himself has prepared us for this, and as a guarantee he has given us his Holy Spirit. While we live in these earthly bodies, we groan and sigh, but it's not that we want to die and get rid of these bodies that clothe us. Rather, we want to put on our new bodies so that these dying bodies will be swallowed up by life. God himself has prepared us for this, and as a guarantee he has given us his Holy Spirit. (2 Corinthians 5:4-5, NLT)

Sometimes people will say, "I know what you're going through." Mostly likely, they *don't* know.

During our time of mourning for Christopher, I really didn't even know what my wife was going through, even though we were together all the time. Her grieving process is different than mine.

I had a person come up to me and say, "I know what you're going through. My grandmother just died." With all due respect, though I am sorry for that individual's loss, the passing of an elderly grandmother is not the same as the loss of a child.

One person said to me, "What doesn't kill you only makes you stronger." That didn't help. Someone else wrote to me, "God always picks His best flowers first." That didn't help, either.

On the other hand, there have been many other things people have said that have been very helpful. So I'm not making a hard and fast rule here that you shouldn't say anything to a grieving person. I'm just saying, take care. And watch out for the old clichés.

People will sometimes ask the question, "Are you at peace with your son's death?" *At peace?* Of course not! Don't ever ask someone that. We should never be at peace about anyone's death. Death is an enemy. The Bible says, "The last enemy that will be defeated is death." Having said that, God is a friend, and I am at peace *with Him.* So we trust the Lord. But no, we will never be at peace with this thing that we call death.

For the believer, however, death isn't the end of the road. It's only a bend in the road…a path that Jesus Himself has walked. Because of what He accomplished on the cross for us, the grave is not an entrance to death but to life, because death has been swallowed up in victory.

Tuesday

Since you became alive again, so to speak, when Christ arose from the dead, now set your sights on the rich treasures and joys of heaven where he sits beside God in the place of honor and power. Let heaven fill your thoughts; don't spend your time worrying about things down here. You should have as little desire for this world as a dead person does. Your real life is in heaven with Christ and God. And when Christ who is our real life comes back again, you will shine with him and share in all his glories. (Colossians 3:1-4, TLB)

Newsweek magazine did an article awhile back called, "Visions of Heaven." The magazine pointed out that 76 percent of Americans believe in heaven, and of those, 71 percent think it's an actual place. But after that, the agreement breaks down. The magazine says that 18 percent imagine heaven to look like a garden, 13 percent think it looks like a city, and 17 percent don't know. The article also said that even those who say they don't believe in heaven at all wish there was such a place.

We need to know what God tells us about heaven…get a lay of the land, so to speak. After all, if you're planning on taking a trip somewhere, you do a little research first. Right? You know… you ask questions like: How should I dress? Where should I stay? Where is the good food? What do you do all day? What's it really like? Things like that.

In Colossians 3:1-2 (NIV), the Bible says, "Since, then, you have been raised with Christ, set your hearts on things above, where Christ is seated at the right hand of God. Set your minds on things above, not on earthly things."

The term that Paul uses here for "set your minds" is an interesting word choice. In fact, it's a command, in the present tense, that speaks of a diligent act of single-minded investigation. So the phrase could be translated, "Keep seeking heaven."

Warren Wiersbe reminds us that, for the Christian, heaven isn't simply a destination, it is a motivation.

Wednesday

"Don't let this throw you. You trust God, don't you? Trust me. There is plenty of room for you in my Father's home. If that weren't so, would I have told you that I'm on my way to get a room ready for you? And if I'm on my way to get your room ready, I'll come back and get you so you can live where I live." (John 14:1-3, THE MESSAGE)

Heaven is an actual place.

It isn't an "idea" or a "state of mind," it's a *location*, like Miami or Chicago or Paris.

We often think of heaven in sort of a mystical way, and our minds gravitate toward the Hollywood version, where people in filmy white robes float around on clouds with little halos over their head, strumming harps.

How boring! That is certainly not the heaven of the Bible. The Bible uses a number of words to describe heaven. One word it uses is "paradise." In the gospels, we're told that Jesus was crucified between two thieves. When one of those thieves in the last moments of life put His faith in Jesus, he said, "Lord, remember me when You come into Your kingdom." And Jesus replied, "Assuredly, I say to you, today you will be with Me in Paradise" (Luke 23:42, 43).

Heaven is also compared to a city. In Hebrews 11:10, we're told that this city's architect and builder is God Himself. And then Hebrews 13:14 (NIV) says, "For here we do not have an enduring city, but we are looking for the city that is to come."

Now we know that cities have buildings, culture, art, music, parks, goods and services, and events. Will heaven have all of these things? We don't know. But we can certainly conclude that heaven will in no sense be *less* than what we experience here on earth—with the exception of all things harmful or evil.

Heaven is also described as a country. Hebrews 11:16 says, "They desire a better, that is, a heavenly country. Therefore God is not ashamed to be called their God..."

Heaven is a paradise, a city, a country...and so much more that we can't begin to wrap our finite minds around it. But one thing I do know: Jesus is expecting me, and He's prepared a place for me. What more could I ask for?

Thursday

Then the high priest asked Stephen, "Are these accusations true?" This was Stephen's reply: "Brothers and fathers, listen to me." (Acts 7:1-2, NLT)

To recognize opportunity is the difference between success and failure. When opportunity knocks, we have to get up and answer the door. And we never know when it will knock. I can tell you this: It won't always be at the most convenient of times. Sometimes, those opportunities will come when we are dealing with pressing trials or heartaches.

The apostle Peter wrote: "But in your hearts set apart Christ as Lord. Always be prepared to give an answer to everyone who asks you to give the reason for the hope that you have. But do this with gentleness and respect" (1 Peter 3:15, NIV). If we as Christians are going to obey the Lord's command to go into all the world and preach the gospel, then we must know what we believe and how to present it. Sadly, many Christians are unable to do that. They have little to no understanding of why or what they believe. The Bible warns that "we should no longer be children, tossed to and fro and carried about with every wind of doctrine, by the trickery of men, in the cunning craftiness of deceitful plotting" (Ephesians 4:14). When we don't know what we believe, we are vulnerable. And because of this spiritual deficiency, we are ineffective witnesses for the Lord.

In Acts 7, we read about a man who was prepared for a significant moment in his life—which turned out to be a defining moment for the young church of Jesus Christ. When Stephen was hauled before the Sanhedrin, he was ready for the opportunity God dropped in his lap. He seized the moment and made a difference.

You can do the same…because you never know when those golden opportunities will come your way. As they would say in the 19th century, "Trust in God and keep your powder dry." Be ready for that opportunity, because you never know when the Lord will drop it in your lap.

Friday

Who is he who condemns? It is Christ who died, and furthermore is also risen, who is even at the right hand of God, who also makes intercession for us. (Romans 8:34)

If you found yourself in a difficult passage in life, would it bring you some measure of comfort if Billy Graham called you? "This is Billy Graham. I wanted to talk to you. I heard you were going through a hard time. I would like to pray for you."

"Please do."

So Billy Graham prays for you, with that unforgettable voice of his, bringing your name and your needs before God. Wouldn't you feel good about that? When it was over, wouldn't you hang up the phone and say, "Wow. That was unreal. I feel so much better now."

Then let's say the phone rings again. "This is Pastor Chuck Smith. I heard you were experiencing some difficulties. I could pray for you if you would like me to." So Chuck Smith prays for you.

The phone rings again. "This is Chuck Swindoll. I heard you were having a tough time. Can I pray for you?" So Chuck Swindoll prays for you.

How would you feel? You would feel good. Why? Because Billy Graham, Chuck Smith, and Chuck Swindoll just prayed for you.

Now all three of those pastors are great men of God, without a doubt, and if the opportunity was there, you would definitely want them praying for you. Yet the Bible teaches that Someone much greater than these is already doing that very thing. *Jesus Christ is praying for you.* The Son of God is interceding for you. What's more, He's not just calling you on the phone, praying, and then leaving you alone again.

Hebrews 7:25 tells us, "Therefore He is also able to save to the uttermost those who come to God through Him, since He always lives to make intercession for them."

He *always* lives to make intercession for you. He *always* prays for you. In fact, He's praying for you right now, at the right hand of His Father in heaven.

And in Hebrews 9:24, we read, "For Christ has not entered the holy places made with hands, which are copies of the true, but into heaven itself, now to appear in the presence of God for us." Jesus is standing for you. He is interceding for you at this very moment.

Weekend

In everything set them an example by doing what is good. In your teaching show integrity, seriousness and soundness of speech that cannot be condemned, so that those who oppose you may be ashamed because they have nothing bad to say about us. (Titus 2:7-8, NIV)

Even after Daniel was stalked by evil men, slandered, and threatened with death for his faith, he wasn't going to back down, no matter what the consequences (see Daniel 6). He didn't change a thing when he was attacked for belief in God. And in prayer, he just maintained his usual habits of meeting with the Lord and openly seeking Him. He kept on keeping on.

People may very well attack us as Bible-believing Christians. Being anti-Christian these days is one of the few politically correct hate groups you can belong to. People call us Bible-thumping bigots. They say that we are narrow-minded and intolerant.

But here's what it comes down to. We can't back down from what we believe. We can't hold back. We need to share the truth of God's Word when He gives us those opportunities—even in the midst of our trials and hardships.

Daniel's enemies had to resort to trickery and deception to get at him, because there was nothing in his life to accuse of. We've all heard the old saying, but it remains relevant: If you were arrested for being a Christian, would there be enough evidence to convict you? If loving God was a crime, would you be an outlaw?

It may sound strange, but I really hope that people who want to harm us would be compelled to make up lies about us. Basically, that would mean they couldn't come up with any truth that could hurt us.

If you are truly attacked or slandered or mocked for being a believer—and not for simply being an annoyance or a jerk—then you have reason to celebrate. That means you're actually accomplishing something as a follower of Christ.

Just keep doing what you're doing. Keep praying. Keep telling others about Christ and living the Christian life. Don't let anyone or anything intimidate you.

Monday

These priests provide only a hint of what goes on in the true sanctuary of heaven, which Moses caught a glimpse of as he was about to set up the tent-shrine. It was then that God said, "Be careful to do it exactly as you saw it on the Mountain." (Hebrews 8:5, THE MESSAGE)

So often we tend to think of heaven as surreal, and earth as real. In other words, our point of reference is earth. "This is earth. This is real. And heaven? Well, who knows?"

In truth, it's the opposite! Heaven is what is real, earth is what is temporary. That is why C. S. Lewis described life on earth as "the shadowlands." Earth is only a pale version of heaven, not the other way around.

God commanded Moses to build a tabernacle *like* the one in heaven. And in Hebrews 8:5, we read that the priests in New Testament days served in a place of worship that was only a copy, a shadow of the real one in heaven. In fact, as Moses prepared to build the tabernacle, God gave him this warning. He said, "Be sure that you make everything according to the design I have shown you here on the mountain" (Hebrews 8:5, NLT).

God wanted to make it clear to Moses that the original was in heaven; the copy was on the earth. To quote C. S. Lewis again: "The hills and valleys of heaven will be to those you now experience not as a copy but an original, nor as the substitute is to the genuine article, but as the flower to the root, or the diamond to the coal."[7]

As earthbound human beings, we tend to start with earth and reason up toward heaven. What we ought to do is start with heaven, and reason down toward earth. Heaven is the real deal, the eternal dwelling place. Earth is the copy, the temporary dwelling place.

When you see that sunset or that panoramic view of God's finest expressed in nature, and the beauty just takes your breath away, remember that it is just a glimpse of the real thing awaiting you in heaven.

Tuesday

Now I know in part; then I shall know fully, even as I am fully known.
(1 Corinthians 13:12, NIV)

People sometimes ask, "What will we know in heaven? Will we recognize each other?"

That question always amazes me. As if we're going to forget everything—or be walking around in a fuzzy cloud of semi-awareness! We will still love, but our love will be perfected. We will still think and remember, but our thoughts will be perfected, too. We certainly will know each other in heaven—and infinitely better than we knew each other on earth.

How do I know that? In Matthew 17 we read the account of Jesus on the mountaintop with Peter, James, and John. In those moments when He was transfigured before them, with His face shining like the sun and His clothes white as the light, He was seen talking to both Moses and Elijah.

From the account, it's obvious that the disciples knew it was Moses and Elijah, though they were never told that fact or introduced to them. I doubt these two visitors from heaven had little name tags on: "Hi. My name is Moses." Do you think Moses was standing with two stone tablets of the Ten Commandments under his arm, just to give them a little hint? No, but there was something about these two that made them instantly recognizable.

The disciples *knew* Moses and Elijah. And when we have been changed and encounter one another on the other side, we will know, too. But I'd like to add just one thing. If you ever want to look me up in heaven, don't look for a bald guy. Look for a guy with lots and lots of hair.

Think of the purest, highest, most ecstatic joy on earth, multiply it a thousand times, and you get a fleeting glimpse of heaven's euphoria. That is why David wrote, "In Your presence is fullness of joy; at Your right hand are pleasures forevermore" (Psalm 16:11).

We will be aware in heaven. More aware than we've ever been before.

You will know more there. You will love more there. Your love for family and friends will be a stronger, sweeter, purer love. Death breaks ties on earth, but they will be renewed in heaven. Heaven is a perfecting of the highest moments of our present Christian experience.

Wednesday

In the same way, our earthly bodies which die and decay are different from the bodies we shall have when we come back to life again, for they will never die. The bodies we have now embarrass us, for they become sick and die; but they will be full of glory when we come back to life again. Yes, they are weak, dying bodies now, but when we live again they will be full of strength. They are just human bodies at death, but when they come back to life they will be superhuman bodies.
(1 Corinthians 15:42-44, TLB)

Y ou will have a new body in heaven.

If you were disabled on earth, you won't be disabled in heaven. If your body on earth was broken by the ravages of age or disease, that won't be the case in your heavenly Father's house.

The Bible says that our resurrection bodies will resemble the resurrection body of Christ. Think of it! In 1 John 3:2 we read: "Beloved, now we are children of God; and it has not yet been revealed what we shall be, but we know that when He is revealed, we shall be like Him, for we shall see Him as He is."

What were the differences between the resurrection body of Jesus and the body that was put to death on the cross? When He walked among us on this earth, He voluntarily exposed Himself to the limitations of humanity. Just like everyone else, He got sleepy, thirsty, tired, and hungry. In His resurrected body there were similarities to the old body, but major differences, too.

His disciples recognized Him, and yet...something in them wondered, "Is it really You, Lord?"

But then again, He could do things He never did in His old body. He would suddenly appear in a room without using a door. And we also know that Jesus ascended through the air, higher and higher, until He disappeared from sight in the clouds. Will we be able to move around like that in our new bodies?

No one can say for sure, but we can know this. The Bible says that "Eye has not seen, nor ear heard, nor have entered into the heart of man the things which God has prepared for those who love Him" (1 Corinthians 2:9).

Thursday

Let us hear the conclusion of the whole matter: fear God and keep His commandments, for this is man's all. (Ecclesiastes 12:13)

If you are seeking fulfillment, purpose, or meaning from this world and from human accomplishments, I have some bad news: you will never find it. There is nothing in the world that will fill the deepest void in your life—not the ultimate car, not the greatest job, not the most beautiful girl or the most handsome guy, not the greatest education, not winning it all on *American Idol.* There is nothing that can even come close.

King Solomon, one of the wealthiest men who ever lived, had everything he wanted. Yet he went on a binge, trying to satisfy his appetites with the wrong things. He went after passion. He went after possessions. He went after things of beauty and buildings and land. He drank and he partied. After all of that, here was his conclusion: "Yet when I surveyed all that my hands had done and what I had toiled to achieve, everything was meaningless, a chasing after the wind; nothing was gained under the sun" (Ecclesiastes 2:11, NIV).

Have you ever been ravenously hungry and tried to satisfy your appetite with snacking? It just doesn't work. You want a real meal. In the same way, we were created with a God-shaped hole in our lives. We have been created to love God, to know God, and to bear fruit. Everything else is secondary.

Think about it: *Everything* else in life, every other responsibility, no matter how significant, must be ordered behind the central purpose of your existence on Earth: knowing, loving, and serving your Creator. Yes, God cares about your career, your marriage, your family, and your ministry. But knowing Him, prioritizing Him, is number one. And when you do, the Bible says you will never be a loser for it!

Jesus said it like this (to paraphrase): *"Your heavenly Father already knows all your needs, and he will give you all you need from day to day if you live for him and make the Kingdom of God your primary concern"* (see Matthew 6:32-33, NLT).

Friday

Now godliness with contentment is great gain. (1 Timothy 6:6)

As you begin to know God's love and purpose for you, you can live a life that overflows with purpose, peace, and joy. This is life as He intends you to live it, and this is exactly what David meant when he said, "The Lord is my shepherd; I shall not want" (Psalm 23:1).

Have you been able to say that? Have you been able to say, "Lord, if You want to give me more, fine. If You don't want to, fine. I shall not want, because I have found my contentment in You."

The apostle Paul found that contentment. Listen to his amazing words as he sat in Roman dungeon, in chains, for telling others about salvation in Jesus Christ: "Not that I was ever in need, for I have learned how to get along happily whether I have much or little. I know how to live on almost nothing or with everything. I have learned the secret of contentment in every situation, whether it be a full stomach or hunger, plenty or want; for I can do everything God asks me to with the help of Christ who gives me the strength and power" (Philippians 4:11-14, TLB).

Paul expressed contentment regardless of his circumstances. But how many of us have thought, I *would be content if I just had a little more money…if I could just land that promotion… if I could get married… if I could only afford that BMW.* But somehow, we never quite reach that place of contentment. We're always looking for something just a little beyond what we have.

There are certain things that only God can give. And when you are in a relationship with Him in which you say, "The Lord is my Shepherd," you can say with David, "I shall not want."

Our contentment doesn't come from what we have. *It comes from Whom we know.* Hebrews 13:5 tells us, "Let your conduct be without covetousness; be content with such things as you have. For He Himself has said, 'I will never leave you nor forsake you.'"

So when you get down to it, everything you need in life is found in a relationship with God.

Weekend

So take courage! For I believe God! It will be just as he said!
(Acts 27:25, TLB)

A pparently, the apostle Paul wasn't above saying, "I told you so."
In a severe storm at sea, after all the cargo had been
jettisoned and the crew had given up hope of even surviving, Paul
reminded them that he had warned them before they ever set out.

The Bible records his words, most likely shouted into the wind
on that wild, stormy day at sea: *"Men, you should have taken
my advice not to sail from Crete; then you would have spared
yourselves this damage and loss" (Acts 27:21, NIV).*

Paul knew a storm was coming when the others didn't. How did
he know that? The Lord's angel had stood next to him at night and
given him that sure word. Initially, the captain and the centurion
in charge rejected Paul's counsel. When the apostle warned them
about the trials and troubles ahead, they blew him off.

But now, in grave danger and at their wits end, they suddenly
found Paul's opinions interesting and relevant!

The truth is, as Christians who believe our Bible, we know
things nonbelievers don't know. We know that circumstances in
our nation and world will eventually go from bad to worse—much
worse. We know that Washington doesn't have the answers, and that
government doesn't have the solutions to life's greatest dilemmas and
needs. And we know that man in his own wisdom will always make a
mess of things.

Yes, because we read and believe our Bible, Christians know
what is coming down in the days to come. And we also know that
earth doesn't have what we are looking for. Not even close. That's
why we, like Abraham, are looking for a city that has foundations,
whose builder and maker is God Himself.

God revealed to Paul something that nonbelievers didn't know,
and He has done the same for us. He is able to take a situation of pain
and hardship and use it as an opportunity to point people to salvation
and new life in His Son. And God gives us that same platform.

Monday

*You will show me the path of life; in Your presence is fullness of joy; at
Your right hand are pleasures forevermore. (Psalm 16:11)*

Do people in heaven know what's happening on earth? This is
an important question to you if you have a loved one who's
gone on to heaven ahead of you. After all, you were connected to
that individual; you walked with them, talked with them, and
now they're gone. And you wonder, "Does he have any idea what's
happening down here since they left?" Or maybe, "Can she see
anything that's taking place on this planet that we're still living on?"

We can at least conclude this much: When people believe in
Jesus on earth, it becomes public knowledge in heaven. Jesus said,
"There will be more joy in heaven over one sinner who repents than
over ninety-nine just persons who need no repentance" (Luke 15:7)

What an amazing verse! Just one individual who puts his or
her faith in Jesus Christ causes a party to break out in heaven. The
residents of heaven are aware of the fact that repentance—a change
of heart—has taken place. In Luke 15:10, Jesus goes on to say,
"There is joy in the presence of the angels of God over one sinner
who repents."

Note that it doesn't say that there is joy *among* the angels in
heaven; it says "there is joy *in the presence* of the angels of God."

The way I see it, that implies that maybe someone else is doing
the rejoicing. Do the angels rejoice, too? I believe that they do. But
could it be that the rejoicing ones Jesus refers to here in Luke 15 are
those who have gone on before us, who are celebrating the salvation
of a loved one? Maybe even a loved one they played a part in
reaching? Is it possible in heaven we would be aware of people who
come to faith because of our testimony or our witness?

That would be exciting, but then…we will eventually know all
such things as we live in beauty and wonder of our Father's House.

Tuesday

Since we have such a huge crowd of men of faith watching us from the grandstands, let us strip off anything that slows us down or holds us back, and especially those sins that wrap themselves so tightly around our feet and trip us up; and let us run with patience the particular race that God has set before us. (Hebrews 12:1-2, TLB)

Are friends and loved ones in heaven watching us right now and cheering us on? What "huge crowd" is this? What is this "great cloud of witnesses," as it says in the King James Bible?

One big hint is the fact that Hebrews 12 comes right after Hebrews 11! Hebrews 11 is a record of the great men and women of faith who died serving God. We sometimes refer to it as the "hall of faith." You read about Abraham, Moses, Joseph, Gideon, Samson, David, Rahab, Daniel, and the list goes on.

So who are the witnesses in Hebrews 12:1? One interpretation says that these are simply people of faith who have gone before us, giving us a model to follow, so we might live and exercise our faith as they did. Reading about the lives of these men and women who have walked with God and trusted Christ and stood strong in the face of trials and persecutions can add steel to our soul.

Another way to look at it is that these men and women aren't simply giving us a template to follow, but are actually observing us and taking note of our progress in the faith. They are the "cloud of witnesses" watching us, and cheering us on, if you will.

Is that the case? Are there heavenly grandstands where people monitor the progress of loved ones living out their lives on earth? It wouldn't surprise me at all, but I don't know. But I do know this much: We are in the race of our life on earth, and we don't how long it will last. And I know for certain that Jesus is watching me, turn for turn, step for step.

Wednesday

The time of my death is near. I have fought the good fight, I have finished the race, and I have remained faithful. And now the prize awaits me— the crown of righteousness, which the Lord, the righteous Judge, will give me on the day of his return. And the prize is not just for me but for all who eagerly look forward to his appearing. (2 Timothy 4:6-8, NLT)

My son Christopher was quite the runner. We would go to his track meets as a family and cheer him on.

I had been a runner in school, too—really more of a sprinter. I wasn't very good at those long distance runs, but I could turn it on for short bursts and do pretty well. So every now and then, I would challenge Topher to a race. We did this a number of times through the years, and though he got faster as he grew older, I could still beat him every time.

My secret was that short burst of energy. I'd just push a little turbo button and I could take off pretty fast and leave him behind. I have to admit it always felt good to beat him. *Ahhh, old Dad can still beat his son. I guess I'm not over the hill yet!*

Then one day when we were racing I pushed the turbo button and—nothing happened. Christopher went cruising by me, and I never won our races again. Actually, I was proud of him and crestfallen at the same time. "Way to go, son. You finally beat old Dad."

In this race called "life," I had always assumed that I would finish my race before my sons, and that I would pass the baton on to them. But my son Christopher beat me again! Beat me to heaven! And now, in effect, he has passed the baton on to me, and I have to finish my race.

We all have a course marked out for us and a race to run and to finish. And we don't know how long this race is going to be; we never know when our lives will end. So we need to be ready, and we need to run our race well.

Thursday

Preach the word of God. Be persistent, whether the time is favorable or not. Patiently correct, rebuke, and encourage your people with good teaching.

For a time is coming when people will no longer listen to right teaching. They will follow their own desires and will look for teachers who will tell them whatever they want to hear. They will reject the truth and follow strange myths.

But you should keep a clear mind in every situation. Don't be afraid of suffering for the Lord. Work at bringing others to Christ. Complete the ministry God has given you. (2 Timothy 4:2-5, NLT)

This was the apostle Paul's last epistle before he left the planet. I read this passage just a few days after my son Christopher went to heaven. And in that moment, I remember thinking how Paul's words applied to both of us; there was a part for me, and a part for Christopher.

That was my part. To me, the passage seemed to be saying that I shouldn't be afraid of suffering, and that I was to continue on in my ministry with an even greater commitment.

And then in verses 6-8, it seemed like I was reading Christopher's part. "As for me, my life has already been poured out as an offering to God. The time of my death is near. I have fought a good fight, I have finished the race, and I have remained faithful. And now the prize awaits me—the crown of righteousness that the Lord, the righteous Judge, will give me on that great day of his return. And the prize is not just for me but for all who eagerly look forward to his glorious return."

Then Paul closes and says, "Please come as soon as you can." And I know he was writing to Timothy to say, "Come visit me," but in my grief I read the words as though Christopher had repeated them, saying, "Come as soon as you can, Dad."

Heaven is closer to me now, since Christopher's passing, and I can't wait to walk through the door of eternity and see him again. But I still have work to do here on earth, and a task to accomplish for the Lord. And, for now, that's what I want to do with all my heart.

Friday

Blessed be the God and Father of our Lord Jesus Christ, who has blessed us with every spiritual blessing in the heavenly places in Christ, just as He chose us in Him before the foundation of the world, that we should be holy and without blame before Him in love, having predestined us to adoption as sons by Jesus Christ to Himself, according to the good pleasure of His will, to the praise of the glory of His grace, by which He made us accepted in the Beloved. (Ephesians 1:3-6)

All that God has done has been because of His grace, which means "unmerited favor." You aren't merely forgiven, not merely justified, not merely cleansed of your sins, but you have been received in love by God Himself. This is because of His deep love for His own Son Jesus. Because His Son lives in you, you have found the Father's favor. You have the approval of God because of what Jesus has done.

Some people have been raised in homes in which their father may have never demonstrated any kind of love toward them. Maybe he was cold and distant, passive or preoccupied. Or maybe they, like me, were raised in a home where there wasn't a father at all. If we're not careful, we can transfer some of those negative emotions or associations to God, our heavenly Father. We can walk around in life feeling as though we don't have the approval of God: *If I just did this, God would notice. If worked a little harder, then God would love me.*

But the truth of Scripture is this: God *does* approve of you. The Bible says, "He made us accepted in the Beloved" (Ephesians 1:6). You are accepted in His own Son—not because you read your Bible a little bit longer, share Christ with more people, or give a little more in the offering. You are accepted in the Beloved when you *don't* do all of that. You are accepted in the Beloved when you fail, when you trip up. You are accepted in the Beloved not because of what *you* have done, but because of what *He* has done.

In understanding this great truth, however, you should want to do these things for His glory—not to earn His approval, because you already have it.

Weekend

"For there stood by me this night an angel of the God to whom I belong and whom I serve…" (Acts 27:23)

Paul spoke of "the God to whom I belong." In the Song of Solomon we read, "My beloved is mine and I am His." As a Christian, you belong to the Lord. You are His.

There are a number of analogies the Lord uses to show how we belong to God. For instance, we are called "the bride of Christ."

My bride is Cathe. I call her my wife, and she calls me her husband. She belongs to me and I belong to her. That's just the way it works. We belong to each other.

The Bible also compares us to sheep that belong to a shepherd. In John chapter 10, Jesus affirmed that He is the Good Shepherd and that we are His sheep. Sometimes we romanticize this wooly little animal, the sheep. They look so charming out there in the green grass, under the watchful eye of the shepherd. But we should also bear in mind that they are one of the stupidest animals on the face of the earth. It should not inflate you with pride to hear that you are compared to a dumb, defenseless sheep.

We are also compared to children belonging to a father. Romans 8:15 says, For you did not receive the spirit of bondage again to fear, but you received the Spirit of adoption by whom we cry out, "Abba, Father. *Abba* was an affectionate cry of a Hebrew child. Even if you go to Israel today you will see a little child cry out, "Abba" to their fathers. We might say, "Daddy," or "Papa." It's a close, affectionate, endearing term. And we have that kind of access and closeness with our Father God.

I belong to God. I've been bought and paid for, and I am His.

I heard the story of an older gentleman who was known for his godly life. Someone once asked him, "Old man, what do you do when you get tempted?"

He smiled and replied, "Well, I just look up to heaven and say, 'Lord, your property is in danger.'"

You are God's bride. You are His child. You are His sheep. You are His property. And like Paul, you too can say, "I belong to God."

Monday

"I will go to him, but he will not return to me." (2 Samuel 12:23, NIV)

K ing David wrote the words above just after the passing of his infant son, and he found comfort in that thought.

I and my family have also found comfort in that truth. Our son Christopher will not return to us, but someday we will go to him. In the same way, you too will eventually join your loved ones and friends who have died in the Lord, and who wait for you on the Other Side.

For me, one of the best pictures in the whole Bible is in 1 Thessalonians 4, where Paul describes a future, incredibly joyous meeting somewhere in the clouds.

> I can tell you this directly from the Lord: that we who are still living when the Lord returns will not rise to meet him ahead of those who are in their graves. For the Lord himself will come down from heaven with a mighty shout and with the soul-stirring cry of the archangel and the great trumpet-call of God. And the believers who are dead will be the first to rise to meet the Lord. Then we who are still alive and remain on the earth will be caught up with them in the clouds to meet the Lord in the air and remain with him forever. So comfort and encourage each other with this news. (vv. 15-18, TLB)

If my son could speak to you right now, I'm sure he would say, "Eternity is real. Heaven is beyond your wildest dreams. And you need to believe the gospel so you can join me here."

Life comes and goes, whether you're in kindergarten or in assisted living. The Bible describes life like a little flower that opens up to the sunlight in the morning and withers that very day before the sun goes down.

James writes: "What is your life? It is even a vapor that appears for a little time and then vanishes away" (James 4:14).

Again and again, the Bible urges us to take the *long* view. If our time on this side of heaven is truly brief (and in comparison to eternity, it is), then we need to invest our lives wisely, laying up eternal treasures for the real and permanent life to come.

Tuesday

That is why we never give up. Though our bodies are dying, our inner strength in the Lord is growing every day. These troubles and sufferings of ours are, after all, quite small and won't last very long. Yet this short time of distress will result in God's richest blessing upon us forever and ever! (2 Corinthians 4:16-17, TLB)

When you're young, life seems to go so s-l-o-w-l-y. It seemed like I was in first and second grade for about thirty years. Every day took forever. Then, as you get a little bit older, the months go by quickly. Years go by quickly. *Decades* go by quickly.

When our granddaughter Stella was two, she hated to hear the words, "Just a minute." She didn't like to wait—not even for a minute. Sometimes she would even cry to hear those words. (But then one day my daughter-in-law Brittany heard little Stella telling the dog, "Just a minute.")

"Just a minute" seems long to a child. But as you get older, just a minute comes and goes. God is effectively saying, "Just a minute, and you will be with Me in eternity, reunited with your loved ones." That's how fast life can go on earth.

We hate to face the fact that we are mere mortals, and that our days are numbered. Death is like a virus that affects everyone. But here is the good news. Jesus Christ overcame death at the cross of Calvary when He died for the sin of the world. The Bible says, "For our dying bodies must be transformed into bodies that will never die; our mortal bodies must be transformed into immortal bodies…. 'Death is swallowed up in victory. O death, where is your victory? O death, where is your sting?'" (1 Corinthians 15:53-55, NLT).

Christ defeated death! Now, I'm not saying we don't die. But I am saying we don't have to be *afraid* of death, because the real you, the real me, is not the body in which we live. The real you is a soul that lives inside of you. That is why when you see the body of a person you had known and loved, it doesn't even look like him or her anymore. Because the real person has moved on into eternity.

And so will we.

Wednesday

Everyone has to die once, then face the consequences. Christ's death was also a one-time event, but it was a sacrifice that took care of sins forever. (Hebrews 9:27-28, THE MESSAGE)

Heaven is not the default destination of every person. You must choose to go there. For instance, you can't just get in your car and drive over to Disneyland and walk in. You have to buy the ticket first. You also have to get your ticket to go to heaven. But you can't buy it. In fact, you could never, ever afford it. The good news is that Jesus Christ bought your ticket to heaven when He shed His blood on the cross of Calvary. And He offers it as a free gift to you right now.

The Bible says, "But as many as received Him, to them He gave the right to become children of god, to those who believe in His name" (John 1:12).

You may be asking, "What do you mean, *receive* Him?" Just this: there has to come a moment in your life when you say, "Jesus come into my heart. Be my Savior. Be my Lord." I can't pray that prayer for you. You must make your own choice. But when you have made that decision, the Bible says that you will go to heaven when you die.

Yes, we will all have to die, but all of us will also live forever. Everyone! It doesn't matter if you're a believer, an agnostic, or an atheist. In effect, we are all immortal. The question is, *where* will you live forever? According to the Bible there are only two options: Heaven or hell.

The believer dies and immediately goes to heaven, but it is a different matter altogether for the nonbeliever. They too, are immortal. They too, live forever. What happens to a nonbeliever when they die? Short answer: They go to hell.

I take no pleasure in stating this, or even in using the word. I don't want anyone to go the place that the Bible describes as "the second death" and "outer darkness." More important, *God* doesn't want anyone to go there. God says, "As I live…I have no pleasure in the death of the wicked" (Ezekiel 33:11). And that is why He made such a radical sacrifice to save us from that horrible destination.

He gave His Son.

Thursday

"Yes, a person is a fool to store up earthly wealth but not have a rich relationship with God." (Luke 12:21, NLT)

A watchmaker who built grandfather clocks inscribed these words on every clock he built: "Lo, here I stand by thee upright to give thee warning day and night, for every tick that I do click cuts short the time thou hast to live."

Jesus told the story of a rich farmer who enjoyed great success. Reflecting on his accomplishments, he said, "I know! I'll tear down my barns and build bigger ones. Then I'll have room enough to store all my wheat and other goods. And I'll sit back and say to myself, 'My friend, you have enough stored away for years to come. Now take it easy! Eat, drink, and be merry!' " (Luke 12:18–19, NLT). But God told him, "You fool! You will die this very night. Then who will get everything you worked for?" (v. 20).

We can find some commendable things about this rich man. He was a hardworking farmer. He probably would have had to work longer and get up earlier and expend more energy than the other farmers of his day to achieve such success. But his mistake wasn't in being successful in his work. His mistake wasn't even in acquiring possessions. His mistake was failing to make plans for eternity. He was living large. But he forgot that the clock was ticking, that life was passing by.

And this man who died, leaving all his possessions behind, is like many people today. They just want to enjoy the moment. "Take it easy!" they say. "Eat, drink, and be merry!" Yet God says that is not the way to live.

In Psalm 5 (NIV), the psalmist describes an arrogant, wicked man. One of the most striking things he says about this man is in verse 10: "In his pride the wicked does not seek him; in all his thoughts there is no room for God."

That says it so well, doesn't it? There was no room for God, no room for the Creator, Lord, and Savior in all this man's many thoughts about this and that.

Our lives on this earth may be very brief, but when we fill our thoughts with the eternal God and His purposes, we prepare ourselves for an endless life in His presence.

Friday

His unchanging plan has always been to adopt us into his own family by sending Jesus Christ to die for us. And he did this because he wanted to! Now all praise to God for his wonderful kindness to us and his favor that he has poured out upon us because we belong to his dearly loved Son.
(Ephesians 1:5-6, TLB)

How often we hear about what we are supposed to do for God. Yet the emphasis of the Bible is not so much on what we are supposed to do for God, but rather on what God has done for us. If we can get hold of that in our minds and hearts, it will change our outlook and actions. The more we understand of *what God has done for us*, the more we will want to do for Him.

This is no small truth. In fact, it's fundamental to our spiritual lives. The devil would love to keep us from praying at all by reminding us how "unworthy" we are—telling us in effect that we have a lot of nerve to even think we could approach a holy God. He whispers, *Do you think that God would hear your prayers after what you've done?* But the real question to ask is this: "Is Jesus Christ worthy to come into the presence of the Father whenever He wants?" Of course He is.

The fact is that we are "accepted in the Beloved" (Ephesians 1:6). Because Christ has open access to the presence of the Father at any time, we have the same access as we come to God the Father through our relationship with Jesus. It's not on the basis of what we have done for God; it is solely on the basis of what Christ has done for us.

Listen to the writer to the Hebrews:

> "And so, dear brothers and sisters, we can boldly enter heaven's Most Holy Place because of the blood of Jesus. By his death, Jesus opened a new and life-giving way through the curtain into the Most Holy Place. And since we have a great High Priest who rules over God's people, let us go right into the presence of God, with sincere hearts fully trusting him" (Hebrews 10:19-21, NLT).

I just can't imagine any better news than that.

Wednesday

As high as heaven is over the earth, so strong is his love to those who fear him. And as far as sunrise is from sunset, he has separated us from our sins.(Psalm 103:11-12, THE MESSAGE)

How much do we really understand about God's grace in Christ? Can we even begin to wrap our minds around it?

Satan doesn't want you to ponder these things. He will whisper in your ear and say, "You've committed that sin one too many times. How many times do you expect God to forgive you? You can't go to Him." And then the guilt and despair will come—guilt that can drive you crazy.

Is all guilt bad, then? No...even guilt has its purpose. You might think of it as a warning system. You're walking down the street barefoot and you step on a little sliver of sharp glass. The pain in your foot shoots right up to your brain, and the warning is instantaneous. *Stop! Don't step down any further.*

It's just a little cut, and not all that bad. But it hurt. It's not bad enough to have you check into emergency, but it's definitely reason to be careful, to back off a little. No, you don't like the discomfort of that initial pain, but it has served you well if it keeps you from more serious injury.

Guilt can be the same way. I say or do something wrong, and almost immediately, I know it. Guilt kicks in to say, "You are not right with God," or "You are not right with that person, and that needs to be rectified."

It's guilt. It's not enough to plunge me into despair or send me into depression, but it's enough to bring me to the cross, where I say, "Lord, I have failed, I have sinned in this, and I'm sorry. Please help me and forgive me."

As far as Satan is concerned, that's the worst. Everything in him wants to keep you from the cross, where Jesus paid the debt for our rebellion and sin with His own blood. It was the cross that sealed Satan's doom, and he doesn't want you anywhere near it. He wants you to feel guilty and condemned, separated from God. But God wants that guilt to bring you to Him, where you will find mercy, forgiveness, healing...and an endless ocean of grace.

Monday

For the wages of sin is death, but the free gift of God is eternal life through Jesus Christ our Lord. (Romans 6:23, TLB)

The big issue on that final day when we step out of this life into eternity won't be a *sin* issue as much as it will be a *Son* issue. The only relevant question on that day will be one that God asks: "What did you do with My Son Jesus Christ, whom I sent to die on the cross for you?"

God has given us the way into heaven. But it's up to us to embrace that way. Here's the hard truth: If you end up in hell, it will be because you effectively sent yourself there. And you did it by rejecting His incredible offer of forgiveness. C.S. Lewis said, "No one will ever go to heaven deservingly and no one will ever go to hell unwillingly." If you end up there you have to practically climb over Jesus to do so.

Every one of us will live forever. But the greatest question of our lives is: *where?* Have you got your ticket? Do you know with certainty?

I heard the story of a Christian father who was terminally ill, and summoned his three sons—two of whom were believers—to his deathbed. To the two young men who had trusted Christ, he said, "Boys, goodbye. I will see you in the morning."

Greatly distressed, his third son said, "Dad, why didn't you say that to me? Why didn't you say that you will see me in the morning, too?"

The father sadly said, "Because son, you have not put your faith in Jesus Christ. And because of that my heart is broken, and I will never see you again." The son began to weep. "Dad, I don't want to be separated from you. I want to be saved. What do I do?" And he said, "Son, put your faith in Jesus Christ, and then one day our family will be complete in eternity." And that's what the boy did.

The fact is, you can be reunited with loved ones who have gone on to heaven, or you can be separated from them forever in hell.

It's your choice.

Tuesday

We must through many tribulations enter the kingdom of God. (Acts 14:22)

We don't always like to read a verse like that. We would rather the passage read, "Through many days of perpetual happiness, we enter the kingdom of God." But that isn't Scripture, and that isn't life. Trials and tribulations will come. Job said it well: "Man who is born of woman is of few days and full of trouble" (Job 14:1, NIV).

Jesus once told a story about two men who built two homes. They may have been built at the same time, close together, and even with the same floor plan. One of the builders, however, erected his home on shifting sand, while the other built on a stable rock foundation.

Then the storms came, hitting both of those houses—hard! The house that had been built on sand collapsed and fell in upon itself, while the one built on the rock stood firm. The obvious moral of the story is to build your life on a foundation that will last, like the one we find in the pages of God's Word.

But here's an application we sometimes miss. The storm came to *both* lives. The wind beat on *both* houses. The rain poured on *both* building sites. The man who was wise and carefully chose a stable foundation got hit with the same hurricane-force winds as the man who foolishly took shortcuts and didn't bother to plan ahead.

We will all experience storms in life. Good things will happen to us, as well as tragic and inexplicable things. Every life will have its share of pain. Even so, we have a God who, despite the worst tragedy, can bring good out of bad! That's not to say that God will make bad good, because bad is bad. But it is to say that good can come out of bad. As Romans 8:28 (NIV) affirms: "And we know that in all things God works for the good of those who love him, who have been called according to his purpose."

Life is a process, and as finite beings who live moment to moment, we can't see around the bend, we can't discern God's ultimate purposes. But we can know that the ultimate result will be good…because He is good.

Wednesday

Because of our faith, Christ has brought us into this place of undeserved privilege where we now stand, and we confidently and joyfully look forward to sharing God's glory. We can rejoice, too, when we run into problems and trials, for we know that they help us develop endurance. And endurance develops strength of character, and character strengthens our confident hope of salvation. And this hope will not lead to disappointment. (Romans 5:2-5, NLT)

As you look at some recent hardship or tragedy that has befallen you, you might well say, "I don't see any good in this." But then maybe a month from now, you will see a little good. And then a little bit later, you will see a little more. Most likely, it won't be until you have departed this life and entered eternity that you will finally see the big picture and the complete good. But until that day, God promises that He can bring good out of bad.

Some people actually believe that as followers of Christ, we are somehow exempt from human suffering. I hate to break it to you, but inexplicable and heartbreaking things happen to good and godly people. Christians get cancer, die in auto accidents, lose their jobs, and experience practically all of the problems that people outside of Christ experience.

Scripture acknowledges that you and I may be surprised by the trials we encounter. The apostle Peter wrote: "Dear friends, do not be surprised at the painful trial you are suffering, as though something strange were happening to you" (1 Peter 4:12, NIV). Even so, we frequently *are* surprised when we encounter problems and difficulties—problems in our career, with our family, with our kids, or in our marriage.

But the Bible never promises a trouble-free, pain-free life.

Now don't get me wrong: that sounds pretty appealing to me, too. And truthfully, we will have many beautiful days of joy, peace, happiness, and good times. But there will also be many tough days. As Jesus said in John 16:33 (NLT), "Here on earth you will have many trials and sorrows. But take heart, because I have overcome the world."

It is Jesus who makes all the difference.

Thursday

Now this is the confidence that we have in Him, that if we ask anything according to His will, He hears us. (1 John 5:14)

I n a broad sense, we should pray about everything. But there are certain things we don't need to pray about. For example, if someone were to say, "Greg, I'm praying about robbing a bank. Would you pray with me?" I will pray *for* that person, but I won't pray that God will bless their efforts. Why? Because the Bible says, "You shall not steal." We don't need to pray about that.

Yet there are certain things God tells us we can pray for. He tells us we can pray for wisdom: "If any of you lacks wisdom, let him ask of God, who gives to all liberally and without reproach, and it will be given to him" (James 1:5).

We can pray for His provision. Philippians 4:19 says, "And my God shall supply all your need according to His riches in glory by Christ Jesus."

We can pray for protection. Psalm 91:5-7 says, "You shall not be afraid of the terror by night, nor of the arrow that flies by day, nor of the pestilence that walks in darkness, nor of the destruction that lays waste at noonday. A thousand may fall at your side, and ten thousand at your right hand; but it shall not come near you."

We can pray for power to meet the challenges of life. Ephesians 1:18-19 (NIV) tells us: "I pray also that the eyes of your heart may be enlightened in order that you may know the hope to which he has called you, the riches of his glorious inheritance in the saints, and his incomparably great power for us who believe."

The key to effective prayer is getting our will in alignment with God's will, as the verse at the top of today's devotional explains.

Nothing lies outside the reach of prayer except that which lies outside of the will of God.

Friday

Now Thomas (called Didymus), one of the Twelve, was not with the disciples when Jesus came. So the other disciples told him, "We have seen the Lord!" So he said to them, "Unless I see in His hands the print of the nails, and put my finger into the print of the nails, and put my hand into His side, I will not believe."

And after eight days His disciples were again inside, and Thomas with them. Jesus came, the doors being shut, and stood in the midst, and said, "Peace to you!" Then He said to Thomas, "Reach your finger here, and look at My hands; and reach your hand here, and put it into My side. Do not be unbelieving, but believing."

And Thomas answered and said to Him, "My Lord and my God!" Thomas said to him, "My Lord and my God!" (John 20:24-28)

Thomas, one of Jesus' disciples, has earned the nickname "Doubting Thomas," but I think that's a bit unfair. I have always thought of Thomas as more of a skeptic than a doubter. After all, Thomas didn't ask for a special revelation from Jesus. He simply asked for the same proof the other disciples had already seen.

Thomas was the kind of guy who wanted to know for himself. He was his own man, and wouldn't let others do his thinking for him.

What did Jesus do with such a man? He made a special resurrection appearance for him. He condescended to Thomas and his desire to know for himself. In other words, Jesus came to Thomas on his level. He didn't rebuke him or humiliate him. He could see that deep down in Thomas's heart, he really wanted to know God.

I like Thomas, because by nature I, too, am a skeptical person. I have never been one to believe something just because someone says it's true.

You might be someone who is a bit skeptical, a bit unsure of your faith. You may have a lot of questions. Deep down inside, you want to know God. You want to know for yourself.

Just as with Thomas, the risen Lord Jesus has something for you, too. He can turn your skepticism into belief.

Just come to Him with your questions and with your doubts. (He knows them, anyway!) And when He has revealed Himself to you in a fresh way, you, too, will be able to say, "My Lord and my God!"

Weekend

"A thief is only there to steal and kill and destroy. I came so they can have real and eternal life, more and better life than they ever dreamed of." (John 10:10, THE MESSAGE)

An interest in life on Mars seems to run in cycles. At this writing, our nation has a new exploration robot prowling around and digging little holes in the dirt near the Martian north pole.

A few years ago, I remember being interviewed for an article about life on other planets. I remember saying, "I don't see anything in the Bible that would indicate there is life on other planets, but if there is, God created it." They closed the article with another of my statements: "Maybe we shouldn't be so worried about life on other planets and ask ourselves the question, 'Is there life on Earth, and are we living it the way God wants us to?'"

We often wonder if there is life after death. But is there life *during* life? That's a question we should all consider.

When I was seventeen, that was my question. I wasn't so concerned with what happened beyond the grave at that age, because I thought I would live a long, long time. My primary concern at that time was, "What's life all about? What's the purpose of life?" I knew in my heart there had to be more than what I'd experienced to that point. I was desperately searching for some kind of meaning in life. I just had to know.

Thankfully, I didn't have to look very far, because there was a group of very outspoken Christians on my high school campus. They practiced what they preached, and they intrigued me. So I began to watch them, and couldn't help noticing that they were experiencing a dimension of life I had never known. Not long after that, I gave my life to Jesus and discovered the truth of Jesus' great statement from John 10:10: "I have come that they may have life, and that they may have it more abundantly." That's what I had been searching for, life during life.

Ask the Lord to point you toward someone today who may be searching for that very thing.

Monday

My troubles turned out all for the best—they forced me to learn from your textbook. Truth from your mouth means more to me than striking it rich in a gold mine. (Psalm 119:71-72, THE MESSAGE)

Here's the problem in a nutshell: Our definition of "good" is what benefits us in the here-and-now, not in our eternal life to come. In other words, we are interested in what will benefit us temporarily, but God is interested in what will benefit us eternally. We are interested in what will make us happy for awhile, but God is far more interested in what will make us holy.

So here is the key. Jesus loves us, and He wants to be glorified through our lives. In view of *that* reality, He won't always remove suffering, because it can make us stronger and bring us closer to Him. Even though we would never choose it, suffering can give us a greater platform for glorifying God and pointing others toward Him.

Adversity levels us, and keeps us humble. Success or prosperity has a tendency to make people proud and self-sufficient. We may not feel an overwhelming need for God when we have our salary, our investments, our career, our 401k, our homes, our health, and our family. But when the economy goes south or the stock market crashes or our home burns, we have the opportunity to turn back to God with all our hearts, being reminded of what really matters in life.

The truth is, you and I shouldn't always be so afraid of pain. There's something worse than pain: it is a prosperity that leads us to forget about God.

Adversity teaches us eternal truths we might not otherwise learn. For most of us, our basic objective in life is to avoid pain at all costs. Bottom line, we just want to dodge pain whenever we can. We want to get in better shape and look cool in our new gym outfit, but we don't want to sweat and strain.

"No pain, no gain?" Alas, it's true. And what is true of the gym or health club is also true of life. Our pain reminds us of a deeper need: the need for God in our lives. And God will teach us lessons in those valleys that we would never have learned on mountaintops.

Tuesday

All praise to the God and Father of our Master, Jesus the Messiah! Father of all mercy! God of all healing counsel! He comes alongside us when we go through hard times, and before you know it, he brings us alongside someone else who is going through hard times so that we can be there for that person just as God was there for us.
(2 Corinthians 1:3-4, THE MESSAGE*)*

C. S. Lewis wrote, "Pain removes the veil; it plants the flag of truth within the fortress of a rebel soul."[8] God wants to plant His flag in your rebel soul. He wants to get control of your life. And with that control comes the deep inner peace and sense of purpose and meaning our hearts crave.

Adversity gives us new compassion for others who are in pain. In case you hadn't noticed, pain, disappointment, and heartache are all around us, as common to the atmosphere of our planet as nitrogen and oxygen. If you preach to people who are hurting, you will never lack for an audience.

It has been said, "Success builds walls, but failure builds bridges." If you have experienced pain, grief, failure, or depression, and by God's grace and help you've come through that valley, your companionship and counsel are like gold for someone who might still be groping their way through that valley.

If I was going to take a hiking trip on a certain trail in the Sierras, I'd want to talk to someone who has actually taken that particular hike, not someone who has only thought about it or read about it in a book.

Paul, who certainly experienced his share of valleys in his earthly journey (and high mountaintops, too!), shared this perspective with the Corinthians when he wrote: "He comforts us in all our troubles so that we can comfort others" (2 Corinthians 1:4, NLT).

When we go through adversity, then, and find our way through it with God's help, comfort, and direction, we need to look around for those who are still wandering, still lost in the woods, still reeling from the pain. Then we can help them in Jesus' name.

Wednesday

"Three times I was shipwrecked. Once I spent a whole night and a day adrift at sea" (2 Corinthians 11:25, NLT).

Writing to the church in Corinth, the apostle Paul says, "Trust me. I've been through it. I know more than I ever wanted to know about shipwrecks."

I have never been literally shipwrecked, but I have been through some pretty rough seas.

I remember years ago being on one of those Bible study cruises with a group of people from our church. We were trying to have an evening service as the ship bounced and rocked on the choppy waves. People were getting sick and lurching out the room. Let's just say the pastor gave an early benediction and ended the service before it ever really got started.

But that wasn't a shipwreck, it was only rough seas.

We've all had our share of rough seas, haven't we? I've had my share of hardships in life. More than many? Perhaps. But not as many as some. I remember thinking not that long ago that maybe the days of big shipwrecks in my life were over. Oh, I know there will always be some difficulties, challenges, and trials in the Christian life. But I'd found myself hoping that I might somehow escape any big traumatic events through my remaining years. You know…relative smooth sailing the rest of the way to heaven. But of course, that was not to be with the unexpected death of our oldest son Christopher in July of 2008.

Anyone who has ever done any sailing can tell you how rapidly the weather can change—how quickly you can find yourself facing stiff winds and rising seas. The fact is, we can't know what's ahead of us in life. We can't see the storms that may be churning just over the horizon. But God can!

And what was true for the psalmist in a time of uncertainty and great storms is true for you and me as well: "God is our refuge and strength, an ever-present help in trouble. Therefore we will not fear, though the earth give way and the mountains fall into the heart of the sea, though its waters roar and foam and the mountains quake…The Lord Almighty is with us; the God of Jacob is our fortress (Psalm 146:1-3, 7, NIV).

Thursday

Now all who believed were together, and had all things in common. (Acts 2:44)

There is nothing in this world quite like Christian fellowship. We know that the early church worshipped, prayed, and studied the Scriptures together. They also ate together, gave their tithes and offerings together, shared the gospel together, helped one another, and stuck together. In short, they loved one another.

The word that describes this phenomenon is the Greek word *koinonia*, which is usually translated "fellowship." But it is also translated into the words "communion," "distribution," "contribution," or "partnership." This means there is something wonderful and supernatural that people in the church experience. It's a bond we share that those outside that fellowship can't begin to understand.

God has a unique purpose and place for the church in the world today. In Romans chapter 1, Paul writes: "And you, dear friends… are among those he dearly loves; you, too, are invited by Jesus Christ to be God's very own—yes, his holy people. May all God's mercies and peace be yours from God our Father and from Jesus Christ our Lord" (Romans 1:6-7, TLB). In the New King James version, it says that we believers are "the called of Jesus Christ."

Called? Yes, God's people are called out of a world system that is hostile to the teachings of Scripture. As Jesus said, "You are not of the world, but I chose you out of the world, therefore the world hates you" (John 15:19).

This doesn't mean we are to isolate ourselves from the world, because Jesus said, "Let your light so shine before men, that they may see your good works and glorify your Father in heaven" (see Matthew 5:16).

We are to be salt and light in this culture. But at the same time, we are called out of the culture and warned not to love it. Called out…and called together. In the world…but not of the world. The apostle Paul called the church "a mystery," and there is nowhere better to be this world than right in the middle of it.

Friday

You keep track of all my sorrows. You have collected all my tears in your bottle. You have recorded each one in your book. (Psalm 56:8, NLT)

When you're hurting and no one else seems to understand, God understands. You can bring a burden before the Lord that may seem insignificant to someone else. *Whatever* weighs on your heart is a concern to Him, and He wants you to talk to Him about it. As it says in the Phillips translation of 1 Peter 5:7, "You can throw the whole weight of your anxieties upon him, for you are his personal concern."

David understood this when he wrote, "You keep track of all my sorrows. You have collected all my tears in your bottle. You have recorded each one in your book (Psalm 56:8, NLT). That is a wonderful insight into the personal compassion that God has for each and every one of us.

We are prone to only pray about the big things. We tend to think of prayer as last resort, like the fire alarms that say, "In case of emergency, break this glass." If it's a little fire, so to speak, we think, *I can handle this*, and we'll put the fire out. But if half the building is burning, then we go ahead and break the glass.

What is God telling us?

Break the glass.

No matter what it may be, run to Him in prayer. Don't wait for a small thing to become a big thing. Your heavenly Father is interested in every detail of your life. Don't reduce the infinite to the finite by placing a limit on God, because He says, "Is anything too hard for the Lord?" (Genesis 18:14).

Philippians 4:6 tells us, "Don't worry about anything; instead, pray about everything" (NLT). Note the word "everything." It doesn't say, "Pray about *some things*." Nor does it say, "Pray about *really big things*." I checked the original language, and guess what? It says "everything" in Greek and "everything" in English. And that's just what God intended.

Pray about everything.

Weekend

After a few days, Jesus returned to Capernaum, and word got around that he was back home. A crowd gathered, jamming the entrance so no one could get in or out. He was teaching the Word. They brought a paraplegic to him, carried by four men. When they weren't able to get in because of the crowd, they removed part of the roof and lowered the paraplegic on his stretcher. Impressed by their bold belief, Jesus said to the paraplegic, "Son, I forgive your sins." (Mark 2:1-5, THE MESSAGE)

The Gospel of Mark gives us the account of a group of men who wanted to bring their paralyzed friend to Jesus for healing. Jesus was teaching in a home, and the men couldn't get in the door with their disabled friend because of the huge crowd. Undaunted, they climbed up on top of the house and dug through the roof to lower the paralyzed man inside…dropping him right in front of Jesus.

When Jesus saw the faith of these men, he looked at their paralyzed friend and said, "Son, be of good cheer; your sins are forgiven you" (Matthew 9:2). Jesus was saying, "You no longer have to be afraid of the penalty for your sin. Your past is behind you. I am giving you another chance in life."

Jesus then told him to get up, pick up his bed, and go to his house. When you think about it, this man had a choice. He could have stayed on his sickbed forever, a perennial "victim of circumstance." He could have said, "I can't," or "I won't," or "I'm just not sure. Let me think about it." He had a choice, and he decided to respond. His brain sent the command to muscles that had never worked before, and he stood to his feet.

There are people today who don't want to change. They don't want to leave their lifestyle or turn from the choices they have made. They refuse to take hold of God's promises and provision and power.

If you want to change, if you want to break free from a vice that has you in its grip, a lifestyle you are trapped in, or an addiction that you can't seem to shake, then Christ has a word of encouragement to you: "Get up and walk. You can do it. Be of good cheer, and arise."

Monday

"We are pressed on every side by troubles, but not crushed and broken. We are perplexed because we don't know why things happen as they do, but we don't give up and quit. We are hunted down, but God never abandons us. We get knocked down, but we get up again and keep going." (2 Corinthians 4:8-9, TLB)

Some of the modern conveniences of the twenty-first century have made traveling a little more safe and convenient, but in some way, shape or form, every one of us will face shipwrecks. That's the reality of life on this planet: you're either coming out of a storm or about to go into one. Yes, of course there will be those wonderful stretches of smooth sailing, when skies are blue and golden sunlight filters through the tree leaves. In God's grace and kindness, you will certainly have your share of beautiful moments in between the storms. Not all the winds that blow in life are necessarily devastating.

In one instance of the ship's log in the book of Acts, the text says, "The south wind blew softly." Thank God for those moments, when the breezes are gentle and the sun is warm on your shoulders. Enjoy those seasons—savor them, live them to the hilt, and thank the Lord for them.

Some believers, however, seem to think that if they're in the will of God, they'll *always* have smooth sailing and calm seas. That certainly wasn't true for the apostle Paul! In the course of his ministry, he seemed to face every kind of adversity imaginable. He had so many enemies jealous of his success that they would actually follow him around and seek to undermine him, hoping to destroy him. He experienced beating after savage beating at the hands of his many adversaries, and spent years of his life in harsh confinement. And on top of it all, he had a personal physical disability that the Lord had declined to heal.

And yet in spite of all this, he wrote to the Corinthians: "Yes, we live under constant danger to our lives because we serve the Lord, but this gives us constant opportunities to show forth the power of Jesus Christ within our dying bodies" (2 Corinthians 4:11, TLB).

For Paul, frequent troubles meant frequent opportunities to show forth the sustaining power of his Lord.

Tuesday

I know that as you pray for me, and as the Holy Spirit helps me, this is all going to turn out for my good. (Philippians 1:19, TLB)

Sometimes I think that today's "prosperity preachers" have hijacked a legitimate biblical term. After all, God does want His sons and daughters to prosper. But what does that really mean? That you'll never get sick? Never have problems? Never run out of money? Never have strains in your relationships? No, that's not what the Bible means by "prosperity."

Five years before making his journey to Rome, Paul wrote the believers there and said in Romans 1:10, "… making request if, by some means, now at last I may find a way in the will of God to come to you." In other words, "Hey, would you guys pray for me? I'm coming your way. And pray that the Lord gives me a prosperous journey by the will of God."

Did God answer his prayer? Yes. He did make it to Rome, and had an amazing ministry there of preaching, teaching, discipleship, and writing. He just hadn't understood that *getting* to Rome would mean false accusations, arrest, incarceration, and chains. He couldn't have foreseen that it would involve hurricane force winds at sea, shipwreck on an island, and the bite of a poisonous viper on the way.

The reality is you can live a prosperous life in the will of God and still face fierce personal conflict and adversity. Paul went through shipwreck on his way to Rome, but he had a prosperous journey by the will of God *because of what it ultimately accomplished.*

Facing storms and shipwrecks in our lives really isn't a matter of "if," it is a matter of "when." So it's time for us to get our sea legs under us. Rather than trying to avoid the storms of life, we need to learn how to get *through* them. How to survive them. And how to learn the lessons that we can only learn in such times and such places.

It has been said, "You can't direct the wind, but you can adjust your sails." In other words, I can't control all the elements of my world—or even very many of them at all. But I can control my *reaction* to them. I can adjust my sails. And adapt.

Wednesday

A huge storm came up. Waves poured into the boat, threatening to sink it. And Jesus was in the stern, head on a pillow, sleeping!
(Mark 4:37-38, THE MESSAGE)

As I write these words, our nation suffers from a deeply troubled economy, and many are losing hope. And some of those discouraged, disillusioned people out there will begin to reevaluate what really matters in life and their relationship with God. This can be an opportunity for us to speak up, offer a word of true and lasting hope, and point people to Christ.

On one occasion, Jesus said to His disciples, "Let's go over to the other side." So they boarded their little boat to cruise across the Sea of Galilee. Suddenly, a storm came roaring out of nowhere. This one was a doozy, because even the seasoned sailors despaired of life. And what was Jesus doing? He was sound asleep in the stern. Waking Him, they yelled, "Teacher don't you care that we are perishing?" (See Mark 4).

It was really more like an accusation. "Hey Lord, are You paying attention? Don't You care that we're going through this? Wake up and do something!" Jesus stood up, and rebuked both the storm *and* His boys. To the storm He said, "Peace! Be still!" And of course it instantly obeyed. But to His own followers He said, "Why are you so fearful? Why is it you have no faith?" Or literally, "Why are you so timid and fearful? Boys, haven't you learned anything? Remember what I said? *'Let's cross over to the other side.'* I didn't say, 'Let's go to the middle of the Sea of Galilee and drown!'"

The fact is, Jesus never promised calm seas and smooth sailing. But He did promise a safe passage. He told them they would make it to the other side.

Listen…it's better to be in a storm with Jesus than anywhere else without Him! I would rather be in a row boat with Jesus in the middle of a hurricane than a thousand miles inland without Him. I would rather be in a lion's den…or a prison…or a hospital…or even a shipwreck with Jesus than in any other situation without Him. As long as I know the Lord is there, I can get through *anything*.

Thursday

Do two people walk hand in hand if they aren't going to the same place?
(Amos 3:3, THE MESSAGE*)*

There are a number of things included in the concept of walking with God. The Bible says that we need to walk in the Spirit (Galatians 5:16). We should walk rooted in Him (Colossians 2:6-7). We should walk humbly with Him (Micah 6:8). The book of 1 John promises us that "if we walk in the light, as he is in the light, we have fellowship with one another, and the blood of Jesus, his Son, purifies us from all sin" (v. 7, NIV). Walking with God means moving in harmony with Him, staying close to Him. This phrase "walking with God" speaks of a joint effort.

If you go into business with someone, it means pooling your resources. Maybe you both have small businesses, even competing businesses, and one day you go to that person and agree to work together. You draw up the contracts and pool your resources. He has his clients, you have your clients, and suddenly you broaden your base.

Walking with God is like going into business with God. This means that I take all of my resources, which obviously are quite limited, and say, "Lord, here is what I have to bring. I give myself to You."

Then God says, "Here is what I bring to the table. I bring My omniscience. I bring My unlimited power. I bring My grace. I bring My knowledge of the future and My perspective of the present and past. I bring all that I have."

Essentially it would be like a billionaire going into business with a homeless person. That's a pretty good deal. The homeless person will benefit because all the billionaire's resources are now at his or her disposal. But it also means that all of his or her resources (such as they are) will now be at the billionaire's disposal.

When we walk with God, He brings all He has, all He is, to the table...but He also asks us for all we are and all we have. Through all of time and eternity, we are the ones who get the better end of that arrangement!

Friday

Then I looked and heard the voice of many angels, numbering thousands upon thousands, and ten thousand times ten thousand. They encircled the throne and the living creatures and the elders. In a loud voice they sang: "Worthy is the Lamb, who was slain, to receive power and wealth and wisdom and strength and honor and glory and praise!"
(Revelation 5:11-12, NIV)

A number of words in the Bible are translated "worship." The one used the most often means "to bow down and do homage." Another biblical word for worship means "to kiss toward." Put the two words together, and you will have a good idea of what real worship is.

We worship God because He is worthy, bowing down in reverence and respect before Him. But we also "kiss toward" Him, which speaks of tenderness and intimacy.

We ought to be learning all we can about worship, because it will be one of the primary activities of heaven. And Jesus made it clear that there is a right and a wrong way to worship. There is true and false worship.

The Pharisees, who considered themselves the worship gurus of their day, missed the target by a mile. Jesus said of them, "'These people draw near to Me with their mouth, and honor Me with their lips, but their heart is far from Me. And in vain they worship Me, teaching as doctrines the commandments of men'" (Matthew 15:8-9).

Some people are too flippant and casual with God. They seem to think of Him as their celestial Big Buddy and approach Him that way in prayer: "Hey, Lord, how are You doing?" We need to be careful about that. In the Old Testament, God once said to a group of distracted and careless worshipers: "'A son honors his father, and a servant his master. If I am a father, where is the honor due me? If I am a master, where is the respect due me?' says the Lord Almighty" (Malachi 1:6, NIV).

Still others may recognize God as holy and all-powerful and may even tremble before Him, but they don't realize that God wants to be known in an intimate and personal way.

Yes, we are to revere and honor God. But we're also to embrace Him in closeness. We are to engage our hearts, with no hypocrisy. And that's where true worship begins.

Weekend

"Let your light so shine before men, that they may see your good works and glorify your Father in heaven." (Matthew 5:16)

The religious leaders thought they had eliminated the problem when they crucified Jesus. But now, His disciples were preaching and performing miracles. It was as though Jesus had returned. And so He had—in the hearts and lives of His people.

This reminds us that one of the best arguments for the Christian faith is a transformed life. New believers are the best advertising God could have because their lifestyles change, their attitudes change, and even their countenances change. The greatest biography of Jesus is written in the words and actions of His people. Your godly lifestyle is a testimony, just as if you were a walking miracle, like the lame man whom Peter and John healed.

Jesus told us we are to be the light of the world and the salt of the Earth. There is a place to let our lights shine and proclaim the truth of God. And there is a place for us to be salt.

Even if you don't tell people you are a Christian, they will sense something different about you, and they will watch you. As a representative of Christ, you're like a walking light bulb. If you continue to keep a sweet and patient spirit while you're going through times of hardship and suffering, that light will burn even brighter, catching the eyes and the curiosity of even more people.

If you are being the kind of follower of Jesus that God wants you to be, if you are being a "salty" Christian, then your lifestyle will stimulate a thirst for God in others. The greatest compliment is when someone wants to know more, when he or she approaches you and says, "What is it about you?" That is your opportunity to…turn on the light.

One paraphrase of Scripture puts it this way: "Through thick and thin, keep your hearts at attention, in adoration before Christ, your Master. Be ready to speak up and tell anyone who asks why you're living the way you are, and always with the utmost courtesy" (1 Peter 3:15, THE MESSAGE).

Monday

To keep me from getting puffed up, I was given a thorn in my flesh, a
messenger from Satan to torment me and keep me from getting proud.
(2 Corinthians 12:7-9, NLT*)*

Paul's "thorn in the flesh" that he mentions in 2 Corinthians 12 could have been some kind of disability, something he'd been born with. More likely, it was something he incurred later in life as a result of his many beatings, his shipwrecks, or the time he was stoned and left for dead.

Whatever it was, it bothered him greatly—to the point that he asked the Lord to take it away on three separate occasions. Each time, however, the Lord said "no," telling Paul, "My grace is sufficient for you." Effectively Jesus was saying, "Paul, I'm not giving you healing this time. I'm giving you Me. I'm giving you My presence, and that is My answer to you."

Sometimes when we have physical afflictions, the healing will come. By all means pray for it, and pray more than once. Ask the Lord to touch you, heal you, restore you. But there are times in our lives, too, when He will say, "My grace is sufficient." And instead of a healing He will personally be there for you in a unique and sufficient way.

God is with you regardless of what hardship, heartache, or storm you may be enduring right now. You are not alone.

I remember teaching my granddaughter Stella Bible verses when she was only two and a half. One was: "Jesus said, 'I will never leave you or forsake you.'" Stella did pretty well with it, even though she said "forsake" instead of "forsake." I don't think she even understands what it means yet. But that's okay; she is hearing God's Word and getting it into her little heart.

What a truth to hang onto! What a handhold in any storm. He will never leave or forsake you...even when tragedy hits...even when your company downsizes and you get the dreaded pink slip... even when the doctor calls and says, "The test results are back, and I need you to come to my office immediately"...even when the phone rings and someone says, "There's been an accident."

You are not alone. The Lord is standing next to you. He cares. He will be there.

Tuesday

Don't let the world around you squeeze you into its own mould, but let God re-mould your minds from within, so that you may prove in practice that the plan of God for you is good, meets all his demands and moves towards the goal of true maturity. (Romans 12:2, PHILLIPS*)*

Paul could have a calm heart in the middle of the mother of all storms because he knew he in the center of God's will for his life. He was on business for God.

In his prison cell back in Caesarea, Jesus Himself had stood by Paul and said, "Be of good cheer, Paul; for as you have testified for Me in Jerusalem, so you must also bear witness at Rome" (Acts 23:11). Then, in the middle of the storm out at sea, an angel stood by Paul with this message from God: "Do not be afraid, Paul; you must be brought before Caesar...." (Acts 27:24).

Bear witness at Rome... Brought before Caesar....

Paul knew that God would get him to where he was supposed to be—at the right time, in the right place, and with whatever he needed to complete the job at hand. With these things in mind, Paul could even relax in the middle of a hurricane...just before a shipwreck. He knew he had heaven's business to transact in Rome, and he knew that God would get him through any difficulty along the way. He was walking in God's plan, and he could rest in the fact that it was *God's* responsibility to get him through—rough seas or not!

The same is true of our service to the King. No, we aren't assured of smooth sailing, and we're not promised immunity from shipwrecks (or viper bites!) along the way. But we are definitely assured of a safe arrival. Know this: *As long as God has work for us to do here on earth, we will be here to do it.* God will preserve us to do it. And when that work is done, it is done, and He'll bring us home to heaven...not a moment too soon, and not a moment too late.

Wednesday

So take courage! For I believe God. It will be just as he said.
(Acts 27:25, NLT)

I love those words. These aren't the words of a person in denial, but one who is very much in touch with reality. Paul said this as they were still in the storm, still being tossed around like a cork on those massive waves.

The Lord Himself had reassured Paul, and Paul believed in God! This wasn't mind over matter, it was faith over circumstances. Paul was fully convinced of the faithfulness of God, and was sustained by that conviction. I'm reminded of the story in Luke 5:4–5:

> When He had stopped speaking, He said to Simon, "Launch out into the deep and let down your nets for a catch." But Simon answered and said to Him, "Master, we have toiled all night and caught nothing; nevertheless at Your word I will let down the net."

When Simon Peter addressed the Lord, he used a nautical term that could have been translated, "We have toiled all night and caught nothing; nevertheless, *Master or Captain of this boat*, we will do it."

Was he being sarcastic or reverential? Did he really think this "landlubber" rabbi called Jesus would know more about fish and the Sea of Galilee than he did, a seasoned fisherman?

I don't know what his tone of voice might have been as he said those words. But I know this much: When they launched out into the deep, there were so many fish in their nets that the nets began to break and the boat began to sink.

Totally blown away, Peter fell on his knees before Jesus and said, in effect, "Lord, don't waste Your time on me. I'm going to disappoint You and let You down. I'm not going to measure up. Don't even bother with me, Jesus."

And Jesus replied: "Do not be afraid. From now on you will catch men" (v. 10).

Is Jesus the Captain of your boat? Let Him be that for you. Let Him take control. Row where He says to row, fish where He says to fish, and trust Him to get you through the roughest of seas. Jesus was the captain of Paul's boat—*even in the storm*—and that gave Paul complete confidence.

Thursday

And you also were included in Christ when you heard the word of truth, the gospel of your salvation. Having believed, you were marked in him with a seal, the promised Holy Spirit, who is a deposit guaranteeing our inheritance until the redemption of those who are God's possession—to the praise of his glory. (Ephesians 1:13-14, NIV)

What does the Bible mean when it says that we are sealed with the Holy Spirit? In the apostle Paul's day, when goods were shipped from one place to another, they would be stamped with a wax seal, imprinted with the signet ring of the owner. This was a unique mark of ownership. People could look at the crate, see its wax seal, and know they had better not open it.

The same was true with a document from a king. It would be sealed in wax and imprinted with the royal seal. People knew if they opened it and weren't the intended recipient, they might very well be signing their own death warrant.

In the same way, God has put His royal seal on us: "Now He who establishes us with you in Christ and has anointed us is God, who also has sealed us and given us the Spirit in our hearts as a guarantee" (2 Corinthians 1:21-22). The seal is the presence and work of the Holy Spirit in our hearts and lives. Upon our conversion, we are sealed with the Holy Spirit.

Let's say that a thief wanted to steal a briefcase. Then he notices a nametag on it, bearing the name of a famous boxer. Most likely, the thief wouldn't steal that briefcase. Why? He would be afraid of what would happen to him if that famous fighter ever caught up with him. And since he doesn't want to suffer serious bodily harm, he leaves the briefcase alone and looks for an easier target.

In a similar way, the devil wants to come and destroy us as Christians. He wants to wreak havoc in our lives. But he sees our ID tag: "Owned by Jesus Christ. Sealed and insured by the Holy Spirit." So he backs off, because he fears the One to whom we belong.

Friday

*But the Lord is faithful, who will establish you and guard you from the
evil one. (2 Thessalonians 3:3)*

We are living in a time when we love to blame someone or
something else for the things we do. It's convenient to have
a scapegoat—especially when no one likes to take responsibility for
his or her own actions anymore. We can make a million excuses
for our wrong behavior, but we never seem to say, "The problem is
looking back at me in the mirror...I'm responsible for my actions"
or "I have sinned against God."

Tragically, even in the church today, psychology is in many
cases placed on the same level as the Bible (and sometimes above
it). Many in the church know more about self-esteem than they do
about self-denial. They know more about inner healing than they do
about outward obedience. But is low self-esteem the source of our
problems today? Is it the fault of others? Is it our family? Our culture
or upbringing? Global warming? Our excuses are legion.

James gives us the answer, telling bluntly and accurately the source
of our problems: "Where do wars and fights come from among you?
Do they not come from your desires for pleasure that war in your
members? You lust and do not have. You murder and covet and
cannot obtain. You fight and war. Yet you do not have because you do
not ask" (James 4:1-2).

James was saying, "Your problems come from your desire for
pleasure that battles within you." The Bible isn't saying that pleasure
in and of itself is necessarily wrong. There are certain pleasures that
have been given to us by God Himself.

James is warning us about possessing a pleasure-mad mentality...
about making pleasure number one in our lives. He is saying that the
source of our problems lies in a selfish pursuit of pleasure. And then he
points us back to our heavenly Father, who loves us and will meet our
legitimate needs if we humble ourselves to ask Him. James reminds us
that "Every good gift and every perfect gift is from above, and comes
down from the Father of lights, with whom there is no variation or
shadow of turning" (James 1:17).

When we seek Him first, everything else in our lives—including
our wants and desires—begin to fall into line.

Weekend

A man who has friends must himself be friendly, but there is a friend who sticks closer than a brother. (Proverbs 18:24)

We can't choose all of our coworkers. For that matter, we can't choose all the members of our family. But we can choose our friends. And we need to be very careful as we do so.

The apostle Paul wrote: "Do not be misled: 'Bad company corrupts good character'" (1 Corinthians 15:33, NIV). Knowing what an influence a close friend can have on our outlook and our lives, we need to look for godly friends. Look for friends who love God, who will speak the truth to you, who will help to build you up, and who will be godly influences on you.

Shadrach, Meshach, and Abed-Nego, those three Hebrew teenagers we read about in the book of Daniel, appeared to be great friends, supporting one another in times of trial. When everyone else turned against them and everyone else was worshiping a false god, these three stuck together as godly friends, even in the fiery furnace. We need friends like this.

So how do we find out which of our friends are true friends? Here is one way: wholeheartedly commit your life to Jesus Christ, and you will find out who your true friends are. Before I was a Christian, I thought I had a lot of friends. Then when I asked Christ to come into my life, I realized that I didn't have any real friends. They all deserted me, because they had no desire to follow the God I had chosen to follow.

Here's another way to determine who your friends are. These are the ones who will stand by you when a hardship or crisis comes. When trouble rolls in, look to your right and to your left; those standing with you are real friends.

Jesus had a lot of fair-weather friends. They were there when He was doling out bread and fish, speaking words of love and compassion, and sticking it to the Pharisees. But where were they when He was arrested and taken away? They were gone. A true friend will be loyal to the end.

Do you have such a friend? More important, are *you* such a friend?

Monday

"So take courage! For I believe God. It will be just as he said. But we will be shipwrecked on an island". (Acts 27:25-26, NLT)

I love the way that Paul always ended up running everything! There he was, a *prisoner* on a Roman ship, and he ends up giving orders to the centurion and the soldiers (see verse 30-36). They listened to Paul because he spoke as one who had authority beyond his own. Everyone had seen how God was with him.

No matter how desperate or dire his situation, Paul never seemed to be under the control of circumstances. He wrote in Philippians 4:12-13 (TLB), "I know how to live on almost nothing or with everything. I have learned the secret of contentment in every situation, whether it be a full stomach or hunger, plenty or want; for I can do everything God asks me to with the help of Christ who gives me the strength and power."

When the ship beached short of the shoreline, everyone swam to shore or rode the surf in on boards. (Was this the first instance of surfing in human history?) Everyone arrived safely on the beach, exactly as God had promised through Paul.

Paul eventually did make it to Rome. And after a peaceful season under house arrest in rented lodgings in Rome (described in Acts 28), tradition tells us that he ended up in the Mamertine Prison—a cold, dark dungeon with no windows, only a hole through which food could be lowered.

Although it isn't recorded in Scripture, tradition further tells us that Paul finally did receive his audience with the emperor—Caesar Nero—just as the Lord said he would.

As Paul's life came to an end in that black dungeon, he might have found himself looking back on imprisonment after imprisonment, beating after beating, rejection after rejection.

Not Paul! In his final epistle, 2 Timothy, the apostle reflected on a life of triumph and victory. He told Timothy, "You take over. I'm about to die, my life an offering on God's altar. This is the only race worth running. I've run hard right to the finish, believed all the way. All that's left now is the shouting—God's applause!" (4:6-8, THE MESSAGE).

Tuesday

"No one is good—except God alone" (Luke 18:19, NIV)

Why does God allow tragedy? Why does He allow babies to be born with disabilities? Why does He permit wars to rage? If God can prevent such hardships and heartaches, why *doesn't* He?

Here is the classic statement of the problem. Either God is all-powerful but He is not all good, therefore He *doesn't* stop evil. Or He is all good but He is not all-powerful, therefore He *can't* stop evil. And the general tendency is to blame all of the problems of the world on God. To say that God is the one who is somehow responsible.

"If God is so good and loving," people will say, "why does He allow evil?" By even stating it in that way, however, what I'm really saying is that I don't believe God to be good and loving.

By questioning God's goodness and love, I am in essence saying that I know more about it than He does. The fact is, God doesn't *become* good because that's my opinion of Him, or because I happen to personally agree with His actions or His words. Nor does He become good because we vote on it and all agree that is the case.

God is good because God says He is good. And it's not up for a vote.

You see, God is good whether I believe it or not, and He alone is the final court of arbitration. As the apostle Paul said, "Let God be true, and every man a liar" (Romans 3:4, NIV).

What, then, is "good"? *Good is whatever God approves.* And by the same token, bad is exactly what God says is bad. Some might say, "That's circular reasoning," but I would describe it as *biblical* reasoning. The Word of God is our source of truth, defining right and wrong and what our values ought to be.

In Isaiah 1:18 we read: "'Come now, let us reason together,' says the Lord." God is saying, "Here's the way I see things. You need to see it the way that I see it." And He goes on to tell us that His thoughts are above our thoughts and His ways are above our ways.

He IS good. If you don't start there, you'll never get anywhere.

Wednesday

God singled out Satan and said, "What have you been up to?" Satan answered God, "Going here and there, checking things out on earth."
(Job 1:7, THE MESSAGE)

The Bible describes Satan as a roaring lion walking about seeking whom he may devour. He never takes a vacation. He never rests. Wouldn't it be nice if the devil took a day off? A devil-free day! But it isn't going to happen. He doesn't take a day off—or an hour off or even a minute off. When he is defeated, he circles around and comes back for more. If you block him at the front door, he'll try to come in the back door, or sneak in through a window. If keep your doors and windows shut, he'll try to come down through the ceiling or tunnel up through the floor. He is so persistent. He doesn't back off. He is a lion constantly pursuing its prey.

Satan walks to and fro, up and down, constantly sizing things up. He says, "There's a Christian who isolates himself from the other Christians. Maybe I'll go after him." Or, "There's someone filled with pride and arrogance. I know I can bring him down." Or, "Oh, that girl over there looks vulnerable right now. I know how I will defeat her. I'm moving in!"

He is always sizing you up. Always looking for a weakness. Always looking for a vulnerability of some kind.

Jesus called Satan the father of lies. But he also tells the truth sometimes, as in Job 1:9-10: "Yes, but Job has good reason to fear God. You have always put a wall of protection around him and his home and his property. You have made him prosper in everything he does. Look how rich he is!" (NLT). The King James Version translates it this way: "You have put a hedge around him."

This brings us to a very important truth. Despite his heartless, wicked agenda, Satan still has to ask permission before he can touch a child of God. Why? Because of the hedge of protection that God has placed around you as His child.

Satan can't simply ride roughshod over you and do whatever he wants, because God has placed limits on his activities. God knows our breaking point, and He will never give us more than we can take.

Thursday

Even though the fig trees have no blossoms, and there are no grapes on the vine; even though the olive crop fails, and the fields lie empty and barren; even though the flocks die in the fields, and the cattle barns are empty, yet I will rejoice in the Lord! I will be joyful in the God of my salvation. (Habakkuk 3:17–18 NLT)

Today's Scripture from the book of Habakkuk is a magnificent description of a heart that holds on to joy by faith. The prophet looked around him, and knew he was in a season of deep trouble and need. But in spite of all the negative circumstances, he said, "I will rejoice in the Lord. I will be joyful in my God."

Solomon said, "For the happy heart, life is a continual feast" (Proverbs 15:15, NLT). The psalmist wrote that in the presence of God there is fullness of joy, and at His right hand pleasures forevermore (see Psalm 16:11). Jesus said, "My purpose is to give them a rich and satisfying life" (John 10:10, NLT). God wants us to experience joy as believers—not a fickle happiness that depends on circumstances or changes with the wind direction, but a joy that remains in spite of what may be taking place around us.

Anyone can be relatively happy when things are going well. But when you face adversity or sickness or hardship and *then* rejoice, you show that something supernatural has occurred in your life. In fact, you show yourself to be a real Christian. This is a unique trait of believers—that we can rejoice when things go wrong.

How do we do it? We find the key in Philippians 4:4: "Rejoice in the Lord always. Again I will say, rejoice!" Paul didn't say to rejoice in circumstances. Rather, he said to rejoice *in the Lord*. In other words, God is still on the throne. You're still going to heaven. You're still forgiven. God still has a plan for your life; He has not abandoned you. We need to take joy in the Lord always. That is the key. I recognize that in spite of what I may be going through right now, His plans for me are still good. And He will never leave or forsake me.

Friday

He has made everything beautiful in its time. (Ecclesiastes 3:11)

When I look back on my life at the things God has allowed me to do and the opportunities He has opened up, I can see the wisdom of His perfect timing.

Our tendency is to rush things. But just because something has never happened in your life to this point, doesn't necessarily mean it won't happen tomorrow. And just because it doesn't happen tomorrow doesn't mean it won't happen a month or a year from now. Maybe one phase of your life is ending and another is beginning. Maybe everything that has happened to you up to this point in your life has been preparation for what is still ahead.

Moses didn't get going until he was eighty. Wandering out there in the desert of Midian with his little flock of sheep, he probably thought his life was pretty much over. In reality, it was just about to begin.

Then there was Caleb, another Israelite who left Egypt in the Exodus. Along with Joshua, Caleb came back full of optimism and belief when they were sent to spy out the Promised Land. But when the Israelites believed the pessimistic report of the ten other spies, God was so displeased that He refused to allow them to enter the land.

Years later, when Joshua led a new generation of Israelites into the Promised Land, Caleb was among them. And at eighty years old, he said to Joshua, "I'm asking you to give me the hill country that the Lord promised me. You will remember that as scouts we found the Anakites living there in great, walled cities. But if the Lord is with me, I will drive them out of the land, just as the Lord said. So give me this hill country that God promised me. You yourself heard the report, that the Anakim were there with their great fortress cities. If God goes with me, I will drive them out, just as God said." (Joshua 14:12, NLT). Joshua gave him his little segment of land as was promised, and Caleb drove out all of its inhabitants. Caleb believed God's promises, and God was faithful. We need to do the same.

David offered the same advice with these words: "Wait on the Lord; be of good courage, and He shall strengthen your heart; wait, I say, on the Lord! (Psalm 27:14,)

Weekend

The fear of the Lord is the beginning of wisdom; a good understanding have all those who do His commandments. His praise endures forever. (Psalm 111:10)

Even the most committed believer has those moments when fear or worry can kick in. Anxiety can overtake us. Maybe we're concerned about our future, feel discouraged about some of our failures and shortcomings, or find ourselves anxious about the lives of our family members.

But far too often, we are afraid of the wrong things in life, and not afraid of the right things—or the right One. Many people don't fear God, giving Him the awe and the reverence that is His due. Yet the Bible tells us that the fear of the Lord is the very beginning of wisdom.

To fear God doesn't mean that we must cower in terror before Him. Rather, the fear of God has been properly defined as *a wholesome dread of displeasing Him.* So if I have sinned, my fear should not be based on the anticipation of what God will do to me, but on what I have done to displease Him. I love Him so much that I would never, never want to grieve His heart by turning my back on Him or going my own way. That is what it is to fear the Lord.

David wrote, "The fear of the Lord is clean, enduring forever" (Psalm 19:9). It is *good* for us to fear Him. The remarkable thing is that when you fear God, you fear nothing else. On the other hand, if you don't fear God, then you fear everything else, and you find yourself running from shadows.

In another psalm, David stated, "The Lord is the strength of my life; of whom shall I be afraid?" (Psalm 27:1). Only the person who can say, "The Lord is the strength of my life" can then say, "Of whom shall I be afraid?"

Maybe you feel that your life has been a failure, or perhaps find yourself discouraged, depressed, or afraid of something. If you're gripped by fear and worry today, then let the Lord be the strength of your life. Trade in all your lesser and destructive fears for the fear that will bring wisdom and peace.

Monday

There was a man named Job who lived in the land of Uz. He was blameless--a man of complete integrity. He feared God and stayed away from evil. (Job 1:1, NLT)

Job was a man of integrity and character.

Character may be the most important thing in any individual's life. How do you determine character? Here's what it comes down to. When you are all alone, when no one is looking, when there's no one around to impress, what does your life look like? *That* is who you really are. The measure of a man or woman's real character is what they would do if they knew they would never be found out.

What if I could give you a foolproof guarantee that you could get away with a certain sin? Would you do it? Would you cheat on your income taxes? Would you be unfaithful to your spouse? If that is the case, then that is who you most truly are.

It really comes down to what you think about most. What saddens you? What makes you mad? What makes you laugh? That is your character.

Bottom line, Job practiced what he preached. He was a man of true integrity. God Himself said so, and no one could have a higher endorsement than that. In a conversation with Satan—overheard by all the angels—God said, "Have you noticed my servant Job? He is the finest man in all the earth. He is blameless —a man of complete integrity. He fears God and stays away from evil" (Job 1:8, NLT).

If we were honest, you and I would have to say that we spend a lot of time wondering what other people might be saying or thinking about us—how we look, what impression we make, how we come across, and so forth. Job, however, put his relationship with God first, and ran everything in life through that filter. *What would God say about this? How would God feel about that? How would God have me respond to this?*

The Bible has a word for this sort of thinking: It's called "fearing the Lord." It doesn't mean we're afraid of Him and run away when He comes near; it just means that we hold Him in such awe, respect, and love that we fear doing anything that would ever disappoint Him.

Tuesday

Job's sons would take turns preparing feasts in their homes, and they would also invite their three sisters to celebrate with them. When these celebrations ended—sometimes after several days—Job would purify his children. He would get up early in the morning and offer a burnt offering for each of them. For Job said to himself, "Perhaps my children have sinned and have cursed God in their hearts." This was Job's regular practice. (Job 1:4-5, NLT)

Job raised his children in the way of the Lord and brought them before God in prayer every day without fail.

So even when his adult kids were having a celebration, he would pray for them. He would offer a sacrifice on their behalf, which was an Old Testament way of saying he was interceding for them. Here was a dad who was concerned about the spiritual lives of his kids, and prayed every day that they would steer clear of sin and walk with God.

Our kids need our prayers—every day of their lives. Especially in the culture in which we live today. While it's true that we need to work toward releasing our sons and daughters, and launching them into independent, self-sufficient lives, we'll always be their parents, and they will always need Mom and Dad's faithful prayers.

Job was a concerned parent, bringing his family before the Lord, praying for their protection and blessing.

When Scripture says Job prayed for his adult children, it underlines the fact that "this was Job's regular custom." In other words, when it came to prayer, Job wasn't hit-or-miss. He had an established routine of coming before the Lord with his requests.

The Bible says that we should "pray without ceasing"…and "in everything give thanks, for this is the will of God in Christ Jesus concerning you." (I Thessalonians 5:17-18). Does that describe your life? Is God first in your list of priorities? Do you pray for your children? Do you set a godly example for them to follow? You've heard the expression, "The apple doesn't fall far from the tree." That is so often true when it comes to loving the Lord and following Him. Your sons and daughters will take their cues from watching how you relate to God, and the priority you give to your spiritual life.

Wednesday

God said to Satan, "Have you noticed my friend Job? There's no one quite like him—honest and true to his word, totally devoted to God and hating evil." (Job 1:8, THE MESSAGE)

God was so proud of Job He was bragging on him!
When I read that statement and then go on to read what happened to Job immediately after God made it, I feel a little nervous about the idea of God ever bragging on me! I almost feel like saying, "Lord if You're ever feeling proud of me just for a fleeting moment, could we kind of keep it between the two of us?"

I wonder if God would ever boast of His servant Greg, or would boast of you with all the angels standing around. I would tend to doubt it in my case. We often will see ourselves one way—maybe in a quick surface way—while God knows us through and through. Over in the book of 1 Samuel, we're told, "The Lord does not look at the things man looks at. Man looks at the outward appearance, but the Lord looks at the heart" (1 Samuel 16:7, NIV).

You and I can be way off in the way we evaluate one another. We might be in a worship service and find ourselves drawing conclusions about how spiritual that person next to us might be. If he's singing loudly, closing his eyes, and raising his hands up high, we might conclude, "Now that is a spiritual person." Then we look around a little more and see someone else who isn't singing at all. Maybe her head is bowed a little, but she's simply holding the chair in front of her and doesn't seem engaged in the worship. And we conclude, "She's not a very spiritual person. I wonder if she's even a believer."

The truth might be the very opposite of what we think!

We don't know what's going on in the heart of another person. So...we had better leave all such conclusions and evaluations with the Lord Himself, where they actually belong. We need to just concentrate on seeking to live a godly life.

Thursday

"Where have you come from?" the Lord asked Satan.

And Satan answered the Lord, "I have been patrolling the earth, watching everything that's going on." (Job 1:6-7, NLT)

Satan is a powerful spirit being...not a myth, not a cartoon character in a red suit with a pitchfork, and not "the dark side of the force," lacking identity or personality. He is real, and Scripture calls him by name.

We're talking about an active personality with an agenda here, not an impersonal force. Satan has something he very much wants to accomplish.

And what is that? *The devil's single, consuming ambition is to turn you and me away from God and all that is good.* His ultimate agenda can be summed up in the statement of Christ in John 10:10, where Jesus said, "The thief's purpose is to steal and kill and destroy. My purpose is to give them a rich and satisfying life" (NLT).

You can immediately see the contrast. Jesus is in effect saying, "I have come to give you life. Satan has come to give you death. I have come to give you freedom. He has come to give you bondage. I have come to build you up, to save you, to restore you. He has come to steal, kill, and destroy." And that is what he wants to do with *you* to this very day, this very hour.

The devil is very effective at what he does. Never doubt that. Never underestimate his capacity to package his wares, making bad things look good, and good things look bad. He is a master deceiver, and we should never dismiss him or treat him lightly.

Even though we shouldn't become overly preoccupied with our adversary and his activities, it's wise for us to understand his methods of operation. Paul wrote to the Corinthians that they should take a certain course of action "in order that Satan might not outwit us. For we are not unaware of his schemes" (2 Corinthians 2:11, NIV).

Being aware of his schemes and how he operates can help us to effectively resist him. And that is exactly what Scripture tells us to do: "Resist the devil and he will flee from you" (James 4:7, NIV).

Friday

*After all, we don't want to unwittingly give Satan an opening for yet
more mischief—we're not oblivious to his sly ways!
(2 Corinthians 2:11,* THE MESSAGE*)*

On a trip to Alaska some years ago, I went fishing for king
salmon. In one spot, our group used bright orange salmon
eggs as bait. But in another place, we used another type of lure.

In the same way, the devil uses different kinds of bait, different
lures to pull us in. And he works with two close allies in our
temptation: the world and the flesh. Every temptation falls under
one of three categories: the world, the flesh, and the devil. The Bible
says, "For all that is in the world—the lust of the flesh, the lust of the
eyes, and the pride of life—is not of the Father but is of the world"
(1 John 2:16).

When Eve was tempted by the devil at the tree of the knowledge
of good and evil, she faced all these temptations. "So when the
woman saw that the tree was *good for food*, that it was *pleasant to
the eyes*, and a tree *desirable to make one wise*, she took of its fruit
and ate. She also gave to her husband with her, and he ate" (Genesis
3:6, emphasis mine).

The lust of the flesh is the gratification of physical desires. Eve
saw that the tree was good for food. The lust of the eyes is mental
temptation; Eve saw that it was pleasant to the eyes. The pride of
life is a craving for honor; Eve took note that it was desirable to
make one wise.

It's good to recognize that these are the temptation strategies,
or bait, the enemy uses in our lives. In 2 Corinthians 2, the apostle
Paul speaks of pursuing a certain course of action "in order
that Satan might not outwit us. For we are not unaware of his
schemes" (v. 11, NIV).

It helps to know what our enemy is up to, because then we can
avoid his lures…and swim right by every disguised hook.

Weekend

Once Jesus was in a certain place praying. As he finished, one of his
disciples came to him and said, "Lord, teach us to pray, just as John
taught his disciples." He said, "This is how you should pray:
"Father, may your name be kept holy,.
May your Kingdom come soon.
Give us each day the food we need.
And forgive us our sins,
just as we forgive those who sin against us.
And don't let us yield to temptation."
(Luke 11:1-4, NLT)

For prayer to be powerful and effective, there have to be at least a few moments of recognizing the One to whom we are speaking.

"What? Isn't all prayer offered to God?" some might ask.

Not necessarily. I think it's entirely possible to pray and never think of God at all! We can rush into God's presence and rattle off our grocery list as though we were talking to Santa Claus, without even taking a moment to contemplate Who it is we are addressing. Often in prayer, there is little thought of God Himself. Instead, our mind is taken up with what we need—or think we need.

Jesus gave us a model prayer that we call the Lord's Prayer. In reality, the Bible doesn't call it that. It could be more accurately called the Disciple's Prayer, because one day the disciples came to Jesus and said, "Lord, teach us to pray, just as John taught his disciples." Notice they didn't say, "Lord, teach us *a prayer.*" Rather, they said, *"Teach us to pray."*

Some people will attach a mystical significance to the reciting of this prayer. They view it as sort of the big-gun prayer to pull out when all else fails. But this isn't a prayer that Jesus gave as much as it was a *model* for praying. No, there's nothing wrong with praying the Lord's Prayer. If you choose to pray it as it is written, that's fine, as long as it's coming from your heart. But more importantly, it's a prayer that gives us a guide to all prayers that we would offer to God.

Check it out! Let every sentence of this prayer—beginning with "Our Father in heaven, hallowed be Your name"—be a launching point to lead you into deeper conversation with the God who loves you.

Monday

No temptation has overtaken you except such as is common to man; but God is faithful, who will not allow you to be tempted beyond what you are able; but with the temptation will also make the way of escape, that you may be able to bear it. (1 Corinthians 10:13)

There is always a way out. There is always a back door. Sometimes it's even the front door, or perhaps a window. You may think you're trapped and that there is no way out of Satan's web. But there always is! The enemy may harass you, but he can never exceed what God in His grace and wisdom allows.

On one occasion Satan came asking for permission to assault Simon Peter. Jesus turned to the fisherman and said, essentially, "Simon, Simon, Satan has been asking for you by name that you would be taken out of the care and protection of God."

It's interesting that Satan asked specifically for Peter. Has he ever asked for me by name? I doubt it. I don't know that I have ever been tempted by the devil himself.

Let me explain. I have certainly been hit with temptations orchestrated by the devil, but Satan can only be in one place at one time. Sometimes we think of him as roughly God's equal, only on the dark side. We know that God is all-powerful, all-knowing, and everywhere-present, and we may imagine Satan to have similar attributes.

He doesn't. The devil is not God's equal. The devil is a powerful spirit being, but he has limitations. He can't be all over the world tempting and harassing everyone at the same time. That's why he employs his vast army of demons. So even though Satan himself may have never tried to tempt me and drag me down, he's had lots of help over the years.

In the case of Peter, however, the devil didn't want to trust an attack to one of his underlings. He came knocking himself. Peter was a big fish, and a direct threat to Satan's kingdom.

Immediately aware of Satan's designs, Jesus warned Peter, assuring him, "I have prayed for you, Peter, that your faith would not fail" (see Luke 22:31-32).

Jesus prays for you, too. He is your Advocate, and speaks in your defense when the evil one tries to slander you before the Father.

Tuesday

Let us then approach the throne of grace with confidence, so that we may receive mercy and find grace to help us in our time of need.
(Hebrews 4:16, NIV)

In the first chapter of Job, Satan says to God, in essence, "Job fears You, God, because You give him a lot of wonderful possessions. But if you took it all away, he wouldn't fear You anymore. In fact, he would curse You to your face. I can prove it to You, if You let me."

The Lord replies, "All right. But you can't touch him physically. Only those things that belong to him." Obviously, that's a loose paraphrase. But it does give us a clear picture of Satan in his role "the accuser of the brethren."

Here's what that might look like in our lives. First, the devil whispers in your ear, "Go ahead and do it. You'll get away with it. No one will ever know. It'll be fun." So you do whatever it is he is enticing you to do. Then he comes back to you and says, "Why you pathetic, miserable, hypocrite! What a loser you are! You're worthless. God doesn't love you anymore, and your salvation is out the window. Don't show your ugly face in the church again. And don't even think about praying or reading the Bible!"

It's very easy to fall for this. And we find ourselves with our chin on our chest, kicking dirt, and saying, "Oh Lord, I failed You. I'm not worthy to worship You and speak for You."

But wait. Hold on a minute here. You were *never* worthy. None of us are. Even on your best day when you were doing everything right and didn't commit any sins that you knew of, you weren't even close to "worthy" on that day.

The devil doesn't want you to know that. He wants you to think, "Well, I've got to work my way back to God. I've got to do a bunch of good things if I'm going to approach the Lord in prayer." But that's a lie!

You can approach God *any* time based on the sacrifice of Jesus on the cross, and His shed blood for you. It has never been about my worthiness. It has always been about His grace extended to me.

Wednesday

Your sons and daughters were eating and drinking wine in their oldest brother's house, and suddenly a great wind came from across the wilderness and struck the four corners of the house, and it fell on the young people, and they are dead...! (Job 1:18-19)

On a dark day when Job lost everything, the darkest news of all was that his children had all been killed. Seven sons and three daughters. Wiped out in a moment.

As my wife and I can attest, the death of a child is the worst thing that can happen to a mother or a father. No parent ever wants to outlive his or her children. We spend our lives caring for them, nurturing them, loving them, and investing our hopes and dreams in them. For most loving fathers and mothers, to lose a child is a fate literally worse than death.

Satan had challenged God, saying, "You just let me take away the things he holds dear and then see how loyal and faithful Job will be. He'll curse You to Your face!"

The Lord granted Satan permission to turn Job's world upside down—within limits. The evil one would not be allowed to lay a finger on Job himself.

And how did Job fare in that attack? Did he curse God as Satan suggested? No. He praised God. *"The Lord gave me what I had, and the Lord has taken it away. Praise the name of the Lord!"* (Job 1:21, NLT)

We have much to learn from this story of Job. In his letter to the church, the apostle James wrote, "As you know, we consider blessed those who have persevered. You have heard of Job's perseverance and have seen what the Lord finally brought about. The Lord is full of compassion and mercy" (James 5:11 NIV).

Persevere. That's the key word here. The book of Job teaches us how to hang in there when we go through heartaches and hard times. Because it's not a matter of *if* some kind of calamity, trial, sickness, or difficulty will strike you or someone you love. It's a matter of *when*.

And even if you feel you don't have the strength to hang on, God will give you that strength, too. Strength for yourself...and strength for those who need you most.

Thursday

For the message of the cross is foolishness to those who are perishing, but to us who are being saved it is the power of God. (1 Corinthians 1:18)

A true story was reported about a couple visiting a jewelry store. As the jeweler showed them various cross necklaces, the woman commented, "I like these, but do you have any without this little man on them?"

That's what so many people want today: a cross without Jesus. They want a cross without any offense…one that will look cool with their outfits. But if we could travel back in time and see the cross in its original context, we would realize that it was a bloody and vile symbol. It would have been the worst picture imaginable to see someone hanging on a cross.

The Romans chose crucifixion because it was meant to be a slow, brutal, torturous way to die. It was designed not only to kill someone, but to utterly humiliate them as they died. Crucifixions outside Roman cities served as warnings to anyone who would dare oppose the rule of Rome.

If there was any other way, do you think that God would have allowed His Son to suffer like this? If there had been any other way we could have been forgiven, then God surely would have found it. If living a good moral life would get us to heaven, then Jesus never would have died for us. But He did, because there was, and is, no other way. He had to pay the price for our sin. At the cross, Jesus purchased the salvation of the world.

Listen to the apostle Paul's description of the divine transaction that took place in those terrible moments when Jesus suffered for our sins: "God made you alive with Christ, for He forgave all our sins. He canceled the record of the charges against us and took it away by nailing it to the cross.. In this way, God disarmed the spiritual rulers and authorities. He shamed them publicly by his victory over them on the cross" (Colossians 2:13-15, NLT).

If you were ever tempted to doubt God's love for you, even for a moment, then take a long, hard look at the cross. Nails did not hold Jesus to that cross. His love did.

Friday

"But he who received seed on the good ground is he who hears the word and understands it, who indeed bears fruit and produces: some a hundredfold, some sixty, some thirty." (Matthew 13:23)

The concept of bearing fruit is used often in Scripture. In the Gospels, Jesus told the story of a sower who went out to sow seed. The seed fell on various types of ground. Some of the ground was rocky and hard. Other ground was receptive, but weeds choked out the seed. But there was a portion of ground that was neither rocky nor weedy, and in that soil the seed took root. Jesus said that this was a picture of the different people who hear the gospel. Those who are true believers will bring forth fruit (see Luke 8:4-15).

What is bearing fruit? Essentially, it is becoming like Jesus. Spiritual fruit will show itself in our lives as a change in our character and outlook. As we spend time with Jesus and get to know Him better, His thoughts will become our thoughts. His purpose will become our purpose. We will become like Jesus.

The Bible gives an excellent description of a life characterized by the fruit of the Spirit. Galatians 5:22-23 says, "But what happens when we live God's way? He brings gifts into our lives, much the same way that fruit appears in an orchard—things like affection for others, exuberance about life, serenity. We develop a willingness to stick with things, a sense of compassion in the heart, and a conviction that a basic holiness permeates things and people. We find ourselves involved in loyal commitments, not needing to force our way in life, able to marshal and direct our energies wisely" (THE MESSAGE).

Is that what others see in your life? If not, then either you don't know God or you are living outside of fellowship with Him. If that is the case, then a commitment or a recommitment to Him would be in order. God isn't asking for a perfect life. But He is asking that these fruits be primary characteristics of a life that is lived for Him.

Weekend

A man's pride will bring him low, but the humble in spirit will retain honor. (Proverbs 29:23)

God hates a proud look. That's interesting to me. I would expect God to start the list of things He hates with "hands that shed innocent blood," or adultery, maybe. But no. Number one on His list is *a proud look* (see Proverbs 6:16-19).

Why is this such a big deal? After all, in our culture today, pride is seen as a virtue. Right? We hear it on all sides. Be proud, we're told. Be proud of your heritage. Be proud of who you are.

But the Bible says that God hates a proud look. What does this mean? Well, a proud look speaks of a person who would want his or her will above the will of God and the will of others. It speaks of people who are arrogant and full of themselves. When push comes to shove, these individuals will always consult their own needs, wants, desires, and good before they consider anyone else's needs, wants, desires, and good.

Our culture thinks that's natural. Maybe even healthy. But our God and Creator *hates* it.

Did you know that pride was the first sin ever committed? Even before Adam and Eve ate the forbidden fruit, Lucifer committed the sin of pride—from which all other sin in the universe eventually grew. Lucifer wasn't satisfied to be an angel serving the Lord. He wanted to be God. And God banished him because of his pride.

So what did he do? He tempted Eve with the forbidden fruit. He basically said, "Go ahead and eat of it, Eve, because when you eat of it, you will be as a god, knowing good and evil. You will know more than everyone else" (see Genesis 3:5). What was he appealing to? Her pride. And she gave in.

You see, pride is probably at the root of most of the problems in our culture today. It is probably at the root of so many of our sins today. When we say, "I don't need to live God's way. I will do what I want to do when I want to do it," that is pride. The world may cheer Frank Sinatra belting out "I did it my way," but those sentiments will draw no applause from heaven.

God hates a proud look. So let's not put our will above the will of God.

Monday

[When I think of the wisdom and scope of God's plan], "I fall to my knees and pray to the Father, the Creator of everything in heaven and on earth." (Ephesians 3:14-15, NLT)

Why does God even allow Satan to exist? Have you ever wondered that? As the evil one says in his own words, he is restlessly going back and forth across the earth, looking for trouble…looking for lives to ruin…looking for saints to trip up. Why does God allow him to carry on? Why doesn't the Lord just take him out, as He could in a nanosecond.

You might be surprised to know that Satan, in his own twisted way, serves the purposes of God. You ask, *How in the world could that be?*

Just consider this. Satan unwittingly played a major role in the cross of Christ. In his enduring hatred for God's Son, the devil thought it would be a great idea to have Jesus betrayed, arrested, beaten within an inch of His life, and then crucified and put to death on a Roman cross.

Everything went according to Satan's plan. As Jesus told the mob who came to apprehend him, *"This is your moment, the time when the power of darkness reigns." (Luke 22:53, NLT)*.

The power of darkness did indeed reign that day, and Satan's plan succeeded. But so did the plan of God! What the evil one didn't realize was that it was the Father's plan all along that the Messiah would die for the sins of the world. In the prophecy of Isaiah, we're told, "It was the Lord's will to crush him and cause him to suffer." (Isaiah 53:10, NIV). Unaware that he was making the biggest blunder since his rebellion against God, Satan played into the plan and purpose of God when, in his rage and hatred, he inspired Judas Iscariot to betray Jesus for 30 pieces of silver (Zechariah 11:12-13).

Satan's "best shot" against God and the people of God was the crucifixion of the God-man, Jesus Christ. And in that act he unwittingly not only sealed his own doom, he opened the door for Jesus to offer redemption and salvation to the whole world.

Remember then, if you hold onto God and trust Him through the dark times, Satan's best shots against you will also end up working for your good…and God's glory.

Tuesday

When they saw Job from a distance, they scarcely recognized him.
Wailing loudly, they tore their robes and threw dust into the air over
their heads to show their grief. Then they sat on the ground with him
for seven days and nights. And no one said a word, for they saw that his
suffering was too great for words. (Job 2:12-13, NLT)

Let's think about Job's situation. Here he is. He has lost his
possessions. He has lost his children. He has lost his health.
He might have wished he had lost his wife after she told him to
"curse God and die," but she was still around, which only added his
misery. And on top of all that, he has broken out in ugly, painful
boils. The one-time wealthiest, most influential man of his world
was reduced to sitting on an ash heap, scraping his scabs with
fragments of a broken pot.

About that time, company showed up.

The Bible names three friends who came to "sympathize with
him and comfort him" (Job 2:11, NIV). As it turned out, Job would
have been better off if these guys had just stayed home.

These three counselors apparently traveled a great distance, and
when they arrived at Job's residence and caught sight of their old
friend huddled out back on top of an ash heap, they were shocked
right down to their sandals.

Shaken and appalled, "no one said a word." They simply sat with
their friend in companionable silence for a long time. It was the
perfect thing to do, and "just what the doctor ordered."

We need to learn from this example. When you spend time with
someone who is suffering or grieving, don't feel that you necessarily
need to say something "wise and profound," or try to explain
the situation. To begin with, you don't know enough to explain
anything, because that knowledge lies with God alone. And besides
that, explanations have never healed a broken heart.

Sometimes the best thing to do is just be there, and say absolutely
nothing. It is your *presence* that speaks

Wednesday

Then Jesus brought them to an olive grove called Gethsemane, and he said, "Sit here while I go over there to pray." He took Peter and Zebedee's two sons, James and John, and he became anguished and distressed. He told them, "My soul is crushed with grief to the point of death. Stay here and keep watch with me." (Matthew 26:36-38, NLT)

Facing imminent arrest and crucifixion, Jesus waited through the night with His disciples in the Garden of Gethsemane. To His three closest companions, Peter, James, and John, He said, "Stay here with Me for awhile and watch with Me."

Watch with Me.

He didn't ask for a sermon, He didn't want an explanation, and He wasn't looking for someone to step in and fix His situation. In His humanity and sorrow, He just wanted a few friends around, to be with Him.

When someone is hurting, you just need to go to them. One of the best things you can say is, "I don't know what to say." Then take your own advice and don't say anything! If you do say something, keep it simple. *"I love you…I'm here for you…I'm praying for you."*

Most of the time, words aren't all that important anyway. I have found that by simply showing up—showing love, and a readiness to listen—I've been able to bring comfort to the grieving.

Years ago, a man I know lost his daughter in a car accident. A month passed, and I happened to find myself in a room with him and a group of other guys. But even though everyone there knew about his daughter, they all tiptoed around the subject. No one said a thing to him or even approached him. It's almost as though he was being punished for suffering.

Why did these men hold back? They may have thought, *Well, if I say anything it might be real uncomfortable. He might even cry.* So no one was willing to even broach the subject.

I remembering thinking to myself, *Something needs to be said.*

So I took him aside, and just bumbled out the words, "I am so sorry about what happened to your daughter."

He looked me in the eyes and said, "Thank you for mentioning it," and began to open up. He just wanted someone to talk to!

Thursday

I don't mean to say I am perfect. I haven't learned all I should even yet, but I keep working toward that day when I will finally be all that Christ saved me for and wants me to be. (Philippians 3:12, TLB)

There is a sign along an airport runway that says, "Keep moving. If you stop, you are in danger and a danger to those who are flying." The same could be said of Christians. We always need to keep moving forward spiritually. We can't rest on our laurels, or take time to make a scrapbook of our press clippings.

Even the apostle Paul said he couldn't live off his past experiences. He needed to maintain his forward momentum. Here was one of the greatest Christians of all time saying that he still didn't have the Christian life wired. He was saying, "I haven't arrived at some higher supernatural plane, unattainable to other believers. I have so far to go."

If anybody ever knew God, it was the apostle Paul. He had led countless people to faith, established multiple churches, and ended up writing much of our New Testament. Yet he said of himself that he had so much to learn and so much ground to cover.

Imagine Paul sitting around with a group of Christians. One person might say, "God inspired me to say something to someone today. It was wonderful." Another might say, "I heard God speak to my heart once."

Paul could say, "God gave me inspired letters to write that will make up half the Bible. Also, I've actually died and gone to heaven, and then I was sent back to Earth again."

Who could top that? If anyone could boast, it was Paul. Yet he didn't. He said, "It's been a long road and a bumpy road, and I've still got a long ways to go." He even said of himself, "For I am the least worthy of all the apostles, and I shouldn't even be called an apostle at all after the way I treated the church of God" (1 Corinthians 15:9, TLB).

So through all of his life, right up until his date with the Roman executioner, Paul kept looking ahead and seeking to move down the trail. And having been to heaven once, he was as happy as he could be to go back…this time to stay.

Friday

You see, at just the right time, when we were still powerless, Christ died for the ungodly. Very rarely will anyone die for a righteous man, though for a good man someone might possibly dare to die. But God demonstrates his own love for us in this: While we were still sinners, Christ died for us. (Romans 5:6-8, NIV)

Two men camping in the forest were enjoying their morning coffee when they suddenly spotted a very large, hungry grizzly bear lumbering toward them. One of the men quickly pulled on his running shoes. "Do you actually think you can outrun that grizzly bear?" his friend asked.

"I don't need to," he replied. "All I have to do is outrun you."

We've all had friends like that, haven't we? At the first threat of danger, hardship, or difficulty, they're out the back door. So what makes for true friendship? It has been said that a true friend is one who walks in when others walk out. Thankfully, there have been people in my life who have stood by me and have been honest friends. But there's one thing of which I'm confident: I have found a true and loyal friend in Jesus Christ.

Jesus Christ offers His friendship to us. In fact, the New Testament goes so far as to say we have been *called* by God the Father into fellowship with His Son (see 1 Corinthians 1:9). But is it all one way? Do we really expect a friendship without a response on our part? A genuine relationship, obviously, is made up of two people committing themselves to one another. I can extend friendship to you, but until you return it to me, I can't legitimately say we're really friends.

Jesus demonstrated His willingness to have a friendship with us by what He did for us. He said, "Greater love has no one than this, than to lay down one's life for his friends" (John 15:13).

Jesus forever proved just how dedicated He was to us when He did just that.

Weekend

Blessed be the God and Father of our Lord Jesus Christ, who according to His great mercy has caused us to be born again to a living hope through the resurrection of Jesus Christ from the dead, to obtain an inheritance which is imperishable and undefiled and will not fade away, reserved in heaven for you, who are protected by the power of God through faith for a salvation ready to be revealed in the last time. (1 Peter 1:3-5, NASB)

A couple from Chicago was planning a vacation to a warmer climate, but the wife couldn't join her husband until the next day, because she was on a business trip. Her husband scribbled down her e-mail address on a little scrap of paper, but upon his arrival, he discovered that he had lost it. He wanted to send off a quick e-mail to let her know he had arrived safely. So trying his best to remember her e-mail address, he composed a brief message and sent it off.

Unfortunately, his e-mail didn't reach his wife. Instead, it went to a grieving widow who had just lost her husband, a preacher, the day before. She had gone to her computer and was checking her e-mail when she let out a loud shriek and fainted on the spot. Her family came rushing in to see what was on the screen: "Dearest wife, I just checked in. Everything is prepared for your arrival tomorrow. P.S. It sure is hot down here!"

The good news is that because of the death and resurrection of Jesus Christ, we don't have to be afraid of that place that's "hot down there." In fact, we don't even have to fear death. Because Christ died and rose again, we know that for us as believers, there is life beyond the grave.

If that were all the resurrection did for us, if all that Christianity offered was the hope of life beyond the grave, it would still be worth it a million times over to be a Christian.

But there is a whole lot more that the resurrection has for us— more in this lifetime! Our risen Lord will give us a new heart and put a new spirit within us (see Ezekiel 36:26). He will give us new knowledge, new comfort, new peace, and a new life in Him.

Monday

Rejoice with those who rejoice, and weep with those who weep.
(Romans 12:15)

Yes, people who are grieving may cry when you speak to them. That's all right! Weeping is part of the mourning process. When you have lost someone—a spouse, a parent, or a child—you don't want their passing to be simply swept under the rug. You don't want that loved one to be forgotten.

Many times, simply because they don't want to be uncomfortable, be rejected, or look silly, people keep their distance from those who grieve. Or if they do spend time with that individual, they will steer clear of mentioning the one who died.

That's no comfort at all. The grieving spouse or parent wants that loved one to be remembered. Sometimes you can simply say something like, "I miss John. I wish he was here with us right now. But thank God we will see him again in heaven."

We have to give people—even fellow believers—time and room to grieve their loss. Sometimes we might say, "She's with the Lord now. She's happier than she's ever been. Don't cry."

What do you mean, "Don't cry"? That's holding people to a higher standard than even the Lord does! The Bible says there is a time to laugh and a time to mourn. Even Jesus wept at the tomb of His dear friend, Lazarus. In the book of Acts, after Stephen was stoned to death by a violent mob, we read that devout men wept over him. It's okay to weep when you lose someone. But as Scripture says, we do not "grieve like the rest of men, who have no hope" (1 Thessalonians 4:15, NIV). We *do* have hope. We have strong, unquenchable hope that we will be with our saved loved ones in heaven, and share eternity together.

Job's comforters always get a bad rap, and deservedly so, but just remember something: *At least they got it right in the beginning.* They wept with their friend, kept their mouths closed, and sat with him on the ground for *seven days* before they said anything. We think we're being a martyr if we sit with someone for seven minutes. At least initially, Job's friends did the right thing. And it must have a real comfort to their broken friend.

Tuesday

When all kinds of trials and temptations crowd into your lives my brothers, don't treat them as intruders, but as friends. Realize that they come to test your faith and produce in you a quality of endurance. And let that process go on until that endurance is fully developed. And you will find you have become men of mature character, men of integrity, with no weak spots. (James 1:2-4, PHILLIPS)

Suffering makes us strong.

God allows hardship in our life so that our beliefs—those handholds of faith in a troubled world—will became more and more real to us, and less and less theory. We can start living out our faith-life in the real world.

I'm reminded of all the people you see on the road these days driving those gleaming new SUVs. Most of these fancy rigs have 4x4 capabilities. In other words, you could drive them through the mud or power up some rocky track up a mountainside.

But how many people really do that? Some guys brag to their buddies, and say, "Yeah, just look at this thing. Look at what it can do. I could drive this baby up the side of a building."

"Well," someone might ask, "do you want to go out in the dirt?"

"Are you kidding? Do you know how much I paid for this thing? There's no way! In fact, I was just on the way to the car wash."

So they never want to actually use that vehicle for its intended purpose—what it was actually designed to do.

We can be that way with our beliefs. We talk about believing this and believing that, and the truths we hold dear. But I can hear God saying to us, "You know, you have a lot of really great beliefs. You talk about them all the time. You talk about how you believe I can provide for your every need. Okay. Let Me put you in a situation where you have no other resources and really *have* to trust Me for that provision."

You see, God can allow these hardships and trials and shortfalls in our lives so that we will exercise our sometimes-flabby faith muscles, and step out on trust alone. We need to transfer our faith from the realm of theory to in-the-trenches reality.

Wednesday

But at midnight Paul and Silas were praying and singing hymns to God,
and the prisoners were listening to them. (Acts 16:25)

A ny fool can be happy and peaceful when the sun shines down
from a blue and cloudless sky. But when those qualities shine
out from the midst of a dark and destructive storm, that's another
matter entirely.

It is a powerful testimony when a believer can praise God
while suffering. Remember the story of Paul and Silas, arrested for
preaching the gospel in the city of Philippi? The Bible tells us that the
jailer had them stripped and flogged—a punishment so severe some
people didn't even survive it. Then they were put in a dungeon, where
their feet were fastened in stocks, causing excruciating pain.

So there they were in this hellhole, this dungeon, and they hadn't
done a thing to merit such terrible punishment! How did they
respond? They "prayed and sang hymns to God." And their fellow
prisoners were listening!

That word "listened" could be translated *listened with great
interest*. Why? Because they had never heard anybody sing praises
to God in such a place. And that's about the time the Lord sent an
earthquake, "At once all the prison doors flew open, and everybody's
chains came loose. The jailer woke up, and when he saw the prison
doors open, he drew his sword and was about to kill himself because
he thought the prisoners had escaped. But Paul shouted, "Don't harm
yourself! We are all here!" (Acts 16:26-28, NIV)

The Philippian jailer responded by saying, "Sirs, what must I do to
be saved?" In effect he was saying, "I've been watching you guys. I've
seen how you have taken such terrible punishment without cursing.
I've seen how you can worship in the worst circumstances, and how
you could have escaped but didn't. All I can say is, whatever you have,
I want it."

Your circumstances may not be as dire as those of Paul and Silas.
But never doubt it, people are watching you. If you're in the midst of
a hardship or a difficulty, they're watching to see how you hold up, if
you will really practice what you preach, and if you will live out what
you proclaim. The way you handle suffering in your life can bring
great glory to God.

Thursday

You have turned for me my mourning into dancing; You have put off my sackcloth and clothed me with gladness. (Psalm 30:11)

It has been said that the best cure for hedonism is an attempt to practice it.

If you chase after pleasure, you will eventually come to the same conclusion as King Solomon: "I said to myself, 'Come now, be merry; enjoy yourself to the full.' But I found that this, too, was futile. For it is silly to be laughing all the time; what good does it do?" (Ecclesiastes 2:1-2, TLB).

The Bible tells us that if the driving desire of our lives is to please ourselves, that very quest will be the source of endless problems and heartaches. "What is causing the quarrels and fights among you? Don't they come from the evil desires at war within you? You want what you don't have, so you scheme and kill to get it. You are jealous of what others have, but you can't get it, so you fight and wage war to take it away from them. Yet you don't have what you want because you don't ask God for it." (James 4:1-2, NLT).

It comes down to this: If you live for yourself and your own happiness and pleasure, then you will be a miserable person. It's ironic that the people who live for happiness never find it, while the people who live for God find happiness as a byproduct. The people who chase after pleasure never really experience it. They may find little bits here and there, but nothing to speak of. Certainly nothing enduring. Yet the people who live for God experience the ultimate pleasure—a joy that bubbles up from deep down in the inmost being.

Pleasure isn't a bad thing in itself, although you might get that impression from some Christians. I think the Christian life is the most pleasurable life around. Why? Because God is the creator of light and laughter and joy…beginning here and now, and stretching on into eternity. The Bible teaches, "You have made known to me the path of life; you will fill me with joy in your presence, with eternal pleasures at your right hand" (Psalm 16:11, NIV).

Cheap thrills are a dime a dozen. True and lasting happiness comes from the hand of God.

Friday

Remember, dear brothers and sisters, that few of you were wise in the world's eyes or powerful or wealthy when God called you. Instead, God chose things the world considers foolish in order to shame those who think they are wise. And he chose things that are powerless to shame those who are powerful. (1 Corinthians 1:26-27, NLT)

In many ways, we have lost the meaning of the word "hero." We throw it around so casually. If you can put a ball through a hoop, you're a sports hero. If you can play eight chords on a guitar, you're a rock' n roll hero. If you can pretend to be something you're not, you're a Hollywood hero. We have a strange concept as to who our heroes really are.

I remember watching a well-known journalist interview an actor about his recent movie, which featured a politically troubled region of the world. When the journalist asked the celebrity what he thought should be done about the political situation there, the actor responded, "Who cares what I think?" and went on to point out that he was just an actor. All too often, we mistakenly think actors really are the people they portray. We think they are heroes when, in fact, they're just people like you and me.

A hero is someone who does something sacrificial, something courageous. There are heroes today, of course. We saw many of them in action on 9/11 and in the days that followed. But often, today's heroes are operating behind the scenes and we never know about them.

As we look at heroes of the faith, those in Scripture and in contemporary history whom God put His hand on, one thing stands out. It seems that God has always gone out of His way to find individuals who did not necessarily look like heroes. And that is precisely the point. God isn't looking for a strong man or woman per se. The psalmist writes: "He takes no pleasure in the strength of a horse or in human might. No, the Lord's delight is in those who fear him, those who put their hope in his unfailing love." (Psalm 147:10-11, NLT).

God is looking for someone who will walk in His strength, no matter what. When He finds that man, that woman, it fills His heart with delight.

Weekend

Stephen, a man full of God's grace and power, performed amazing miracles and signs among the people. But one day some men from the Synagogue of Freed Slaves, as it was called, started to debate with him. They were Jews from Cyrene, Alexandria, Cilicia, and the province of Asia. None of them could stand against the wisdom and the Spirit by which Stephen spoke. (Acts 6:8-10, NLT)

If there is one consistent quality we can see in the lives of men and women God used in the pages of Scripture, it is *faithfulness*. Paul wrote to Timothy: "Be strong in the grace that is in Christ Jesus. And the things that you have heard from me among many witnesses, commit these to faithful men who will be able to teach others also" (2 Timothy 2:1-2). Jesus said, "He who is faithful in what is least is faithful also in much; and he who is unjust in what is least is unjust also in much" (Luke 16:10).

Right now, you may be at a place in life where nothing seems to be happening. You might be thinking, *Lord, come on! Use me. Call on me. I'll turn this world upside down for You.* But the Lord may be saying, "My son, My daughter, you're not ready yet. I have to prepare you first. Be faithful to do what I have set before you today, to the best of your ability."

That's what Stephen did in Acts 6. As a newly appointed deacon, his job was to serve tables. Notice the church leaders didn't say, "Stephen, go out and do miracles and then go preach the gospel to the Sanhedrin. While you're preaching, a guy named Saul of Tarsus will hear you. He ultimately will be converted, and will become the greatest preacher in the history of the church." Instead, Stephen waited on tables. And as the Lord found him faithful in the little things, He gave him more responsibility.

You can never be too small for God to use; only too big. We need to be faithful in what God has set before us. Because if we're not faithful in the little things, then we won't be faithful in greater things, either.

Monday

"Though he slay me, yet will I trust in him." (Job 13:15, KJV)

Sometimes, God will glorify Himself by the way you and I lean on Him and trust Him through our suffering and hardships. At other times, He will glorify Himself by simply removing those things.

He doesn't always say "no," and He doesn't always say "wait." Sometimes, He steps in immediately, bringing help, wisdom, comfort, and provision. I've seen that happen many, many times in my life and ministry.

The gospel of John tells the story of Jesus and His disciples encountering a man who had been blind from birth. The disciples asked their Master, "Why was this man born blind? Was it because of his own sins or his parents' sins?" (John 9:2, NLT).

It sounds a little like a rehash of the accusations Job's counselors tossed out at him, doesn't it? *"Whose fault was this? Why is he sick? Who committed this sin?"* In fact, it may not have anything to do with personal sin. Godly people can suffer, too, and still be right in the middle of God's good plans and purposes.

Jesus had a strong answer for the disciples when they asked, "Who sinned, this man or his parents, that he was born blind?"

"'It was not because of his sins or his parents' sins,' Jesus answered. 'This happened so the power of God could be seen in him'" (John 9:3, NLT).

God wanted to display His power by healing this man—as He did when He raised Lazarus from the dead. But we must also recognize that there are times when God will choose *not* to heal the blind, raise the dead, or do what we plead with Him to do through our anguish and tears.

And it is then that we must trust Him.

It is then that we must do what Job did when his whole world fell apart. He said, "Praise the name of the Lord." He didn't say, "I understand this, I understand You." He simply said, "Lord, I trust You."

Job lived a real life in real time, and in the midst of his suffering, he couldn't read the end of his own story to see how things would turn out. Yet he said, "Praise the name of the Lord." And so must we.

Tuesday

"I am nothing—how could I ever find the answers? I lay my hand upon my mouth in silence. I have said too much already." (Job 40:4-5, TLB)

We can ask God "why" anytime we want to. But I don't know if we will really be satisfied with His answers.

If God came down to you on a shining cloud and explained His purposes to you, would it really make it any better? I don't know that it would. As far as we know, Job was never given the "why" of all the tragedies that befell him. But He was given an incredible revelation of God's wisdom and power.

When Jesus was in great agony, dying on the cross for our sins, and He cried out, "My God, My God, why have You forsaken Me?" (Matthew 27:46). He did ask "why?" But notice that He prefaced it with, "My God, My God." It wasn't an accusation against the Father. Jesus was merely stating the reality of what was taking place in those awful hours, as all of the sin of the world was being placed upon Him who had known no sin. And as the Father turned His holy face away, the Son cried out, "Why have You forsaken Me?"

The fact is, Jesus was forsaken that I might be forgiven. But even in His great cry of grief and loneliness over His separation from the Father, as He bore the sins of the world for all time, Jesus still said, *"My God, My God...."* There was complete trust in the Lord.

You might say, "Well, I have a lot of questions for God. When I get to heaven I'm going to ask Him some things. In fact, I've got a list."

You just keep that list with you. Take it with you everywhere you go, and then if you die unexpectedly, you'll have it handy to pull out and ask God when you stand before Him.

Somehow, I don't think that's the way it will be. I suggest to you that when you arrive in heaven, when you see your Creator, your God, your Savior in all His blazing glory, you'll forget all about your little list of questions. One commentator wrote, "I had a million questions to ask God, but when I met Him, they all fled my mind and it didn't seem to matter."[9]

Wednesday

Being confident of this, that he who began a good work in you will carry it on to completion until the day of Christ Jesus. (Philippians 1:6, NIV)

God will sometimes allow suffering in our lives to prepare us for a special task out ahead of us. That was certainly the case with Joseph in the book of Genesis.

Through unbelievable adversity as a young man, God prepared him for a task beyond his imagination. You remember his story. Abandoned and betrayed by his brothers, and sold into slavery as a teenager, he was eventually elevated to a position of great power. As the Prime Minister of Egypt, the second most influential man in the world, he was given charge of Egypt's food stores during a worldwide famine.

Then the day came when ten of his brothers (who thought Joseph was long dead) came down to Egypt from Canaan to get food for their starving families. The moment Joseph recognized them, he could have had them executed on the spot.

Instead, he forgave them, and made this amazing statement: "But as for you, you meant evil against me; but God meant it for good, in order to bring it about as it is this day, to save many people alive" (Genesis 50:20).

Earlier, he had told them: "But don't be upset, and don't be angry with yourselves for selling me to this place. It was God who sent me here ahead of you to preserve your lives." (Genesis 45:5, NLT).

Did you catch that? Joseph didn't just say "God allowed it," though you could describe it that way, too. He said, "God *did* it." Why? Joseph said, "To save many people alive."

The suffering Joseph endured prepared him for the job that God had for him to do.

Maybe the Lord is allowing you to go through some difficult circumstances right now to prepare you for something He wants you to do tomorrow. That thought may not bring much comfort at the moment. You may be thinking, *No, this suffering doesn't make any sense at all!*

Joseph might have thought that same thing at several points in his life journey. But the truth is, God might very well be preparing you to touch someone else's life in a way no one else could.

Thursday

Therefore He is also able to save to the uttermost those who come to God through Him, since He always lives to make intercession for them. (Hebrews 7:25)

The Bible tells us to keep ourselves in the love of God (see Jude 21). But we are also told in the same passage that *God* will keep us (see v. 1). So who is keeping what for whom? Is this a contradiction? Not at all. The truth is, these verses complement one another, showing us both God's part, and ours. No, we don't keep ourselves saved…but we can keep ourselves *safe*.

God's love is unconditional. And—most happily for us—Jesus Christ loves, preserves, and intercedes for us before the Father. But we can do things that will get us out of sync and out of harmony with His love. That's why we're reminded to keep ourselves in the love of God, which means that we're to keep away from all that is unlike Him. We are to keep our distance from any influence that would violate God's love and bring sorrow to His heart.

We are loved by God, and He will protect His investment. Think about it: If you own an inexpensive pair of sunglasses, you may not be all that concerned about where they are. But if you have a really nice, expensive pair, then you will tend to know their whereabouts. Or, if you went to Disneyland with your children, you wouldn't just forget about them. Instead, you would keep your eye on them, because you want to protect what is dear to you.

In the same way, we are preserved, protected, and kept by the power of God. Peter tells us that we are "protected by the power of God through faith for a salvation ready to be revealed in the last time" (1 Peter 1:5, NASB).

Even so, we too have a responsibility. We need to keep ourselves in a place where He can actively show His love to us. We need to keep ourselves in the love of God.

Friday

Enoch walked with God three hundred years, and had sons and daughters. (Genesis 5:22)

I'm glad the Bible compares the Christian life not only to running a race, but also to walking a walk.

"I am God Almighty; walk before me and be blameless." (Genesis 17:1-2, NIV)

And this is love: that we walk in obedience to his commands. (2 John 6, NIV)

"They will walk with me, dressed in white, for they are worthy." (Revelation 3:4, NIV)

Enoch walked with God for three hundred years, teaching us the importance of pacing ourselves in the spiritual race. In contrast to this, some people have a yo-yo relationship with God—either fully backslidden, or passionate to the point of being obnoxious. They haven't learned to pace themselves.

I learned the importance of this one day on a twenty-five-mile bike ride with some friends. I had a lot of energy, so I would pedal ahead of the pack. But then I'd run out of steam and have to pull back. I would get another burst of energy and pedal ahead of everyone else. Then they would catch up and pass me. Once we reached our destination and were on our way back, one of the guys I'd been cycling with actually had to push me, because I had no strength left. That is *not* the way to do it. The objective is to get there—and back!

The same is true in the spiritual race. The objective isn't just to run fast. It is to run *long*, and to finish. If you want to grow up spiritually, you need to pace yourself in this race of life—because you're in it for the long haul.

Weekend

My little children, let us not love in word or in tongue, but in deed and in truth. (1 John 3:18)

The Bible tells us again and again that we should love one another. Love is like the glue that holds us all together. The apostle John wrote, "Beloved, let us love one another, for love is of God; and everyone who loves is born of God and knows God" (1 John 4:7).

The Bible's definitive chapter on love, 1 Corinthians 13, is the most comprehensive description of love in all of Scripture. In these classic verses, Paul shines love through a prism, so to speak. We see many of its colors and hues, so we can more easily understand love and apply it in a practical way. Each ray gives a different facet of God's *agape* love, as in this passage: *"Love knows no limit to its endurance, no end to its trust, no fading of its hope; it can outlast anything. It is, in fact, the one thing that still stands when all else has fallen" (1 Corinthians 13:7-8,* phillips*).*

The Bible doesn't focus so much on what love is, but on what love does—and doesn't do. The love of God that we are to demonstrate toward one another is not merely feeling or emotion. Nor is it abstract or passive. It is active. It engages. It works. It moves. It rolls up its sleeves, takes risks, and gets busy. God's love doesn't merely feel patient; it *is* patient. God's love doesn't simply have kind feelings; it *does* kind things. Love is fully love only when it is active. As the apostle Paul said to the Romans: "Don't just pretend that you love others: really love them" (Romans 12:9, tlb).

At the same time, the Bible tells us the goal of the Christian is to be conformed to the image of Christ (see Philippians 3:10). This is what God wants you to strive for and aim toward—so that the love He speaks of will work its way into every aspect of your life.

Monday

Indeed, experience shows that the more we share Christ's suffering the more we are able to give of his encouragement.
(2 Corinthians 1:5, PHILLIPS)

If someone has just found out they have cancer and you are a cancer survivor, you have no idea how much encouragement and perspective you can bring to such a person, who feels as though he or she has been handed a death sentence.

If you have alcoholism in your past, and God has graciously delivered you from that plague and kept you from falling back into it again, your life can bring great hope to someone still in the grip of the addiction.

Or maybe a couple you know lost a child through illness or some terrible accident, and they are walking on the ragged edge of sanity, feeling like they can't go on another minute, much less another day. If you have lost a child in the past, and God has brought you healing, you can come along and say, "We lost a child, too, and it was the hardest thing that ever happened to us. Though we still mourn that child, and though we're still dealing with it, and we miss them every single day, we want you to know that God can help you each step of the way. His grace really will be sufficient for you."

You have no idea how much comfort that can bring. *And it would be something that only you could say.* No one else could say those words with the same kind of credibility.

The apostle Paul, who had his own serious issues with suffering, as we have said, wrote: "God is our merciful Father and the source of all comfort. He comforts us in all our troubles so that we can comfort others. When they are troubled, we will be able to give them the same comfort God has given us. For the more we suffer for Christ, the more God will shower us with his comfort through Christ" (2 Corinthians 1:3-5, NLT).

God will give you that comfort—over and beyond what you can personally contain—so that you can share it with others.

Tuesday

For he knows how we are formed, he remembers that we are dust.
(Psalm 103:14, NIV)

Thinking about what Job endured, you might say, "Honestly, I don't see how I could handle one tenth of all the things Job faced. In fact, I can't handle suffering at all."

Don't worry. God knows what you can manage. He knows what you can take, and He will parcel it out accordingly. You just need to trust Him. God will give you what you need when you need it. Not before, never after, but just when it is needed.

Until then, we must simply trust Him.

Corrie ten Boom, author of *The Hiding Place*, was placed in a Nazi concentration camp along with her sister and her father. They were committed Christians, and their "crime" had been hiding Jewish people in their home, trying to protect them from Nazi genocide.

Both Corrie's father and sister died, and Corrie herself went through deep suffering during that time. But she survived, and spent the rest of her life traveling around the world as a self-described "tramp for the Lord," declaring that there is no pit so deep that God is not deeper still.

When Corrie was a little girl, she was reading a story about martyrs for the Christian faith, and was trying to process what these saints of God had endured for the sake of Christ.

She said to her father, "Daddy, I am afraid that I will never be strong enough to be a martyr for Jesus Christ."

"Tell me," said that wise father, "when you take train trip to Amsterdam, when do I give you the money for the ticket? Three weeks before?"

"No Daddy," she replied. "You give me the money for the ticket just before we get on the train."

"That's right," he replied. "And so it is with God's strength. Our Father in heaven knows when you will need the strength to be a martyr for Jesus Christ. He will supply all you need just in time."

As it turned out, God never required Corrie to die as a martyr, as her father and sister did. Even so, Corrie had suffered much in her life, and God always gave her the strength she needed…just as her father had told her.

Wednesday

Dear friends, don't be surprised at the fiery trials you are going through, as if something strange were happening to you. Instead, be very glad— because these trials will make you partners with Christ in his suffering, and afterward you will have the wonderful joy of sharing his glory when it is displayed to all the world. (1 Peter 4:12, TLB).

When the apostle Peter sat down to pen a letter to some churches facing persecution and trials, he had a word of counsel for them.

"Don't let it surprise you."

In other words, don't be taken aback. Don't be thrown for a loop. Don't let it shock you. Don't let it send you into a tailspin. Why? Because it really isn't all that strange or unusual if you find yourself being tempted or tested. It isn't weird or bizarre if you find yourself going through the fire of trials. In spite of what you may have been taught, hardships and difficulties are a normal thing in the life of a committed follower of Jesus Christ.

It was Phillips Brooks who said, "Character may be manifested in the great moments, but it is made in the small ones."[10]

Get used to the idea…there *will* be times in your life when your faith will be tested, when you will be challenged for what you believe. There will be multiple occasions when the temptation for you to go the wrong direction, say the wrong thing, or engage in the wrong activity will be very, very strong.

You might ask the question, "Will I be able to stand strong spiritually when this takes place?"

That's entirely up to you.

The stand you make today will determine what kind of stand you will make tomorrow. So you have to think about it now, as you are laying the foundation for the years that remain ahead of you. The way you exercise your faith and cling to confidence in the Lord today will set a pattern for the week, for the year, and for the rest of your life.

Thursday

"Listen! A farmer went out to plant some seed. As he scattered it across his field, some of the seed fell on a footpath, and the birds came and ate it.... The farmer plants seed by taking God's word to others. The seed that fell on the footpath represents those who hear the message, only to have Satan come at once and take it away." (Mark 4:3-5, 14-16, NLT)

Without question, the devil focuses his attacks on those who are young in the faith and those who seek to make a difference in the kingdom of God.

You probably remember that when you first put your faith in Christ, the enemy was right there to attack you. Maybe the day after you had made that commitment to Christ, you started thinking, "What was that all about, anyway? Has God really forgiven me? Did something really happen to me? Maybe I just psyched myself into this." Or maybe you remember some very strong temptations that came your way right after you became a Christian. Obviously, temptation has to be tempting, so the devil will offer things that look attractive to you.

This is why we should pray for new believers. The enemy will be there, trying to rob them of what God has done. Way back in the fourth chapter of Genesis, we see in the story of Cain and Abel how Satan waits to pounce on a vulnerable individual. The Lord said to Cain, "If you do what is right, will you not be accepted? But if you do not do what is right, sin is crouching at your door; it desires to have you, but you must master it" (Genesis 4:7, NIV).

Then, of course, the devil will attack those who are making a difference in the kingdom, those who seek to walk with God and reach others with the gospel. When believers step up and say, "Use me, Lord. I want my life to make a difference," they should brace themselves. The enemy won't take that sitting down. Expect opposition. It comes to those who have set their heart on following Christ and are making a difference in the kingdom.

Friday

Keep yourselves in God's love as you wait for the mercy of our Lord Jesus Christ to bring you to eternal life. (Jude 21, NIV)

There is a lot of disagreement in the church as a whole over what we call "eschatology," or prophetic events. Most often, it seems, the differences lie in the order of events. Some don't believe Christ could return at any time. Some believe the church will go through the Tribulation.

Here's my bottom line: There is room for honest disagreement as to the timing and order of events in the book of Revelation. But the imminent—at any moment—return of Jesus Christ is a teaching we need to hold onto. The fact that Jesus could come back at any time is a New Testament emphasis that not only fills our lives with hope, it also has a *purifying* effect. As 1 John 3:2-3 says, "Dear friends, we are already God's children, but he has not yet shown us what we will be like when Christ appears. But we do know that we will be like him, for we will see him as he really is. And all who have this eager expectation will keep themselves pure, just as he is pure." (NLT).

A literal translation of this verse would be, "Whoever has this hope continually set on Him is constantly purifying himself." If I live my life in a sense of expectation that Christ could come back at any time, then it will purify me.

Children who are prone to get into trouble will be on their best behavior if they know their parents might walk into the room at any moment. In the same way, if we know that Christ could come back at any moment, it should affect the way we live.

In contrast, however, to disobedient children who dread the arrival of their parents, we should look forward with great excitement to the return of our Lord. Like John, we should be able to say, "Even so, come, Lord Jesus!" (Revelation 22:20). If you can't say this, it could be an indication that something isn't right spiritually.

I enjoy life and the opportunities God sets before me. But if tonight were the night for Christ's return, I would say, "Bring it on!" Wouldn't you? That is the way to live.

Weekend

Because, although they knew God, they did not glorify Him as God, nor were thankful, but became futile in their thoughts, and their foolish hearts were darkened. Professing to be wise, they became fools.
(Romans 1:21-22)

Though God's love toward us is undeserved, unconditional, and even unsought, it's still possible for us to fall out of harmony with Him. To keep ourselves in the love of God, as Jude 21 urges us, means *to keep ourselves in a place where God can actively show His love toward us.*

Take the prodigal son, for example. He rebelled against his father, went to a distant land, and did things he shouldn't have done. Was he still his father's son? Of course he was. Was he in a place where his father could actively show his love to him? No, he was not.

Though this loving father missed his son, longed after his son, and grieved over the young man's rebellion, the prodigal was in a far country. He had removed himself from his father's love, provision, and protection. The father had many, many blessings to give, but the son had placed himself out of reach for those blessings.

We, too, can do the same thing. We can still be children of God, but if we are out of fellowship with Him and His people, pursuing a path that we know violates His Word and breaks His heart, then we are not in a place where God can actively demonstrate His love toward us. In the book of Isaiah, the Lord said, "But my own people—though I have been spreading out my arms to welcome them all day long—have rebelled; they follow their own evil paths and thoughts" (Isaiah 65:2, TLB).

The key is to keep ourselves in a place where God can pour His love and blessing into our lives. One way to do that is to simply keep yourself from all that is unlike God. Keep yourself from any influence that would violate His love or possibly bring sorrow to His heart. Enjoy His richest blessings by making yourself "bless-able."

Monday

*Then Nebuchadnezzar flew into a rage and ordered that Shadrach,
Meshach, and Abednego be brought before him. When they were
brought in, Nebuchadnezzar said to them, "Is it true, Shadrach,
Meshach, and Abednego, that you refuse to serve my gods or to worship
the gold statue I have set up?" (Daniel 3:13-14, NLT)*

If you had been the mother of Shadrach, Meshach, or Abednego, you
would have never prayed that your boy would be taken captive into
Babylon and placed in the service of a pagan, bloodthirsty king. (See the
book of Daniel.)

And you certainly would have never prayed, "Lord, I'm hoping that
before they get out of their teens, they'll end up in a fiery furnace." But
the Lord had a plan for these young men—a plan that included testing,
defiance of the established order, and deadly danger. But in the process,
He would gain great glory through their lives. And here we are some
2,500 years later, still telling the story of their courageous choices.

Had you been the mother of Daniel, you never would have prayed,
"O Lord, let our nation be taken captive and let my son one day be put
into a den of hungry lions." No loving parent would pray such a thing.
And yet the Lord allowed it, and look how He was glorified through the
life of Daniel.

Had you been Mary, you never would have prayed, "Lord, I hope
my Son will one day be falsely accused, stripped, beaten, and crucified
between two thieves." Could anything be more heartbreaking?
Nothing is harder for a parent than to see their child suffer. In her worst
nightmare, could Mary have foreseen or visualized the young Man
who had been her pride and joy so beaten and bludgeoned that His face
was beyond recognition?

If you were His mother and saw such things, you would have to cry
out in your heart, "This is the worst thing that could possibly happen!"

And yet, through His sacrifice, through His death and resurrection,
He would become the salvation of the whole world—including hers!

As dads and moms who love the Lord, then, we need to pray that
God will gain great glory through our sons' and daughters' lives. Yes,
Lord, please protect them. Bless them, guide them, and keep Your hand
on them.

But use them for Your glory.

Tuesday

Then King Nebuchadnezzar was astonished; and he rose in haste and spoke, saying to his counselors, "Did we not cast three men bound into the midst of the fire?"

They answered and said to the king, "True, O king."

"Look!" he answered, "I see four men loose, walking in the midst of the fire; and they are not hurt, and the form of the fourth is like the Son of God." (Daniel 3:24-25)

Not many of us, perhaps, will face tests as great as Shadrach, Meshach, or Abednego faced, on the day when the king threw them into a fiery furnace. Even so, tests will come. Temptations will come. And many of those moments of great testing will come when you are alone, with no one looking.

We're foolish if we think we can stand up to temptation—the lure of the world, our own flesh, and the devil—in our own strength and wisdom. We need help from on high.

The key to the courage and serenity of these three teenagers in the midst of those flames was their Companion! Nebuchadnezzar said it best. "The fourth looks like the Son of God."

I don't know that Nebuchadnezzar necessarily realized that this fourth person in the flames was Jesus Christ. I don't know what he thought. All he knew was that he tossed three men in a blazing furnace and they were walking around in the fire like it was a Sunday stroll in the park.

And Someone Else was walking with them.

Just that quickly, the king didn't want to mess with these guys anymore. He had great respect--not necessarily belief at that point--but yet respect for the God they represented.

Are you in a fiery trial right now? Are you in the hot waters of temptation? Know this. You are not alone in life. Jesus is there with you each step of the way. Jesus said, "Surely I am with you always, to the very end of the age." And again, "I will never leave you nor forsake you." (Matthew 28:20, NIV; Hebrews 13:5).

Take your stand for the Lord, in things great and small, and even though you may feel the heat, your Companion will never leave your side.

Wednesday

So at last the king gave orders for Daniel to be arrested and thrown into the den of lions. The king said to him, "May your God, whom you serve so faithfully, rescue you." A stone was brought and placed over the mouth of the den. The king sealed the stone with his own royal seal and the seals of his nobles, so that no one could rescue Daniel. (Daniel 6:16-17, NLT)

King Darius immediately realized he had been duped by these devious administrators. He recognized what a fool he had been…but even he could not change the decree that he had authorized and signed.

Daniel was arrested for breaking the new law, and he was well aware of the penalty. Death by hungry lion. At least if it's my time to go, he might have reasoned, the end will be quick.

To me, the situation is almost humorous. There was a seal on the stone…as if that was going to stop God from working! Can't you just hear the God of the universe saying, "Oh no. A seal on the stone!" Do you think things like this concern the Lord? Didn't they put a seal on the stone of our Lord when He was placed in the tomb after His crucifixion?

That didn't work too well, either.

We need to remember whatever deadly plots have been hatched against us—no matter how well thought out or "foolproof"—will fail because we are going to live as long as God wants us to live. A Christian is indestructible until the Lord is through with him.

Listen, when you die you die, and you step into the presence of the Lord. If you live you live, and you serve the Lord. It's a win-win situation.

This doesn't mean we should be foolish or careless with our lives in a way that puts God to the test. But it does mean that we trust God, knowing we are safe in His hands, come what may.

Somehow I imagine that Daniel had a good night's sleep. Once he saw that God's angel was protecting him, he probably used one of those lions for a pillow.

Thursday

Daniel answered, "Long live the king! My God sent his angel to shut the lions' mouths so that they would not hurt me, for I have been found innocent in his sight. And I have not wronged you, Your Majesty."
(Daniel 6:21-22, NLT)

So Daniel was in the lions' den, but the lions left him alone. It wasn't because these were godly lions. They were very normal lions. Even hungry lions. But none of them wanted to mess with the Lord's angel. And Daniel probably got a solid seven hours that night.

Real peace is being able to lay your head down on your pillow at night at peace with God. Committing your life to the Lord, and every detail of your life. No longer plagued with guilt. Saying the words, "Lord I trust You" as you drift off to sleep.

David, who had good reason for a lot of sleepless nights in his life, wrote, "In peace I will both lie down and sleep, for You alone, O Lord, make me to dwell in safety" (Psalm 4:8, NASB). I think Daniel could do that through most of his long life.

Do you find yourself in a "lion's den" today? As with Daniel, you may have some enemies out there plotting your destruction. And you certainly have an adversary who "prowls around like a roaring lion looking for someone to devour." (1 Peter 5:8, NIV). You feel like the heat's on, and you wonder if you can hold onto your sanity—and your faith—in this time of pain and perplexity.

Daniel refused to be distracted from the purpose in his heart. He maintained his priorities and kept his cool in the face of opposition and intimidating circumstances. So did Shadrach, Meshach, and Abednego, when ordered to betray the Lord or die. And so did Job, when Satan stole everything from him but that which he cherished most—his relationship with the living God.

These real people from the pages of Scripture teach us to keep our eyes of faith locked on our faithful God…no matter what. Keep on praying…keep on living a godly life…keep on claiming the promises of God's Word…keep on trusting the Lord to come through for you, and to continue working for your best and His glory.

Friday

*"When two of you get together on anything at all on earth and make
a prayer of it, my Father in heaven goes into action. And when two or
three of you are together because of me, you can be sure that I'll be there."*
(Matthew 18:19-20, THE MESSAGE*)*

We live in a time in which our society is becoming more and more disjointed and divided. Rather than celebrating what we have in common, it seems nowadays we emphasize the things that separate us. You hear strong, strident political and social views on one cable channel, turn to the next one, and hear the exact opposite take on the very same events.

In fact, I don't know of a time, at least in my brief life, when our culture has been more divided (perhaps with the exception of the tumultuous 1960s).

Families are falling apart like never before, and the result is that people are looking for a place where they can belong, a community where they can feel safe, a family they can belong to...a place where they can genuinely love and be loved in return. And that is exactly what the church is. It is a warm refuge in a cold, impersonal, and often hostile world.

I know the church isn't perfect. The church is made up of imperfect people, but foibles and all, it is the only organization that Jesus Christ Himself ever established. And after two thousand years, it's still going strong.

Millennia ago, the Roman emperor Diocletian set up a stone pillar as a monument, boasting that he had exterminated the word "Christian" from the Earth. That was the aim of Diocletian, and needless to say, he failed miserably in his endeavor.

Any attempt that has ever been undertaken to eradicate the church that Jesus established and maintains has met with utter failure, because Jesus said of His church, "I will build My church, and the gates of Hades shall not prevail against it" (Matthew 16:18). He is with His church, and it is still going strong!

Weekend

"In the same way, anyone who holds on to life just as it is destroys that life. But if you let it go, reckless in your love, you'll have it forever, real and eternal." (John 12:25, THE MESSAGE*)*

Most of us have had mixed experiences when it comes to our trade-in on a car deal. The salesperson will say, "Trade that in, and I'll give you a deal." Then you tell your friends, "I got this great deal for my trade-in." The real question, however, is what they charged you for the new one you bought. In other words, what they give you with one hand, they most likely will take back with the other.

In spite of what they might tell you on the TV used car ads, you can't get something for nothing—even on those mythical days when "the boss is away" and the employees are "practically giving cars away."

Nevertheless there is an exchange that seem too good to be true—but really is true! God Almighty says to us, "I will give you eternal life. I will forgive all of your sins." So we say, "What's the catch? Surely there's something I need to do." It's hard for us to accept that God could simply forgive us.

God says, "No, you have broken all the laws. There is no way you could earn My grace or forgiveness. Nevertheless, I offer it to you for free. I give you everything. Now you give Me your life. I don't care what shape it's in. I'm in the restoration business. You watch what I can do." So you bring your life to Him.

Jesus said, "Whoever loses his life for My sake will find it" (Matthew 16:25). You will be a new creation, because in Him, all things have become new (see 2 Corinthians 5:17).

"Do you want to find life?" Jesus says to us. "You won't find it by looking within yourself. You won't even find it by looking for life. You will find it by looking to Me. And as you trade your life in, I will give you life. The very thing you want, you'll find by coming to Me."

This is God's trade-in deal.

Monday

And now dear friends of mine. I beg you not to be unduly alarmed at the fiery ordeals which come to test your faith, as though this were some abnormal experience. You should be glad, because it means that you are called to share Christ's sufferings. One day, when he shows himself in full splendor to men, you will be filled with the most tremendous joy. If you are reproached for being Christ's followers, that is a great privilege, for you can be sure that God's Spirit of glory is resting upon you.
(1 Peter 4:12-14, PHILLIPS)

Throughout history, God has given special grace and courage to millions of Christians who were persecuted for the faith or who lost their lives. They were unwilling to renounce the Lord, unwilling to deny the One who had so radically changed their lives.

We may hear the stories of these Christians and say, "What a tragedy." But I don't think that's a tragedy, because everyone has to die. These believers not only lived well, but they died well. They died for the greatest cause on the face of the Earth: the cause of Jesus Christ.

Sometimes we might think, *I don't know if I could handle it if my life were actually threatened for the sake of the gospel.* But if God allowed you to be put into such a situation, then I am confident He would give you the grace and strength you would need—in that moment—to face it.

Jesus told His followers, "Now when they bring you to the synagogues and magistrates and authorities, do not worry about how or what you should answer, or what you should say. For the Holy Spirit will teach you in that very hour what you ought to say" (Luke 12:11-12).

This doesn't mean you shouldn't be prepared for such a day. You simply shouldn't worry about it, knowing that God won't give you more than you can handle. He will give you just the right words for just the right situation. And not only will God give you the right words, He will also give you the power to stand up for your faith— even it means harassment or hardship or persecution.

Tuesday

Brothers, we do not want you to be ignorant about those who fall asleep, or to grieve like the rest of men, who have no hope. We believe that Jesus died and rose again and so we believe that God will bring with Jesus those who have fallen asleep in him. (1 Thessalonians 4:13-14, NIV)

It's a funny thing how we find sleep more and more appealing as we get older. When I was a kid, I hated to go to sleep. I still remember kindergarten, with the lukewarm milk in little cartons and having to lie down and take naps in the middle of the day. Sleep is usually the last thing kids want to do, but as we start getting older, the idea of sleep becomes more attractive.

Interestingly, the Bible describes death for a believer as sleep. You close your eyes to the only life you've ever known—life on earth—and in the next instant, you open your eyes and find yourself in the very presence of the Lord. Scripture teaches that there is no delay at all between life here on Earth and life in heaven.

In Acts 7, we read these words about Stephen's final words, as he was martyred for the sake of Jesus: "Then he knelt down and cried out with a loud voice, 'Lord, do not charge them with this sin.' And when he had said this, he fell asleep" (Acts 7:60).

Stephen's statement indicates that he expected to enter the Lord's presence as soon as he died. And that's just what happened, as the Lord Jesus personally received Him into heaven.

Again, in 2 Corinthians 5:8, we're told that a believer will enter immediately into the presence of God following death: "We are confident, yes, well pleased rather to be absent from the body and to be present with the Lord."

John Bunyan said, "Death is but a passage out of a prison into a palace."[11] You see, when death strikes a Christian down, he or she falls into heaven.

Wednesday

"The shepherd walks right up to the gate. The gatekeeper opens the gate to him and the sheep recognize his voice. He calls his own sheep by name and leads them out. When he gets them all out, he leads them and they follow because they are familiar with his voice. They won't follow a stranger's voice but will scatter because they aren't used to the sound of it." (John 10:2-5, THE MESSAGE)

Does God still speak to people today? Is He interested in what happens to us as individuals? Does He really have a master plan for our lives?

God truly is interested in us as individuals. He *does* have a master plan for our lives, and He *does* want to speak to us. Jesus described Himself as our Good Shepherd. And as His sheep, we can hear and recognize His voice.

So how can we know when it is God speaking? First, we need to remember that God primarily speaks to us through His Word, and He will never lead us in a way that contradicts that Word. We don't have to go any further than the Bible to know the will of God for our lives.

God also speaks through circumstances that can include failure or even hardship. We don't enjoy it when God speaks to us through tragedy and hardship, but, as C. S. Lewis said, "God whispers to us in our pleasures, speaks in our conscience, but shouts in our pain: it is His megaphone to rouse a deaf world."[12]

Often I have found that if something is the will of God, then it will be confirmed. There are times when I feel the Lord has been speaking to me through circumstances, such as an opportunity that has opened up. But I never make decisions by looking at circumstances alone.

Lastly, God speaks to us through His peace. Colossians 3:15 tells us, "Let the peace of God rule in your hearts..." God is the author of peace, not of confusion.

Maybe we hear the voice of God more often than we think. Then again, maybe we're not giving Him the opportunity to speak. Today would be a good day to take your Bible and get alone with Him, away from the noise and confusion, and ask, "Lord, what do you have to say to me today? I am listening!"

Thursday

But whatever was to my profit I now consider loss for the sake of Christ. What is more, I consider everything a loss compared to the surpassing greatness of knowing Christ Jesus my Lord, for whose sake I have lost all things. I consider them rubbish, that I may gain Christ and be found in him. (Philippians 3:7-9, NIV)

When you become a Christian, one of the more notable changes is that you will give up many of the things you once did. Of course, this depends on your lifestyle prior to your conversion. But for many of us, a dramatic change will take place.

I have heard people share their stories of how they came to Christ and the great sacrifices they made to follow Him, saying things like, "I had a great life...I went to parties...I had so much fun...But I gave it all up for Jesus Christ, hallelujah! I left it all for the glory of God!"

When I hear statements like that, I feel like asking, "What in the world are you talking about? *You gave it all up?* What did you give up?"

If they were to look at those things honestly and realistically, they would come to the same conclusion that Paul did. He said, "But what things were gain to me, these I have counted loss for Christ. Yet indeed I also count all things loss for the excellence of the knowledge of Christ Jesus my Lord..." (Philippians 3:7-8).

Paul was saying that the stuff that used to be so important, the stuff he once valued so highly, meant *nothing* to him now in comparison with the awesome privilege and value of belonging to Jesus.

We might do well to bring certain activities or habits in our lives under the same scrutiny. It's a good idea to periodically ask ourselves, "Is this thing that I am doing slowing me down or speeding me along in my walk with God? Is it building me up spiritually, or is it tearing me down?"

The conclusion has to be the same: If anything is keeping you from an intimate, open-hearted relationship with God through Jesus Christ, whatever that thing may be, you must count it as a *loss*.

Friday

To everything there is a season, a time for every purpose under heaven...
A time to keep silence, and a time to speak. (Ecclesiastes 3:1, 7)

I can think of so many times when I should have kept silent, but I just had to speak. On more than one occasion I have said something, and the moment it left my lips, I thought, *Why did I just say that?* And I have found myself instantly wishing I could have those words back.

Have you ever been in a situation where you wanted to say the perfect thing, but instead, you ended up saying the lamest thing possible? It reminds me of when Peter, along with James and John, witnessed the Transfiguration of Jesus. What an awesome privilege these three men had been given! Their eyes were the only ones who got to see Jesus' face and clothes suddenly become shining like the sun. And then they had the privilege of having a front row seat as Moses and Elijah appeared and spoke with Jesus about His upcoming trials. Even as this conversation was taking place, however, Peter blurted out, "Rabbi, it is good for us to be here..." (Mark 9:5). Mark includes this interesting commentary: "He did not know what to say, for they were greatly afraid" (verse 6).

But Peter wasn't quite finished. He said, "Let us make three tabernacles: one for You, one for Moses, and one for Elijah" (verse 5).

I wonder if Moses turned to Jesus and asked, "Who is that guy?"

"Oh, that's Rock. Never mind."

How easily thoughts can jump into our minds, and we just say them without thinking. But how much better it is to think about it a moment and ask ourselves, *Is this the right thing to say? Would this be an appropriate statement to make? Would this glorify the Lord?*

Ephesians 4:29 (NIV) says, "Do not let any unwholesome talk come out of your mouths, but only what is helpful for building others up according to their needs, that it may benefit those who listen."

If we applied that filter to our conversations—"Will this comment build this person up? Will these words benefit this person?"—imagine what a difference there would be in the content of our words.

Weekend

For this is the love of God, that we keep His commandments. And His commandments are not burdensome. (1 John 5:3)

A lot of us don't care much for commandments, because we see them as restrictive. CNN founder Ted Turner once made this statement about the Ten Commandments: "We're living with outmoded rules...Today, the commandments wouldn't go over. Nobody around likes to be commanded."

I agree with Turner that people don't like to be commanded. But if we want to live full and happy lives, we have to recognize and live within a structure, parameters, and absolutes.

It would be like someone saying, "I don't like traffic laws. I'm not into stoplights. I don't believe in speed zones. And by the way, I think I should be able to drive on whatever side of the road I feel like driving on. I want my freedom." Now there's a freedom that might be...short lived! Those traffic laws and rules of the road are there for our protection. Those stoplights and traffic lanes are there so we can get to where we need to go.

The Bible does indeed command us not to do certain things or act in certain ways. But it also tells us what we *should* do—what will bless our lives and bring grace and goodness into the lives of others. When it tells us to stay away from one thing, it tells us to do another thing in its place.

For example, the Bible says, "And do not be drunk with wine" (Ephesians 5:18). There's the don't. But here's the *do*: "But be filled with the Spirit, speaking to one another in psalms and hymns and spiritual songs, singing and making melody in your heart to the Lord" (verses 18-19). God says, "Don't do this, but do this instead."

God's plan is always better. Sure, He tells us to stay away from certain things. But it's for our own good. And as the apostle John reminds us in today's opening verse...God's commands are not burdensome. And the pleasure and benefit that flows from walking in His love makes the requirements seem ever lighter still.

Monday

"What do you think? If a man owns a hundred sheep, and one of them wanders away, will he not leave the ninety-nine on the hills and go to look for the one that wandered off? And if he finds it, I tell you the truth, he is happier about that one sheep than about the ninety-nine that did not wander off. In the same way your Father in heaven is not willing that any of these little ones should be lost." (Matthew 18:12-14, NIV)

Jesus, the Good Shepherd, is a familiar and comforting picture of God's feelings for us and His outlook toward us. In John we read, "I am the good shepherd; and I know My sheep, and am known by My own" (John 10:14).

It is a picture echoed throughout the pages of Scripture. Isaiah 40:11 tells us, "He will feed His flock like a shepherd; He will gather the lambs with His arm, and carry them in His bosom, and gently lead those who are with young."

In the story of a shepherd who left his flock of ninety-nine and went after one stray sheep, Jesus declares God's heart toward the person who strays from the flock. How easily He could write off the one who strays. But He doesn't. Instead, He goes out and looks for that sheep. When He finds it, He brings it back with great joy.

The Shepherd knows His sheep. He knows us by name. He knows our personalities, our strengths and weaknesses, our secret dreams, and what frightens us the most.

Not only does God know our natures, but He knows our needs. Don't forget that this God we serve and follow knows also what it's like to be human. He knew what it was like to face the limitations of humanity. He knew what it was like to feel the pressure of temptation and to experience loneliness, sorrow, and joy. As Hebrews 4:15 says, "For we do not have a High Priest who cannot sympathize with our weaknesses, but was in all points tempted as we are, yet without sin."

Our Good Shepherd cares about us. He knows sheep—and people—inside out. And He knows what you are going through today, down to the smallest detail.

Tuesday

"To him the doorkeeper opens, and the sheep hear his voice; and he calls his own sheep by name and leads them out." (John 10:3)

As you get to know your Shepherd, you will come to realize that when He calls you, it is always worth obeying. When He says something, it is for your benefit. If He says, "Go this way," it's because He has green pastures and still waters for you. If He says, "Stop! Don't do that," it's because He's trying to protect you from potential danger.

The fact that God speaks to us is clear throughout the pages of Scripture. To some, like Moses, God spoke audibly. To others, like the prophet Elijah, He spoke quietly on at least one occasion:

> And behold, the LORD passed by, and a great and strong wind tore into the mountains and broke the rocks in pieces before the LORD, but the LORD was not in the wind; and after the wind an earthquake, but the LORD was not in the earthquake; and after the earthquake a fire, but the LORD was not in the fire; and after the fire a still small voice. So it was, when Elijah heard it, that he wrapped his face in his mantle and went out and stood in the entrance of the cave. (1 Kings 19:11-13)

Often we look for the big events, the earth-shaking circumstances in which God speaks. And many times He is speaking to us, but it is in a still, small voice. We should try turning off the television, the radio, and the telephone and just listen. With all the noise in our world and all the information that bombards us, we might very well miss the most important voice of all. Maybe one reason we don't hear Him is because we never stop and listen. We should heed the words of Psalm 46:10, which says, "Be still, and know that I am God."

Once we have heard the voice of God, we need to follow. Jesus said, "The sheep follow him, for they know his voice" (John 10:4). The word "follow" means to deliberately decide to comply with instruction. It is a deliberate choice for sheep to follow the shepherd. We need to deliberately decide to follow our Shepherd, to listen for His voice, and to do what He tells us to do.

Wednesday

As he was walking along, he saw a man blind from birth. "Master," his disciples asked him, "why was this man born blind? Was it a result of his own sins or those of his parents?"

"Neither," Jesus answered. "But to demonstrate the power of God."
(John 9:1-3, TLB)

Sometimes the question comes up whether our physical suffering on Earth is the result of sin. *Who sinned?* That's the question the disciples asked Jesus in John 9. Was it the blind man or his parents? Jesus responded by clearly pointing out there was no specific correlation here. In other words, the blind man wasn't being punished for his own sin or the sin of his parents.

One Scripture paraphrase puts it like this: Jesus said, "You're asking the wrong question. You're looking for someone to blame. There is no such cause-effect here. Look instead for what God can do" (THE MESSAGE).

But notice this. Jesus did not say that suffering is just a random event that has nothing to do with sin. In a broad sense, all sickness, disabilities, and the limitations that come with the physical body are a result of sin. God's original plan was that our physical bodies would never get sick, wear out, or die. God's original purpose was for this body to live forever. But because of the sin of Adam, because he disobeyed God in the Garden of Eden, sin came into human life and spread to all of humanity.

But let me add this. You *can* experience physical hardship as a result of your own sin. If you are an alcoholic, that will affect you physically. If you're a drug addict, that will affect you physically. In a sense those physical problems could be directly linked to sin. So yes, you can bring problems into your life as a result of breaking the commandments of God.

There is a reason that He gave us these guidelines in His Word. It was for our own good. God had a plan and a purpose for each rule to protect us in life that we might live life to its fullest. Every day, we have the ability to choose between right and wrong. Choose life!

Thursday

God wants you to be holy, so you should keep clear of all sexual sin.
(1 Thessalonians 4:3, NLT)

When wildfires swept through Southern California a number of years ago, I noticed a photograph in the newspaper of an entire neighborhood that had been leveled by the flames. All that was left were the foundations. In the midst of all the burned, charred rubble, however, one house remained completely untouched, even by smoke. This gleaming white house stood in stark contrast to all of the ruin around it.

When asked why his house was left standing when all the others fell, the homeowner explained how he had taken great care to make his house flame-retardant. This included double-paned windows, thick stucco walls, sealed eaves, concrete tile, and abundant insulation. This man went the extra mile and, as a result, his house survived when the fires came. Undoubtedly he had also taken the time and effort to remove pine needles, leaves, small branches, brush, and other flammables from the immediate vicinity of his home.

Today, our country is being devastated by the wildfires of immorality. Satan, a master arsonist, is causing massive devastation. Sexual infidelity and immorality destroy homes and devastate families. And if we aren't careful, we could become its next victims.

The writer of Proverbs asked, "Can a man scoop fire into his lap without his clothes being burned? Can a man walk on hot coals without his feet being scorched?" (6:27-28, NIV). The answer is "no." If you think you can play around with fire or juggle hot coals without paying the price, you have been deceived. And once started, such fires can so easily burn out of control—with devastating results.

If we as believers allow temptation to infiltrate our lives and permit our sinful natures to prevail, we will likely fall, as surely as the hungry flames of a wildfire consume dry wood and grass. But if we take practical steps to guard ourselves and stay close to the Lord, then we don't have to fall. Let's go the extra mile to protect our families and our lives against the wildfires of immorality.

With God's help, we can make our homes "fire free" zones.

Friday

Therefore we also, since we are surrounded by so great a cloud of witnesses, let us lay aside every weight, and the sin which so easily ensnares us, and let us run with endurance the race that is set before us, looking unto Jesus, the author and finisher of our faith.
(Hebrews 12:1-2)

In the ancient Greek games, a judge would stand at the finish line holding, in plain sight, the laurel leaves that would be rewarded to the victor. As runners came down the final stretch, they were exhausted, perhaps in agony, and feeling as though they couldn't go another step. But suddenly there was the prize in sight, and a new burst of energy would kick in.

This is the picture behind the phrase "looking unto Jesus" in Hebrews 12:2. We have to keep our eyes on Jesus Christ. And our prize is the privilege of standing before Him and receiving the crown of righteousness that He will give us.

That is why we try to live godly lives, and why we try to reach people for Him. It isn't for brownie points. It isn't for applause. It isn't for notoriety. It's so we can hear Jesus say to us on that final day, "Well done, good and faithful servant." No, we can't earn our salvation, because He has already provided it. But we want to please the One who laid down His life for us. Ultimately, we want to be able to say, "Lord, I took the life You gave me and tried to make a difference. Here it is. I offer it to you."

"Looking unto Jesus. . ." That keeps you going, doesn't it? After all, you can get discouraged at times. People will let you down. They will disappoint you. They won't appreciate your hard work or notice your efforts. Not bothering to understand your real motives, they'll criticize that which they don't (or won't) understand. And that is when you need to remind yourself, *I am not running my race for this person or that person. I am running for You, Lord. And I will keep running. . .with my eyes fixed on You.*

Weekend

Where is another God like you, who pardons the guilt of the remnant, overlooking the sins of his special people? You will not stay angry with your people forever, because you delight in showing unfailing love. Once again you will have compassion on us. You will trample our sins under your feet and throw them into the depths of the ocean! (Micah 7:18-19, NLT)

Have you ever done anything that you're ashamed of? Have you ever done things you wished you hadn't? If you have repented of those sins and have turned your back on them, the Bible clearly teaches that you are forgiven.

There is something in us, however, that wants to keep dredging up our sins. Maybe we feel that by doing so, we are somehow making amends for the wrong that we've done. Maybe by punishing ourselves, we think we are somehow appeasing God. But this is wrong—and thoroughly unscriptural.

The book of Acts tells us: "Brothers, listen! We are here to proclaim that through this man Jesus there is forgiveness for your sins. Everyone who believes in him is declared right with God— something the law of Moses could never do." (Acts 13:38-39, NLT).

Speaking of our sins, God said, "And I will forgive their wickedness, and I will never again remember their sins" (Hebrews 8:12, NLT).

In the verse that opens today's devotional, the prophet speaks of God throwing our sins into the depths of the ocean. Have you ever lost anything in a lake or in the ocean? It's pretty much a lost cause. Once it goes down, it goes *way* down. And that's what God has done with our sins: He has thrown them into the deepest part of the ocean.

In the Psalms, David celebrated his forgiveness with these words: "He doesn't treat us as our sins deserve, nor pay us back in full for our wrongs. As high as heaven is over the earth, so strong is his love to those who fear him. And as far as sunrise is from sunset, he has separated us from our sins" (Psalm 103:10-12, THE MESSAGE)

Simply put, our sins are G-O-N-E…and you and I shouldn't choose to remember what God has chosen to forget.

Monday

And He said to him, "Go, wash in the pool of Siloam" (which is translated, Sent). So he went and washed, and came back seeing.
(John 9:7)

We've all heard people say, "Seeing is believing. Show me and I will believe." But the Bible essentially teaches us that *believing is seeing*. When we say, "Show me and I will believe," God says, "Believe, and I will show you."

In John 9, we read that Jesus opened the eyes of the blind man in more ways than one. The man received his physical sight, but he had his spiritual eyes opened as well. He was able to understand who God was, what right and wrong were, and what the purpose of life was.

Jesus used a very unusual method to heal him: Spitting in the dirt, He made clay with the saliva, and placed it on the man's eyes. Then He told him to go wash in the pool of Siloam. Notice that Jesus didn't say, "Go wash in the pool of Siloam and you'll receive your sight." That's important, because He offered this man no promise whatsoever, or said that something wonderful would happen if he went. He just told him to go and do it.

Yet something activated this blind man's heart and mind and caused him to want to obey the words of Jesus as quickly as possible. And as we follow his example, we, too, can have our spiritual eyes opened.

Those who know God have come to realize that His words and commands can be trusted and immediately followed. The Psalmist wrote: "Oh, how I love your law! I meditate on it all day long. Your commands make me wiser than my enemies, for they are ever with me. I have more insight than all my teachers, for I meditate on your statutes. I have more understanding than the elders, for I obey your precepts" (vv. 97-100, NIV).

If God tells us to do something, it's for a reason, and it's for our own good. *Obey Him.* Great blessings await those who wait on the Lord.

Tuesday

And I heard a loud voice from the throne saying, "Now the dwelling of God is with men, and he will live with them. They will be his people, and God himself will be with them and be their God. He will wipe every tear from their eyes. There will be no more death or mourning or crying or pain, for the old order of things has passed away."

He who was seated on the throne said, "I am making everything new!" (Revelation 21:3-5, NIV)

One day, for those who have received Jesus Christ as Savior and have gone on to heaven, sickness and sorrow, pain and tears, heartaches and disappointments will fade away like a bad dream, and never return. But even today, in this troubled world of ours, God can work in spite of sickness.

He still answers prayer and heals people today, and He still does miracles. In sickness and in hardships, He can work in a person's life. Even if a person still has the sickness or problem, God can work in spite of it and give them a special strength. And no matter what happens to our physical bodies here on earth, we have the promise of heaven and ultimate healing in heaven. At that time, God says He will wipe away all our tears. There will be no more death, sorrows, crying, or pain.

What a glorious promise! There is more—so much more!— beyond this life on earth. Whatever our limitations, whatever our problems, God promises us that we will one day receive a new body that will not have the shortcomings we experience today.

And God can also use sickness to bring a person to Himself, can't He? I know of many people who have come to the Lord in the hospital or when facing death. Suddenly they reevaluate their lives. They wonder, *What am I living for? What's really important in my life? What's going to happen to me when I die?* And they begin to think about eternity.

As the psalmist says, "Before I was afflicted, I went astray, but now I keep Your word" (Psalm 119:67). God can work in spite of sickness, and He can work through sickness, and—if He chooses, for His glory—He can remove sickness altogether. Nothing is impossible for Him.

Wednesday

Peter was therefore kept in prison, but constant prayer was offered to God for him by the church. (Acts 12:5)

In some of the old TV westerns of the 1950s, the desperados (always in black hats) would be making their escape with the stolen loot from the stagecoach robbery. Suddenly someone on the posse chasing them (usually in white hats) would shout, "We have 'em now! They've ridden into a box canyon!" And everybody knows there's no way out of a box canyon.

There are box canyons in life, too. Seemingly impossible situations where there seems to be now way out and nowhere to turn. Surrounded by insurmountable obstacles, you find yourself temporarily paralyzed, not knowing what to do.

Those are the very times when God invites us to pray.

In Acts 12, we find the story of how God took a tragic, even hopeless, situation and turned it around. It was accomplished by the power of prayer, the kind of prayer that storms the throne of God and gets an answer: Both James and Peter were in prison. Tragically, James was put to death. But Peter was still incarcerated, awaiting his fate. Though all doors were closed, one remained open: the door of prayer. The church recognized that "We use God's mighty weapons, not worldly weapons, to knock down the strongholds of human reasoning and to destroy false arguments (2 Corinthians 10:4, NLT).

Prayer was and is the church's secret weapon. Although the devil struck a blow against the church, the church gained victory through prayer as Peter was miraculously released.

Sadly, we don't pray often enough. Yet it is essential that Christians learn more about effective prayer, because all of us will certainly face difficulties, hardships, problems, and more than a few box canyons. So we need to discover what God can do through the power of prayer.

Prayer for the Christian should be second nature, like breathing. We should automatically pray, lifting our needs and requests before the Lord. Jesus said that we should always pray and not lose heart (see Luke 18:1).

Prayer is something we should never avoid and never grow tired of. Prayer should be woven through our day like a bright gold thread woven through a piece of fabric. The more we pray, the more we will see the kingdom of God break through the darkness of seemingly "impossible" situations.

Thursday

Whatever you do, work at it with all your heart, as working for the Lord, not for men, since you know that you will receive an inheritance from the Lord as a reward. It is the Lord Christ you are serving. (Colossians 3:23-25, NIV)

Some people come to church expecting "something profound" to happen in the church service, and then, when they don't see it happen, they're disappointed. They conclude it must the church's fault...or the music team's fault...or the lackluster people in the congregation. The question is, did they ever stop and think the problem might be with them? The truth is, if they haven't been worshiping God for the last six days, they can't effectively worship Him on Sunday. The worship in the sanctuary is largely meaningless, unless it's preceded and prepared for by a life of worship.

The word *worship* comes from an old English word that means "worth-ship." It means to worship something because it merits your love and adoration. But worship isn't just when we sing a song or possibly raise our hands.

Living a life of worship means that we live to glorify God in all we say and do. Classical guitarist Christopher Parkening has said there are two things he can do well: fish and play the guitar. Now you may not be proficient at either. Fine...but what *can* you do? Can you program a computer? Frame a house? Tune an engine? Cook a good meal? Do you have artistic ability? Great! You can take whatever you have and do it for the glory of God. Whatever you do, you can honor the Lord with it. God can use you in whatever vocation you are in. One paraphrase of Scripture quotes the apostle Paul saying, "And don't just do the minimum that will get you by. Do your best. Work from the heart for your real Master, for God, confident that you'll get paid in full when you come into your inheritance. Keep in mind always that the ultimate Master you're serving is Christ" (Colossians 3:22-24, THE MESSAGE).

You can do your job well and effectively as a testimony and a witness for Jesus. In doing so, you can live a life of worship.

Friday

Therefore, whether you eat or drink, or whatever you do, do all to the glory of God. (1 Corinthians 10:31)

I remember when, as a young Christian, I would sit in the pews at Calvary Chapel of Costa Mesa and listen to Senior Pastor Chuck Smith speak. I would think to myself, *I wonder if God would ever use me. I wonder if the Lord would ever speak through me.* Never in my wildest dreams did I ever think that God would allow me to be a pastor, proclaiming the gospel. It was beyond my dreams—beyond my aspirations, even.

If you are planning your future right now, perhaps thinking about what course you want to follow in life, begin with God. Ask for His direction. Seek His counsel. Take time to listen for His voice. You might pray something like this: "Lord, I want to be the person that You want me to be. I want to marry the person You want me to marry. I want to be in the center of Your will." God's plans for you are better than anything you have ever planned for yourself.

God has given each of us certain abilities, talents, and resources. The question is, what are you doing with them? Are you seeking to use them for His glory? Are you offering your resources and future to Him?

Paul wrote: "If our gift is preaching, let us preach to the limit of our vision. If it is serving others let us concentrate on our service; if it is teaching let us give all we have to our teaching; and if our gift be the stimulating of the faith of others let us set ourselves to it. Let the man who is called to give, give freely; let the man who wields authority think of his responsibility; and let the man who feels sympathy for his fellows act cheerfully" (Romans 12:6-8, PHILLIPS).

I'm not saying that you have to be a pastor. But whatever you do, whether you're a doctor, an architect, a secretary, a computer programmer, a builder, a musician, or something else, you should want to serve the Lord and do it for the glory of God. That's what matters. Your life can be a bright and radiant light for Jesus, in whatever corner you may find yourself.

Weekend

It's not the one who plants or the one who waters who is at the center of this process but God, who makes things grow. Planting and watering are menial servant jobs at minimum wages. What makes them worth doing is the God we are serving. You happen to be God's field in which we are working. (1 Corinthians 3:7-9, THE MESSAGE)

A man who was doing a little cleaning went up to his attic, trying to weed out and throw away a bunch of old junk. Then he came across an old vase that he thought might be worth something, and took it to an antique dealer who knew a bit about these things. He was shocked when he walked out with a check for $324,000. It turns out that the vase was a piece of 15th-century art from the Ming dynasty. And all that time it had been sitting there in his attic.

There are people who faithfully labor in obscure places and behind the scenes for the Lord whom we don't know of. But their heavenly Father who sees them in secret will one day reward them openly. In fact, you might be one of those people. No one knows your name. No one knows what you do. But you are faithful to what the Lord has asked you to do, trying to do the best with what He has given you.

So don't be jealous of what someone else has. Don't worry about what God has called someone else to do, because you won't be judged for that. And they won't be judged for what He has called you to do. Be faithful with what God has put before you. Be thankful you have a life to use for God's glory, and use it for Him.

You may think that what you do for the Lord doesn't have any real value. But what is so valuable here (on earth) will be worthless there (in heaven). And what may not seem valuable here may be priceless there, when we stand before God.

Monday

You want what you don't have, so you scheme and kill to get it. You are jealous of what others have, but you can't get it, so you fight and wage war to take it away from them. Yet you don't have what you want because you don't ask God for it. (James 4:2, NLT)

It is my firm conviction that some Christians today don't have God's provision, healing, or blessing in their lives *simply because they haven't asked for it.*

I'm not saying God will give us everything we ask for. But I am saying that many of us are going through life missing out on many of the things God has for us. The Bible says, "You do not have, because you do not ask God."

Some Christians pray only as a last resort, when everything else fails, after they've called all their friends and all their relatives. When no one can help them, they say, "What else can I do? All I can do now is pray." But prayer should not be a last resort. It should be our first resort. The very first way we turn.

The old William Cowper hymn says, "And Satan trembles when he sees, the weakest saint upon his knees." The simple fact is the devil doesn't want you to pray. He will do everything he can to distract you, divert you, or discourage you from turning the Lord in prayer. Why? Because he is afraid of the power that can be exercised through prayer. He whispers, "Don't pray. Try this. Try that. You aren't worthy to pray. God won't hear you. Prayer is boring, anyway, and you're no good at it." He will do anything to keep you from approaching the throne of God.

The Lord gave us this invitation in the book of Jeremiah: "Call to me and I will answer you and tell you great and unsearchable things you do not know" (Jeremiah 33:3, NIV).

Prayer is a privilege given to the child of God. God will hear the prayer of an unbeliever who calls out to Him for forgiveness, but only a person who has put his or her faith in Christ can have a prayer life. So pray with fervor. Pray with energy. Pray continually. Don't give up, because you never know what God will do.

Tuesday

So teach us to number our days, that we may gain a heart of wisdom. (Psalm 90:12)

It's hard to explain when someone's life has been cut short, dying at a relatively young age. We expected that person to live a much longer life. But who is to say that it wasn't his or her appointed time to go? Who is to say that it wasn't the exact length of life that God had preordained for that man or woman from the very beginning?

In the book of Acts, the apostle Paul says of King David: "For when David had served God's purpose in his own generation, he fell asleep; he was buried with his fathers" (Acts 13:36, NIV). David, great a man as he may have been, served his purpose in his own generation, and then was taken off the scene.

That is why we want to make every day count. To paraphrase the words of Moses in Psalm 90:12, "Lord, help us to realize our lives can end on any day, so please show me how to use each day wisely."

We don't know when our day will come. We don't know when we will have "served our purpose in our own generation." When God calls you home, you're going home! You can live on vitamin C, zinc, and Echinacea. You can drink green tea, eat tofu, and avoid all the toxins you can, but when your number is up, your number is up.

On the other hand, you will be around until God is done with you. You won't go before your time. You may or may not be the healthiest person, but you will live to the time that God has appointed for you...and worrying about it won't extend your life for one moment.

At the same time, however, we are not to take foolish risks and "put the Lord to the test."

We can be assured that we are here until God is done with us. As the apostle Paul said, "For to me, to live is Christ, and to die is gain" (Philippians. 1:21). So let's make the most of the lives God has given us.

Missionary Jim Elliot once wrote: "Wherever you are, be all there. Live to the hilt every situation you believe to be the will of God."[13]

Wednesday

Jesus said to her, "I am the resurrection and the life. He who believes in Me, though he may die, he shall live." (John 11:25)

The older we become, the more this question will gnaw away at us: Is there life after death? Sometimes we ask that question earlier in life, when someone close to us dies without warning, and we come face-to-face with the uncomfortable fact of death.

Some Christians will say, "I'm going to go to heaven, so when I die, don't weep for me." But death is hard for everyone, and there's nothing wrong with feeling sorrow over the loss of someone you care about. It's a natural part of the grieving process. As the Bible says, there is "a time to weep, and a time to laugh" (Ecclesiastes 3:4).

Death even brought tears to the eyes of Jesus when His friend Lazarus died (see John 11:35). Yes, we know there is life beyond the grave for Christians. We know that life is not limited to this time on earth, and that our stay on this planet is temporary. Even so, we will feel sorrow and a sense of loss for a Christian who has died.

The apostle Paul wrote about an incident where his friend and fellow worker Epaphroditus fell gravely ill. Paul wrote in a letter: "Indeed he was ill, and almost died. But God had mercy on him, and not on him only but also on me, to spare me sorrow upon sorrow" (Philippians 2:27, NIV). So even Paul, who certainly had strong faith and his theology straight, could hardly bear the thought of being separated from a close friend by death.

Nevertheless, as believers, we know we will see that person again in heaven. That is God's great gift to us. His Son Jesus personally intervened and turned death into victory.

The writer of the book of Hebrews put it like this: "Because God's children are human beings—made of flesh and blood—the Son also became flesh and blood by being born in human form. For only as a human being could he die, and only by dying could he break the power of the devil, who had the power of death. Only in this way could he set free those who have lived all their lives as slaves to the fear of dying" (Hebrews 2:14-15, NLT).

Thursday

To all who mourn in Israel, he will give a crown of beauty for ashes, a joyous blessing instead of mourning, festive praise instead of despair. (Isaiah 61:3, NLT)

I have been amazed at the testimonies of some people when they tell me the way they used to be. I've looked at them and thought, *There is no way they used to be that way.* Jesus Christ has so radically changed them.

Isaiah 61:3-4, (NLT) promises that God "will give a crown of beauty for ashes, a joyous blessing instead of mourning, festive praise instead of despair. In their righteousness, they will be like great oaks that the Lord has planted for his own glory. They will rebuild the ancient ruins, repairing cities destroyed long ago..."

For the person who has made a mess of his or her life—a pile of ashes, so to speak—God says, "I will bring beauty." For those who mourn because of the wrongs they have done and the sins they have committed, God says, "I will bring joy out of it."

Only God can do that. Only He can take a tangled mess of a life, turn it around, and transform it in such a way that you wouldn't even know that individual used to be a very different person. As Paul wrote: "When someone becomes a Christian, he becomes a brand new person inside. He is not the same anymore. A new life has begun!" (2 Corinthians 5:17, TLB).

That's the best news ever for the person being transformed, but the change in that life also gives great hope to others, who may still despair over the condition of their lives.

If you come to Christ and say, "Lord, here I am. Forgive me of my sin," He can transform you and change you. He can take your mistakes and your sins, turn them around, and even use them for His glory. When you commit your life to Christ, putting the broken, stained, twisted pieces into His hand, He will transform it into a thing of beauty.

Friday

Serve the Lord with reverent fear; rejoice with trembling.
(Psalm 2:11, TLB)

Have you ever been semi-listening in on someone's conversation? Not intentionally, of course, because you would never do that. But maybe you were in a restaurant and your table was right next to someone else's, or maybe you were in an adjoining booth. And then (even though you didn't mean to hear) someone said, "What I'm about to tell you now is a secret. I need you to hold this in complete confidence…"

What did you do then? Did you put your hands over your ears? No. If you're like most people, you listened more carefully. Maybe you even leaned a little closer to hear what that person was saying in hushed tones. We all love to hear secrets! We all want to know the inside story. Even if someone is a complete stranger, we're still interested and intrigued by what his or her secret might be.

God has a secret that He wants to declare to you. The Bible says, "The secret of the Lord is with those who fear Him" (Psalm 25:14). In many ways, this isn't really a secret, because it is plainly declared in Scripture. Unfortunately, because so few people have opened up the Bible to see what it says, they have missed out.

This is the secret of making your days on earth more full and meaningful. It is a secret that can help you avoid untold misery and heartache. It's the secret that will point you toward heaven, and the unimaginable joy of eternal life in the presence of God. You might even say it's the secret of life itself. Solomon said much the same in the concluding chapter of Ecclesiastes: "Let us hear the conclusion of the whole matter: Fear God and keep His commandments, for this is man's all" (Ecclesiastes 12:13).

That's what it all comes down to. A deep reverence for God and His Word, a strong aversion to disappointing or grieving Him in any way, and a strong, motivating desire to walk that particular path He has marked out for your life.

Weekend

"And whoever does not bear his cross and come after Me cannot be My disciple. For which of you, intending to build a tower, does not sit down first and count the cost, whether he has enough to finish it..."
(Luke 14:27-28)

When Jesus was in Jerusalem during the Passover, John's Gospel tells us that many believed in His name after they saw the signs He did. But Jesus would not entrust Himself to them, because "He knew all men, and had no need that anyone should testify of man, for He knew what was in man" (John 2:24-25).

To put it simply, many believed in Him, but He didn't believe in *them*. Many believed in Him in a shallow, superficial sort of way, without any real commitment attached. They were interested in Him, curious about Him, drawn by Him, and perhaps even felt affection for Him. But the loyalty of these crowds was a mile wide and an inch deep. Jesus knew that when push came to shove, the multitudes would simply drift away. For that reason, Christ did not commit Himself to them.

There are many people who say they want to follow Jesus. And that's good. But that commitment will be challenged. We must decide to follow Jesus—not because our best friend is, not because our boyfriend or girlfriend is, not because our parents are, but because we have chosen in our own heart of hearts to follow Christ.

Many of us can get caught up in the moment. It's like watching an Olympic medal ceremony. We see someone representing their nation standing up on that pedestal. As the gold medal is placed around the athlete's neck and the flag of his or her country is raised while the national anthem plays, we say, "I want to be an Olympic athlete. That's what I want to do." But do we realize the hours, days, months, and *years* these athletes dedicate to one competition?

We get excited about the medal ceremonies. But are we willing to go through the training? Are we willing to count the cost? Is our commitment to Him and Him alone? Are we willing to be real followers of Jesus?

Monday

Jesus said to her, "Mary!" She turned and said to Him, "Rabboni!"
(John 20:16)

Mary Magdalene was one of the most devoted followers that Jesus ever had. The book of Luke tells us that she and others ministered to Him out of "their substance," which simply means that she financially supported Him. She traveled with Him, wanted to be near Him and hear Him, and had the courage to stand at the foot of the cross after most of the disciples had run for their lives. Imagine how her heart broke at His crucifixion.

She was the last one at the cross, and early Sunday morning, she was the first at the tomb. She wasn't there to see a risen Lord, but to anoint His dead body. But she was in for a great surprise, because Jesus came to her in the midst of her sorrow.

And Jesus comes in the same way to the grieving person today. Maybe you feel desperate in your own grief. Maybe it's over a death. Maybe it's the breakup of a marriage or child who has gone astray spiritually. But you are broken and grieving.

The good news is that things can change. Circumstances in your life may look absolutely bleak today, but that husband or wife may return. That prodigal child may come back to God. And as a believer, you will again see that Christian loved one who has died. No matter what your circumstances, Jesus will be there with you. Maybe He will resolve your problems immediately. Or maybe your problems will continue. But you will never, never be alone.

That is the message of the resurrected Lord to us. He knows what we are going through. He understands. And He cares. Peter, who walked with Jesus through His earthly ministry, and also knew the strong encouragement of His resurrected Lord, put it like this: "So, humble yourselves under God's strong hand, and in his own good time he will lift you up. You can throw the whole weight of your anxieties upon him, for you are his personal concern" (1 Peter 5:6-7, PHILLIPS).

Tuesday

"Since his days are determined, the number of his months is with You; You have appointed his limits, so that he cannot pass." (Job 14:5)

The Bible says our days are numbered, which means there is a day coming (we don't know when) when we are *out of here*. We can worry about that, or we can simply trust that God knows when that day will be. It doesn't mean we take up bungee jumping off of bridges or swimming with sharks, putting our lives at unnecessary risk. But it does mean we recognize the fact that our lives belong to God. We're in His hands.

This is a very comforting thought, because it means that until God is finished with us, nothing will happen to us. That's great to know. But it also means when our number is up, it's up. When that day comes, there is nothing we can do to turn the clock back.

So what are we to do? As we have already read in these pages, the apostle Paul said, "For to me, to live is Christ, and to die is gain" (Philippians 1:21). So we should praise God for each new day, thank Him for the opportunities He provides, for the blessings He gives us, and for our family and friends. We should take time to smell the flowers, bounce a little one on our knee, and savor the sight of a rainbow, a tree painted with the colors of autumn, or the blue surf rolling in across a sandy beach. And of course we should be available and willing to serve Him in whatever plans He has for us.

God values you. He loves you. But if death came for you today, would you be ready? If not, you would face a certain judgment. That's the last thing God wants to happen to you. That's why He sent Jesus to die on the cross and shed His blood for every sin you have ever committed.

Only the person who says, "To live is Christ" can then say, "To die is gain." That is a person whose soul is right with God.

Wednesday

And I am convinced and sure of this very thing, that He Who began a good work in you will continue until the day of Jesus Christ [right up to the time of His return], developing [that good work] and perfecting and bringing it to full completion in you. (Philippians 1:6, AMPLIFIED)

Are you discouraged today? Afraid of an uncertain future? The Bible tells the story of a time when Jesus' disciples were not only discouraged, but were actually in terror for their very lives.

Jesus had told them to get into a boat and go over to the other side of the Sea of Galilee, and they obeyed. But when they were a considerable distance from land, a fierce storm arose that terrified them. Jesus, who had been on a mountain praying, went to meet the disciples, walking on the water. Thinking He was a ghost, the disciples cried out in fear. So Jesus immediately told them, "Take courage! It is I. Don't be afraid" (Matthew 14:27, NIV).

There are two simple reasons the disciples didn't have to be afraid: First, Jesus would help them weather the storm. And second, He had told them to go to the other side, which meant that they *would* reach the other side. Where God guides, God provides.

Jesus knows where you are at this very moment. As complicated and tangled as your situation might seem to you right now, it's all perfectly clear to Him. He knows what you are thinking, feeling, experiencing. He's telling you to be courageous, because He is with you and there is a brighter tomorrow for you. Even if you've failed, even if you've made a mistake, it isn't over. You can still learn from that mistake and get out of the situation in which you find yourself.

God has a future for each of us. Jeremiah 29:11 (NIV), one of my all-time favorite verses, says, "For I know the plans I have for you... plans to prosper you and not to harm you, plans to give you hope and a future." God will complete the work He has begun in your life.

Take courage!

Thursday

Therefore I, a prisoner for serving the Lord, beg you to lead a life worthy of your calling, for you have been called by God. Always be humble and gentle. Be patient with each other, making allowance for each other's faults because of your love. (Ephesians 4:1-2, NLT)

The ancient Greeks didn't put much stock in humility. In classical Greek, humility was a derogatory term suggesting low-mindedness and groveling servanthood. It was looked upon as an undesirable, negative trait. Sometimes humility doesn't fare much better in our culture, as evidenced by attitudes that say, "Look out for number one" and "What's in it for me?"

The Bible, however, makes it clear that God expects us to put the needs of others above our own. And in the language of Scripture, "meek" doesn't mean weak. The biblical term literally means "strength under constraint." Think of a mighty racehorse here, controlled by a bit in his mouth...or maybe a powerful car with a huge engine being driven ever-so-carefully in a school zone.

A person who is meek in the biblical sense may be a very strong individual with a high capacity to hurt you...but he chooses not to.

Some through the years have described Jesus as "meek and mild." Was God's Son weak, then? Not on your life! In His great strength, however, He chose not to return insult for insult or blow for blow. He gave us an example to follow—a powerful man who chose the path of humility, and dealt with others in gentleness.

To walk that path means humbling ourselves. Sometimes, it means going to an individual and saying, "I don't know if I have said or done something to offend you, but if I did, I'm truly sorry. Let's try to work it out." And it means saying these things even if you're convinced you're right and the other person was wrong from the get-go. That's where humility and meekness come in.

We need to get rid of any me-first attitudes and start thinking biblically. And we need to be asking, *What can I do to help others? How can I learn to resolve conflicts?* It can change your life.

Jesus said, "Blessed are the meek, for they will inherit the earth" (Matthew 5:5). They will also bring pleasure to the heart of God Himself, and that's about as good as it gets.

Friday

Now when the devil had ended every temptation, he departed from Him until an opportune time. (Luke 4:13)

In a broad sense, temptation can come to us at any time. Of course, it often happens after times of great blessing. Jesus was tested, or tempted, in the wilderness for 40 days and nights, right after His baptism in the Jordan River when the Spirit of God came upon Him in the form of a dove. After the dove came the devil. After the blessing came the attack. Often after great times of blessing, the enemy will be there, wanting to rob us of what God has done.

Maybe you have experienced a sweet season of blessing in your life recently. Enjoy it, savor it, thank God for it. But keep your guard up! The enemy will be there. He will attack you, and he will tempt you. He waits for the opportune time to confront us, and we are often the most vulnerable when we think we are the strongest.

If you think that weak believers had better be careful, then I have a thought for you: Strong believers had better be careful, too. The Bible says, "Therefore let him who thinks he stands take heed lest he fall" (1 Corinthians 10:12).

Many times temptation can come when we're relaxing. Take David for example. He was tempted when he was up on the rooftop taking a little rest and relaxation, at the time when kings usually go out to battle. He sent his commander Joab into battle, probably reasoning, "Joab can handle it. I don't have to fight *every* battle. Hey, I'm the king. I may as well kick back and enjoy myself a little." And that's how he came to be wandering around on his palace rooftop one night, just as the beautiful Bathsheba was bathing on her rooftop. David lowered his guard, and…we know the rest of that tragic story.

There is no rest from spiritual battle. There are no holidays from warfare with Satan and his evil legions. Always keep your guard up, because the moment you think, *It won't hit me here*, that is where it will hit you. The enemy is just waiting. He is looking for an opportunity. So keep your armor on.

Weekend

We despised him and rejected him—a man of sorrows, acquainted with bitterest grief. We turned our backs on him and looked the other way when he went by. He was despised, and we didn't care.

Yet it was our grief he bore, our sorrows that weighed him down. And we thought his troubles were a punishment from God, for his own sins! But he was wounded and bruised for our sins. He was chastised that we might have peace; he was lashed-and we were healed! We-every one of us-have strayed away like sheep! We, who left God's paths to follow our own. Yet God laid on him the guilt and sins of every one of us! *(Isaiah 53:3-6, TLB)*

I heard a true story about a man who operated a drawbridge. At a certain time every afternoon, he raised the bridge for a ferryboat to go by, and then lowered it in time for a passenger train to cross over. He performed this task precisely, according to the clock.

One day, he brought his son to work so he could watch. As his father raised the bridge, the boy got excited and wanted to take a closer look. His father realized his son was missing and began looking for him. To his horror, his son had come dangerously close to the bridge's gears. Frantic, he wanted to go rescue him, but if he left the controls, he wouldn't be back in time to lower the bridge for the approaching passenger train.

He faced a dilemma. If he lowered the bridge, his son would be killed. If he left it raised, hundreds of others would die. He knew what he had to do. With tears streaming down his face, he watched the passenger train roll by. On board, two women chatted over tea. Others were reading newspapers. All were totally unaware of what had just transpired. The man cried out, "Don't you realize that I just gave my son for you?" But they just continued on their way.

This story is a picture of what happened at the cross. God gave up His beloved Son so that we might live. Most people, however, don't give it a second thought. How about you? Are you conscious of the ultimate sacrifice God made on your behalf?

Monday

While Jesus was still speaking, some men came from the house of Jairus, the synagogue ruler. "Your daughter is dead," they said. "Why bother the teacher any more?"

Ignoring what they said, Jesus told the synagogue ruler, "Don't be afraid; just believe." (Mark 5:35-36, NIV)

Jairus was a well-known, powerful, wealthy individual who was the head of the local synagogue. When his twelve-year-old daughter, his only child, was in great need, hovering between life and death, he sought out Jesus to heal her.

We don't know whether Jairus was a believer in Jesus. As the head of the synagogue, he would certainly have been a religious man. He'd probably heard about Jesus. Maybe he had already put his faith in Him. The Scripture doesn't say. Nevertheless, Jairus believed that Jesus could save his daughter's life. So he went and found the Lord and begged Him to heal his desperately sick girl. He placed complete trust in Jesus to care for the greatest treasure in his whole life.

As they were on their way to his house, however, the news came that his daughter had died. The reason they hadn't arrived at his daughter's side more quickly was because a woman in need of healing came along and touched Jesus, and He stopped and demanded to know who it was that touched Him.

Jairus, however, didn't complain. He had committed himself and his situation to Jesus, believing that God knew what He was doing. His faith was dramatic, especially because at this particular time in Jesus' ministry, He hadn't raised anyone from the dead. Granted, He had healed people. But there had been no resurrections.

Jairus had to wait, and sometimes we have to wait. A lot of us grow impatient with God, and in our impatience, we may foolishly take things into our own hands and make them far worse. Know this: God's delays are not necessarily His denials. We need to wait on the Lord. He's worth waiting for! God's timing is just as important as His will. He doesn't ask for us to understand, He just asks us to trust.

Tuesday

For men are not cast off by the Lord forever. Though he brings grief,
he will show compassion, so great is his unfailing love. For he does not
willingly bring affliction or grief to the children of men.
(Lamentations 3:31-33, NIV)

In the much-loved Psalm 23, David wrote: "Your rod and Your staff, they comfort me." The rod and the staff were shepherd's tools. The staff was a long, crooked instrument the shepherd would use when a sheep was going astray. But the rod was simply a club, which was used when the staff wasn't working anymore.

We may think that a club is extremely cruel to use on a poor sheep. But better to get whacked with a club than eaten by a wolf! Sheep are incredibly dumb. They will actually line up to die. If one sheep goes over a cliff, the other sheep will say, "Get in line. We're all going to die today. Let's go. Single file." The shepherd sometimes has to use extra corrective measures on a wayward sheep that could otherwise lead others astray.

I have seen the Lord use the rod of suffering or sickness to get someone's attention. He will say, "You really shouldn't do that," and then convicts them by His Spirit. But they might ignore Him. So He tells them, "Don't do that. I don't want you to do that." If they continue to ignore Him, BAM! God will use His rod: "I told you… don't do that." I have met a lot of people in hospitals who have come to Christ. Unfortunately, a lot of them don't stay with Christ. But others continue to walk with the Lord.

Maybe God has recently whacked you with His rod to get your attention. Maybe He has given you a wake-up call in the form of suffering or sickness, and you've been wondering why.

The book of Hebrews tells us: "My dear child, don't shrug off God's discipline, but don't be crushed by it either. It's the child he loves that he disciplines; the child he embraces, he also corrects" (Hebrews 12:5-6, THE MESSAGE).

Don't ever doubt it: If God has allowed hardship or suffering into your life for a season, it is because He loves you.

Wednesday

After this, the armies of the Moabites, Ammonites, and some of the Meunites declared war on Jehoshaphat. Messengers came and told Jehoshaphat, "A vast army from Edom is marching against you from beyond the Dead Sea. They are already at Hazazon-tamar." ... Jehoshaphat was terrified by this news and begged the Lord for guidance. He also ordered everyone in Judah to begin fasting. So people from all the towns of Judah came to Jerusalem to seek the Lord's help.
(2 Chronicles 20:1-4, NLT)

Jehoshaphat, King of Judah, faced a terrifying dilemma. His enemies greatly outnumbered him...and they were already on the march, with little Judah in their sights.

From a human perspective, the situation was hopeless. There was no way he could meet this mighty army with what he had. It looked for all the world like doomsday for God's people.

What did Jehoshaphat do? The Bible says that he prayed: "O our God, won't you stop them? We are powerless against this mighty army that is about to attack us. We do not know what to do, but we are looking to you for help." (2 Chronicles 20:12, NLT).

The Lord told Jehoshaphat, "Do not be afraid! Don't be discouraged by this mighty army, for the battle is not yours, but God's... But you will not even need to fight. Take your positions; then stand still and watch the Lord's victory. He is with you, O people of Judah and Jerusalem. Do not be afraid or discouraged. Go out against them tomorrow, for the Lord is with you!" (2 Chronicles 20:15, 17, NLT).

Jehoshaphat and his army went out to meet their enemies, but they put the worship team out in front of the soldiers! The Bible says that when they began to sing and praise the Lord, the enemy started fighting amongst themselves and destroyed each other.

Maybe you are facing what seems like an impossible situation right now. You may not be able to see a way out. But God can. Call on Him. Then stand still and see what He will do.

Thursday

God lifted him high and honored him far beyond anyone or anything, ever, so that all created beings in heaven and on earth—even those long ago dead and buried—will bow in worship before this Jesus Christ, and call out in praise that he is the Master of all, to the glorious honor of God the Father. (Philippians 2:9-11, THE MESSAGE)

There are people today who teach that Jesus never claimed to be God; it's just something people dreamed up. But that is a lie. Jesus indeed claimed to be God, and any group who says that Jesus is not God is not a Christian group, no matter how big their Bibles or how much they might look like Christians.

Jesus made clear claims to deity. He said, "For if you do not believe that I am He, you will die in your sins" (John 8:24). When Moses saw the burning bush and walked up to it, he heard a voice speaking to him that said, "Do not draw near this place. Take your sandals off your feet, for the place where you stand is holy ground....I am the God of your father—the God of Abraham, the God of Isaac, and the God of Jacob" (Exodus 3:5, 6). It was a claim to deity. So when Jesus said, "Unless you believe that I am He, you will die in your sins," it means that Jesus claimed to be God.

To suggest otherwise is ludicrous. We know, for instance, that on many occasions He accepted worship, something absolutely reserved for God alone. He said to Satan during the temptation in the wilderness, "'You shall worship the Lord your God, and Him only you shall serve'" (Matthew 4:10). Yet on other occasions, Jesus personally accepted worship.

When Thomas saw the risen Lord, he fell down before Him and said, "My Lord and my God!" (John 20:28). Jesus never corrected Thomas or refuted him for that worship. Instead, He simply accepted it, because He is indeed the Lord and God, and all worship belongs to Him.

Friday

He who says he abides in Him ought himself also to walk just as He walked. (1 John 2:6)

The word "walking" speaks of regularity, of moving at a certain pace. The Bible tells us in Genesis 5 about Enoch, who walked with God. But what does it mean to "walk with God?" Is it just a religious cliché?

The prophet Amos asked, "Can two walk together, unless they are agreed?" (Amos 3:3). The idea is to be walking in pace or harmony with another.

I have a problem with this when I walk with my wife. I always walk a little faster than she does. Every time, I find myself walking out ahead of her. Then I'll stop, and wait for her to catch up. So I'll try to walk more slowly, but the next thing I know, I'm walking fast again.

When it comes to walking with God, some of us want to run ahead of Him. Others lag behind. What we need to do is move in harmony with Him. We need to stay close to Him, and make a continual commitment to do so. Referring to our daily relationship with God's Holy Spirit, the New Testament says, "Since we live by the Spirit, let us keep in step with the Spirit" (Galatians 5:25, NIV).

But what does this mean in practice? How do we do this? What does it look like to "keep in step with the Spirit"? It means we take time for the things of God. It means when we get up in the morning, we take time to read the Bible. If we neglect the Word of God, it will show in our lives. Abiding in Jesus also means that we spend time in fellowship with God's people.

Make time for the things of God. And don't wait for time to simply materialize; deliberately carve out room in your schedule. If it means an hour less of sleep, fine. If it means skipping a meal, okay. If it means missing a television program, so be it. Do what you need to do, because these things are essential to spiritual growth, to abiding with God, and to bearing spiritual fruit.

And this walk with God is a walk—the best of all walks—that will bring indescribable richness to your daily life.

Weekend

And He said to them, "He who has ears to hear, let him hear!"
(Mark 4:9)

It is possible to hear God's Word with our ears, but not with our hearts. Jesus knew that we can often hear without understanding. That is why He would so often say, "He who has ears to hear, let him hear!" If we were to paraphrase that in our modern language, Jesus would be saying, "Pay attention to what I'm saying. Listen carefully to what I'm telling you right now." *He who has ears to hear, let him hear...*It is attention with intention.

I do quite a bit of traveling. When I get on a plane and take my seat, I really don't listen carefully to the safety message that the flight attendants give before every single flight. They have a long list of information to give out, pointing out the exits and the location of oxygen masks and life vests. But often I don't pay attention. I may look at a magazine instead. Why? Because I've heard it so many times, I think I don't need to listen.

But what if a few minutes after takeoff the pilot came on the intercom again and said something like this? "We are currently experiencing some technical difficulties, and the flight attendant is going to go through that safety message for you one more time," I can guarantee you that I would be listening. Why? Because my life would depend on it. I would really want to know where those exits are, how to use my seat as a flotation device, and what steps I might need to take to survive an emergency.

When you think about it, that's how we need to be reading the Word of God. Not as a ho-hum morning routine where we're skimming a passage and not really even thinking about it. No, we need to listen carefully. It is attention with intention, listening with the desire to apply what we have read to our own daily situations, because so much depends on that infusion of wisdom and life. Probably more than we'll ever know.

Monday

"Let not your heart be troubled; you believe in God, believe also in Me."
(John 14:1)

H ave you ever felt troubled in your heart—agitated, stressed-out, or uncertain about tomorrow?

There's a lot to be afraid of these days, isn't there? You check the news headlines in the paper or online in the morning, and it seems like disaster after disaster, tragedy upon tragedy. Or maybe something has happened to you recently that has turned your world upside down. Perhaps you've received news that has tied your stomach in a knot. Maybe you've found yourself wondering whether God really is aware of the (multiple) problems you're facing right now.

That's exactly how the disciples of Jesus felt. They were downhearted and discouraged. When they were all gathered in the Upper Room for the Passover feast, Jesus told them that one of them was going to betray Him. Then He identified Judas Iscariot as the betrayer. Not only that, but Jesus also said Simon Peter would deny Him—not once, not twice, but three times. Peter? Could it really be? The whole world had turned upside down for these men. And then, worst of all, Jesus began talking about leaving them, about being crucified. Can you blame them for wondering, *What in the world is going on here?*

Maybe you feel that way. Maybe there is uncertainty in your future. As you survey your fears and concerns today, take a few minutes to consider what Jesus said to His disciples and to us in that tense Upper Room: "Let not your heart be troubled; you believe in God, believe also in Me" (John 14:1). This verse could also be translated, "Let not your heart be agitated, or disturbed, or thrown into confusion…"

In other words, "Don't let these things throw you! Put your full trust and faith in Me!" It was good advice for some deeply troubled believers two thousand years ago and I can tell you right now with complete confidence…it's the best counsel anyone will give you all day today.

Tuesday

And we know that all things work together for good to those who love God, to those who are the called according to His purpose. (Romans 8:28)

There are times in our lives as Christians when God will do things, or fail to do things that we want Him to do, and it won't make a bit of sense to us. And because we don't see the big picture, we may falsely conclude that God has abandoned us. But we need to trust Him during these times, remembering that Jesus Christ is the author and finisher of our faith. In other words, what God starts, He completes.

Remember that wonderful word from the first chapter of Philippians? "There has never been the slightest doubt in my mind that the God who started this great work in you would keep at it and bring it to a flourishing finish on the very day Christ Jesus appears" (Philippians 1:6, THE MESSAGE).

It seems as I get older, I get distracted and forget things all the time. But what if God forgot about us? What a frightening thought. Imagine being in the midst of a fiery trial as God is watching and waiting for that moment to take us out of it. Then the phone rings, and He's gone for a decade! Thankfully, God never forgets about us. He remains—forever and ever—in full control. He knows exactly what He is doing. He will complete what He has begun.

Sometimes in the middle of that process, we may think the Lord is missing it. But He isn't. We're the ones who are missing it. From our limited human viewpoint, we think of the temporal, but God lives in the eternal. We are thinking of today, but God is planning for tomorrow...in fact, He's already been there. We are thinking of comfort, but God is thinking of character. We are thinking of an easy time, but God is thinking of how to make us better people.

So let's trust Him. Whatever our circumstances or hardships, let's believe His promise to His children... All things *are* working together.

Wednesday

"In My Father's house are many mansions; if it were not so, I would have told you. I go to prepare a place for you." (John 14:2)

We don't have to be stressed-out or troubled in our hearts, because as Christians, our destination is eternal life in heaven. No matter what happens, no one can rob us of that great hope. Maybe you've lost your job or your car won't start. Maybe you have all kinds of problems in your life right now. But you are still going to heaven.

The apostle Paul encouraged the church with these words: "That is why we never give up. Though our bodies are dying, our inner strength in the Lord is growing every day. These troubles and sufferings of ours are, after all, quite small and won't last very long. Yet this short time of distress will result in God's richest blessing upon us forever and ever! So we do not look at what we can see right now, the troubles all around us, but we look forward to the joys in heaven which we have not yet seen. The troubles will soon be over, but the joys to come will last forever" (2 Corinthians 4:16-18, TLB).

Jesus promises there is a real place called heaven, and you have His word on it—the surest word in all the universe.

Now when Jesus said, "In My Father's house are many mansions," I don't believe He was speaking of a celestial Beverly Hills with beautiful, palatial mansions for those who live really godly lives on earth. The Amplified Bible renders this verse: "In My Father's house there are many dwelling places (homes)."

Who can begin to imagine what these "homes" or "dwelling places" will be like? All I know is that Jesus Himself—the One who created the universe with all its wonders—has been working on preparing a place for us for over 2,000 years.

I agree with Paul when he wrote: "No mere man has ever seen, heard, or even imagined what wonderful things God has ready for those who love the Lord" (1 Corinthians 2:9, TLB).

Jesus has promised us that we will be together with Him in heaven, for eternity, in the place He has prepared for us. And He will keep His word.

Thursday

So, my very dear friends, don't get thrown off course.
(James 1:16, THE MESSAGE)

In many—if not most—cases, temptation enters through the doorway of our minds. When Satan wanted to lead the first man and woman into sin, he started by attacking the woman's mind. That's why Paul warned the Corinthian believers, "But I fear that somehow you will be led away from your pure and simple devotion to Christ, just as Eve was deceived by the serpent" (2 Corinthians 11:3, NLT).

We need to protect our minds, because that's where the enemy will hit us. To advance his attack, he has the ability to reach into the past through our memories and into the future through our imaginations.

When the children of Israel were in the wilderness, their first step into trouble began with looking back. God had miraculously delivered them from Egypt. He fed them with manna from heaven every day. For some, that was a little too much manna. They had tried all of the recipes in Moses' cookbook, *101 Ways to Eat Manna*. But they remembered the food they had in Egypt. Isn't it interesting that they thought it was a lot better than it had really been? They let their imaginations run wild as they remembered the scraps of food they had been given by the slave masters in "good old Egypt." In their imaginations, they magnified those paltry scraps into feasts.

That's how the devil will work against us. He will make a few good moments we had way back when seem like the greatest times we ever had. But he is a liar. Jesus said, "No one, having put his hand to the plow, and looking back, is fit for the kingdom of God" (Luke 9:62).

So don't look back.

Temptation starts with a thought, and—please take careful note of this—*from that point on, the tempter needs cooperation from the tempted.* That's why we need to guard our minds.

An old quote that has sometimes been attributed to Martin Luther says: "You can't stop the birds flying over your head, but you can stop them from nesting in your hair."

Friday

Therefore we also, since we are surrounded by so great a cloud of witnesses, let us lay aside every weight, and the sin which so easily ensnares us, and let us run with endurance the race that is set before us.
(Hebrews 12:1)

When I was a kid, I had all kinds of ribbons on my walls for races I had run, but not one of them was blue. Not one of them had the words "first place." They were all purple. Purple represented "honorable mention." An honorable mention is not first, second, third, or fourth place. It means "also ran." In other words, "We don't want him to feel bad, so we'll give him a purple ribbon."

Of course, everyone wants first place. Everyone wants to win the gold medal. That's where the prestige and popularity are. That's where you get all the strokes and the "atta-boys."

But let me say this. I am running this race of life, and the Bible tells me that one day in heaven there will be a reward waiting for me. It won't be based on how much I have done or how much recognition I have gained in the course of my life. It will be based on how faithful I was to what God called me to do. The same is true for you. Your reward will be based on how faithful you have been through the days of your life to the calling you have received from God.

Let me also say that I am not running this race for the reward. Nor am I running it for other people or to score points. I am running this race for Jesus. He is the One we all should be running for.

The apostle Paul presents the same principle in Philippians 3:10: "That I may know Him and the power of His resurrection, and the fellowship of His sufferings, being conformed to His death...." Paul was saying, "This is why I'm doing it. My purpose for running this race is to know Jesus Christ." That's what mattered to him. And that's what should mean the most to us.

Weekend

One thing I have desired of the Lord, that will I seek: that I may dwell in the house of the Lord all the days of my life, to behold the beauty of the Lord, and to inquire in His temple. (Psalm 27:4)

David wrote, "*One thing* I have desired of the Lord, that will I seek…." In other words, the one thing that really excited him was spending time in the presence of God.

Mary knew this one thing, too, when Jesus came to visit her and her sister Martha in the little village of Bethany. She sat down at His feet, absolutely riveted by everything He had to say.

Martha, a diligent, hardworking woman, wanted to impress the Lord with the fine meal she was preparing. Who wouldn't, if you had a guest like Jesus? Can you imagine Jesus showing up at your house? You would want to offer Him your best, right? You wouldn't give Him a microwave dinner or last night's leftover spaghetti. You would want to prepare a special meal.

As Martha was working away in the hot kitchen, she undoubtedly kept looking for Mary. *Where's Mary? I can't believe she's not in here.* Finally in frustration, she came out—probably with her hands on her hips—and said, "Lord, do You not care that my sister has left me to serve alone? Therefore tell her to help me."

Jesus replied, "Martha, Martha, you are worried and troubled about many things. But one thing is needed, and Mary has chosen that good part, which will not be taken away from her" (Luke 10:41-42).

Mary figured out one thing, and that was the importance of sitting at Jesus' feet. What is your "one thing"? What gets you out of bed in the morning? What keeps you going, even through heartaches and trials and disappointments?

In Philippians 3:13-14, the apostle Paul said: "But one thing I do, forgetting those things which are behind and reaching forward to those things which are ahead, I press toward the goal for the prize of the upward call of God in Christ Jesus.

Paul said, "*But one thing I do.*" He didn't say, "Twelve things I dabble at." In other words, Paul's life had a strong focus that helped him prioritize everything else.

Monday

Having loved His own who were in the world, He loved them to the end.
(John 13:1)

We have all probably heard someone say at some time, "God loves you." And sometimes we may wonder, *Is that actually true? Does God really love me?* Maybe you've been let down and sorely disappointed by people. Maybe someone said he loved you and then turned against you. Maybe someone said she was your closest friend, but ultimately betrayed you.

When it comes to God's love, we tend to ask ourselves whether it's for real. We wonder whether He, too, will turn away from us if we let Him down.

Our Lord knew what it was like to be betrayed. As Jesus celebrated the Feast of the Passover with His disciples, the devil had already put it into the heart of Judas to betray Him. The other disciples didn't stand by Jesus, either. They forsook Him, but He did not forsake them. They denied Him, but He did not deny them. He loved His own who were in the world, and He loved them to the end.

The story is told of a little boy who was troubled one night by a thunderstorm. He cried out from his room, "Daddy! I'm scared!"

The father responded, "Son, don't worry. God loves you, and He will take care of you."

The boy replied, "I know God loves me, but right now I need someone with skin on."

Jesus is God with skin on. Jesus is God demonstrating His love for His own. I love the passage from the book of Hebrews that speaks about God "going the distance" to relate to us in our weak humanity:

> "Since we, God's children, are human beings-made
> of flesh and blood--he became flesh and blood too by
> being born in human form; for only as a human being
> could he die and in dying break the power of the devil
> who had the power of death. Only in that way could he
> deliver those who through fear of death have been living
> all their lives as slaves to constant dread"
> (Hebrews 2:14-15, TLB).

Aren't you glad that God doesn't treat us the way we so often treat Him? Aren't you relieved He doesn't reciprocate that way? No matter what you do, no matter where you go, God will always love you.

Tuesday

See how very much our Father loves us, for he calls us his children, and that is what we are! Dear friends, we are already God's children, but he has not yet shown us what we will be like when Christ appears. But we do know that we will be like him, for we will see him as he really is. (1 John 3:1, 2, NLT)

What do you think God's love is? Do you envision a permissive love that allows you to do whatever you want? That doesn't describe the love of God. You see, God loves you enough to put restrictions in your life. He loves you enough to say, "Do this. It will help you. And don't do this. It's bad for you."

Suppose a child asks his mother, "Mommy, can I play in the street?" Of course she would say, "No, you may not. I love you and don't want you to be in a place where you would be endangered. One day, you will realize that I did this not from a lack of love, but because I do love you."

It's the same with us. When God says "no" to us, it's not because He doesn't love us. It's just the opposite.

In the Garden of Eden, God told Adam, "'Of every tree of the garden you may freely eat; but of the tree of the knowledge of good and evil you shall not eat, for in the day that you eat of it you shall surely die'" (Genesis 2:16-17). So the devil tempted Eve: "Has God indeed said, 'You shall not eat of every tree of the garden?'" (Genesis 3:1). Essentially he was saying, "If God really loved you, then He would let you do whatever you want." The truth was that because God loved Adam and Eve, He didn't want them to fall into sin. Yet they disobeyed God and that's exactly what happened.

Those limits that you find in the pages of the Bible are there for your own good. God has put a fence around you, so to speak. But it's not to keep you confined—it's to keep you safe from the many dangers in this world—and in the invisible spiritual world that surrounds us.

Wednesday

If you, O Lord, kept a record of sins, O Lord, who could stand? But with you there is forgiveness; therefore you are feared. (Psalm 130:3-4, NIV)

Before the Passover meal, Jesus took off His outer robe. He got down on His hands and knees, picked up the basin, and began to wash the disciples' feet.

As Jesus made His way around the room, Peter was watching. Always one to speak his mind, he blurted out, "Lord, are You washing my feet?" (John 13:6). It's almost as though he didn't want to humble himself in this way. Perhaps he saw that it had symbolic meaning and, in spite of the fact that he had already bathed, the implication was that he was dirty again.

There are people like that today who say, "I haven't sinned. I haven't done anything wrong. I'm a good person. I don't need God's forgiveness." But *everybody* needs it.

Jesus told Peter, "He who is bathed needs only to wash his feet, but is completely clean..." (verse 10). In other words, once you have received Jesus Christ as your Savior and Lord, you don't need to be saved again and again. You don't have to shower over and over. Once you have received Christ into your life and have asked Him to forgive you, then you are forgiven. Christ has already come into your heart...but you do need regular cleansing.

In 1 John 1:8-9 (NLT), we read: "If we claim we have no sin, we are only fooling ourselves and not living in the truth. But if we confess our sins to him, he is faithful and just to forgive us our sins and to cleanse us from all wickedness."

I know that my sin is forgiven; I know my final destination is heaven, but on a daily basis I do need to say, "Lord, forgive me." As David prayed: "Search me, O God, and know my heart; test me and know my anxious thoughts. See if there is any offensive way in me, and lead me in the way everlasting" (Psalm 139:23-24, NIV).

So it's a good thing to say, "Lord, cleanse me. Forgive me." Because we need constant cleansing.

Thursday

For the kingdom of God is not eating and drinking, but righteousness and peace and joy in the Holy Spirit. (Romans 14:17)

Jesus calls us His sheep, and we know that the Shepherd's primary objective for His sheep is that they flourish. He wants His sheep to be well-fed, well-cared for, content, and satisfied. It is the joy of the Shepherd to lead His sheep to green pastures and still waters.

Jesus also has given His sheep a great promise. He said, "My sheep hear My voice, and I know them, and they follow Me. And I give them eternal life, and they shall never perish; neither shall anyone snatch them out of My hand" (John 10:27-28). There is great security in knowing that the Lord is our Shepherd, and that we are under His protection.

Did you know that God loves to bless you? Delights to pour His grace out upon you? Truly enjoys working in your life? He wants to bless you more than you want to be blessed! He wants to answer your prayers more than you want them answered. He wants to speak to you even more than you want to be spoken to. And He wants to use you even more than you want to be used. He loves you. Jesus said, "Do not fear, little flock, for it is your Father's good pleasure to give you the kingdom" (Luke 12:32). It is His joy, His pleasure, to give you the kingdom.

And what is that kingdom? The Bible says the kingdom of God is "righteousness and peace and joy in the Holy Spirit" (Romans 14:17). He wants His righteousness, peace, and yes, overflowing *joy* to permeate every level of your life.

Our world today doesn't really grasp the concept of joy. Our culture speaks of "happiness" as a temporary condition when the random happenings of our lives fall into a pleasing alignment. But then, when something happens to upset or disturb that balance, happiness goes out the window. The joy of the Lord is completely different. It is a gift of God, a beautiful fruit of the indwelling Holy Spirit. It can even quietly bubble up in our hearts—like water from an artesian spring—in the midst of hardships or difficult circumstances.

That is a taste of heaven on earth, and that's what God desires for you today.

Friday

The Lord isn't really being slow about his promise, as some people think. No, he is being patient for your sake. He does not want anyone to be destroyed, so he is giving more time for everyone to repent. (2 Peter 3:9, NLT)

As we look at this world we're living in, and consider the path our culture has taken, we find ourselves glancing up at the sky from time to time, whispering, "Lord, isn't it about time? Please come back. Please return soon." But God has His own schedule: He isn't late, and He isn't early. He will be right on time.

When Jesus came to earth the first time, it was according to God's perfect plan. Paul wrote in the book of Galatians: "But when the fullness of the time had come, God sent forth His Son, born of a woman, born under the law, to redeem those who were under the law, that we might receive the adoption as sons" (Galatians 4:4-5). I love that expression, "the fullness of time." In other words, when the time was just right, at the appointed hour, Jesus Christ—the Son of God—fulfilled the prophecies of Scripture and was born in a stable in Bethlehem. And so it will be at His return. When the time is just right, at the hour already determined in the councils of eternity, Jesus Christ, the Son of God, will return to the earth.

But don't get the idea that God is just "marking time" until that day arrives. No, He has a plan He wants to accomplish in the interim. The Shepherd is still looking for lost, wandering sheep to bring into the fold. As we saw in 2 Peter 3:9, the Lord is waiting for those last people to come into His kingdom and put their faith in Him. Can you imagine if you knew the one person for whom God was waiting? Wouldn't you be tempted to put a little pressure on that individual?

We need to remember that as Christians, our numbers are relatively small. But the task is immense. And the time is short.

Weekend

I don't mean to say that I have already achieved these things or that I have already reached perfection! But I press on to possess that perfection for which Christ Jesus first possessed me. No, dear brothers and sisters, I have not achieved it, but I focus on this one thing: Forgetting the past and looking forward to what lies ahead, I press on to reach the end of the race and receive the heavenly prize for which God, through Christ Jesus, is calling us. (Philippians 3:12-14, NLT)

Everyone who has run a race knows that you can break your stride by looking over your shoulder to check out how your opponents are doing. Many races have been lost when the leader looked back. When you see that finish line, that's the time to give it everything you've got…because sometimes it's mere inches that separate one runner from another. You must stay focused.

This is the idea behind Paul's statement in Philippians 3:13. The apostle was saying, "Don't look back. Don't look behind you."

When God promises, "I, even I, am He who blots out your transgressions for My own sake; and I will not remember your sins" (Isaiah 43:25), He isn't predicting a lapse in His memory. God is saying, "I will no longer hold your sin against you, because my Son has paid for it at the cross."

In the same way, then, we need to do what God does: forget our past. Yes, we certainly need to learn from our mistakes and remember some of the bitter lessons we've learned. But we no longer need to be *controlled* by our past.

That's what Paul meant by "forgetting what is behind…" Think about the horrible things Paul had done. He shared responsibility for the death of Stephen, and had to carry that in his conscience until his final day. He knew that he was responsible for terrible deeds. But he was able to put his past in the past. And we need to do the same.

Monday

Then the angel said to me, "Write: 'Blessed are those who are invited to the wedding supper of the Lamb!'" And he added, "These are the true words of God." (Revelation 19:9, NIV)

I like that word *supper*. That's what they call dinner in the South. We say, "Let's have dinner." But in the South they say, "Let's have supper." My grandmother, we called her "Mama Stella," was a great southern cook, who knew how to throw down all those southern goodies—fried chicken, black-eyed peas, collard greens, and mashed potatoes made from scratch. And of course her crowning achievement was the biscuit. (It seems perfectly reasonable to me that God would utilize my grandmother's skills in the wedding supper of the Lamb!)

Not only will we be eating together at the wedding supper of the Lamb, but we will be in some pretty good company as well. In Matthew 8:11, we read that "Many will come from the east and the west, and will take their places at the feast with Abraham, Isaac and Jacob in the kingdom of heaven" (NIV).

Can you imagine that? Can you picture yourself sitting down for lunch with Abraham and Isaac—or the apostle Paul or C. S. Lewis or C. H. Spurgeon?

Heaven will be amazing beyond description. And that's why the Bible tells us we should all be a lot more heavenly-minded. In Colossians 3, Paul wrote: "Since you have been raised to new life with Christ, set your sights on the realities of heaven, where Christ sits in the place of honor at God's right hand. Think about the things of heaven, not the things of earth. (vv. 1-2, NLT).

Think about that last sentence again. *"Don't think only about things down here on earth."* Yet that is exactly what we spend the majority of our time doing! We think about things that we're concerned about or stressed over. The Bible isn't saying, "Don't think about these things," it's saying, "Don't *stress* and worry about these things. Let heaven fill your thoughts instead! Because when you do, everything on earth gets placed in its proper perspective.

Tuesday

Don't love the world's ways. Don't love the world's goods. Love of the world squeezes out love for the Father. Practically everything that goes on in the world—wanting your own way, wanting everything for yourself, wanting to appear important—has nothing to do with the Father. It just isolates you from him. The world and all its wanting, wanting, wanting is on the way out— but whoever does what God wants is set for eternity. (1 John 2:15-17, THE MESSAGE)

E. M. Bounds once said: "Heaven ought to draw and engage us. Heaven ought to so fill our hearts and hands, our conversation, our character, and our features that all would see that we are foreigners and strangers to this world. The very atmosphere of this world should be chilling to us and noxious. Its sun has eclipsed and its companionship dull and insipid. Heaven is our native land and home to us, and death to us is not the dying hour but the birth hour."[14]

The truth of heaven should give us great hope, even in the midst of devastating circumstances here on earth. Earth is a temporary place where we decide our eternal destiny. Heaven is our real home.

Death for the believer is not the end of life, but the continuation of it in another place. You and I tend to get our thoughts wrapped around the affairs of today—the worries, fears, desires, and preoccupations—and sometimes imagine that everything of consequence has to happen during our short span of years on earth. But the Bible says that we will live forever, and much that we will do is out ahead of us, beyond this life, beyond our conception.

I think of my own son Christopher, who died at age thirty-three, and is in heaven right now. On earth, he was a talented designer, as well as a loving son, brother, husband, father. Does God still have plans for him to design—something out there in eternity, or during the thousand year reign of Christ on earth? We will certainly have work to do in our new resurrection bodies, and tasks to accomplish in the life to come. It may very well be that the dreams you never realized on earth will be realized in heaven.

Let some of those thoughts fill your mind today. It's good to think about heaven!

Wednesday

He who dwells in the secret place of the Most High shall abide under the shadow of the Almighty. I will say of the Lord, "He is my refuge and my fortress; my God, in Him I will trust". (Psalm 91:1-2)

Without question, Psalm 91 is a real gem among the psalms. Next to Psalm 23, it has probably brought more encouragement and comfort throughout the centuries than any other psalm.

It's worth noting, however, that the blessings promised in Psalm 91 aren't for just anyone. They are specifically given to believers—and not just to believers in general. These benefits are targeted toward believers who specifically meet the *requirements* found within the psalm. Psalm 91 is full of what Bible teachers call "conditional promises." In other words, God promises to do certain things for us, hinging on *us* doing certain things.

Verse 1 begins, "He who dwells in the secret place of the Most High…" The word "dwells" could be translated as "quiet and resting, enduring and remaining with consistency." It's very similar to the word "abide," which we see often in the New Testament. Jesus said, "He who abides in Me, and I in him, bears much fruit" (John 15:5). That word "abide" means, "to stay in a given place, to maintain unbroken fellowship and communion with another."

And what is the "secret place"? One way of looking at it is simply a time and place where you get alone with God, to enjoy His nearness and companionship, and to converse with Him.

So here's what God is essentially saying: If you want to experience the promises of Psalm 91—My protection, provision, and blessing—you must dwell in the secret place of the Most High. You must remain in constant fellowship with Me."

We have relationship with God because we have put our faith in Jesus Christ and have turned from our sin. But are we living in constant fellowship with God? Many believers are not.

God is interested in a relationship with you, not just on Sundays, but throughout the week. He wants you to dwell in the secret place of the Most High. Matthew Henry, a Christian commentator from 400 years ago, wrote: "He that by faith chooses God for his guardian shall find all that in him which he needs or can desire."[15]

Thursday

Give unto the Lord, O you mighty ones, give unto the Lord glory and strength. Give unto the Lord the glory due to His name; worship the Lord in the beauty of holiness. (Psalm 29:1-2)

King Herod was a shrewd and clever tyrant, and a great builder. Today, some 2000 years later, the remains of his incredible structures, including his fortress of Masada, are still visible in Israel. He built Masada because he was afraid that someone would try to take his kingdom. He even had his own sons executed because he perceived them as a threat to his kingdom.

When wise men from the East came to Jerusalem asking, "Where is He who has been born King of the Jews?" (Matthew 2:2), Herod suddenly realized there was another king in town, and the Bible says he was troubled. He told them, "When you have found Him, bring back word to me, that I may come and worship Him also" (Matthew 2:8). Just as the wise men were true worshipers, Herod was a false one. He was hostile toward God, yet he masqueraded as a true worshiper.

Herods by the dozens sit in the pews of many churches today. Outwardly, they appear devout and deeply religious, but inwardly they're living a lie. They don't really know God or have a relationship with Him. They may sing the songs, give to the offering, and do all the right things, but it doesn't mean they're true worshipers, because God looks on the heart.

If your life isn't right with God when you come to worship Him, not only does it fail to please God, but it's offensive to Him. In the book of Malachi, we read about a time in Israel's history when the worship had become so robotic, so cynical, that God told the priests they might as well board up the temple. He would rather have no worship at all than an artificial, perfunctory worship absent of all heart and passion.

What does God see in your heart? There are plenty of false worshipers today. Are you a true one?

Friday

Away then with sinful, earthly things; deaden the evil desires lurking within you; have nothing to do with sexual sin, impurity, lust, and shameful desires; don't worship the good things of life, for that is idolatry. God's terrible anger is upon those who do such things. You used to do them when your life was still part of this world; but now is the time to cast off and throw away all these rotten garments of anger, hatred, cursing, and dirty language. Don't tell lies to each other; it was your old life with all its wickedness that did that sort of thing; now it is dead and gone. (Colossians 3:5-9, TLB)

Spring means many things to us. But one of the most notable things that comes with spring is spring cleaning, when we go through our houses and take care of all the messes that have built up over the months.

I heard about an interesting custom in Italy for New Year's Eve. At midnight, the windows of every house open and everyone pitches out whatever they absolutely hate—furniture, clothes, dishes, unwanted wedding presents—they all come crashing to the ground. Now I would call that serious housecleaning!

I have to confess here that I'm not the tidiest person on the planet. Ironically, I like to be in tidy surroundings. But in contrast, my wife Cathe is Mrs. Clean. She just loves to clean, and does it all the time.

In our spiritual lives, too, some of us allow messes to develop. Becoming neglectful, we allow anger, bitter attitudes, lustful fantasies, or unconfessed sin to remain in our hearts. Before we know it, we find ourselves reaping the inevitable results of sin. Before long, we're crying out, "Oh God, get me out of this mess!"

And then there are others who live their spiritual lives the same way that my wife cleans house. They're careful to cultivate and maintain their relationship with the Lord, constantly asking God to search their hearts, and confessing their sins before God (as David did in Psalm 139:22-23).

You and I need to be cleansed from sin on a daily basis. How much better it is to ask for forgiveness on a regular basis than to allow a major problem to develop in your life.

We need a professional. Essentially, we need God himself to come and clean house.

Weekend

For you are the temple of the living God. (2 Corinthians 6:16)

God wants to clean your house. Or, to put it in another way, He wants to cleanse your temple. Under the old covenant, the temple was either a tabernacle in the wilderness or a great building in Jerusalem where the high priest, representing the people, met God.

But ever since the crucifixion and resurrection of Jesus, God doesn't live in a temple. John wrote in Revelation 21:3: "And I heard a loud voice from heaven saying, "Behold, the tabernacle of God is with men, and He will dwell with them, and they shall be His people. God Himself will be with them and be their God."

Under the new covenant, God lives in the hearts and lives of His own people.

We are so careful about cleaning the outside of our bodies, aren't we? Some of us can't stand going camping even for a couple of days, if it means skipping a shower or two. But what about the inside? Do we have that same level of concern about our inner person? The Bible tells us: "Or do you not know that your body is the temple of the Holy Spirit who is in you, whom you have from God, and you are not your own? For you were bought at a price; therefore glorify God in your body and in your spirit, which are God's" (1 Corinthians 6:19-20).

When we give our lives to Christ and put our trust in Him, He comes in and cleans house. He throws out old clothes, old furniture, even the old food in the refrigerator. Then He lays down beautiful new carpet. He puts in new furniture. He fills the refrigerator with the finest gourmet foods. And we realize that He took the old things away only to put something better in their place.

God wants to clean house. Let Him do that. Invite the Spirit of the living God to do whatever He needs to do to make your life—your inner temple—a place where He will feel at home.

Monday

For He shall give His angels charge over you, to keep you in all your ways. (Psalm 91:11)

The angels of God are nearer than you may think. Even though we're rarely aware of their presence, they're around us all the time, caring for us and ministering to us. Working in secret is fine with them, because essentially they are God's secret agents, doing His bidding and the work He has called them to do. Many, many times they have intervened in our lives, and we didn't even know they were doing so.

According to Psalm 91 and other passages of Scripture, angels are actively involved in the life of the believer. Hebrews 1:14 says that they are ministering spirits, sent forth to minister to those who will inherit salvation. Hebrews 13:2 tells us not to be forgetful to entertain strangers, for in doing so, some have entertained angels without even knowing it. There are so many stories in the Bible of angels who delivered the people of God—we read about Jacob, Lot, Daniel, Peter, and Paul, among others.

But as wonderful as the promise of angelic involvement in our lives is, we must first recognize what the conditions are for this promise to be activated in our lives: "For He shall give His angels charge over you, to keep you in all your ways" (Psalm 91:11). Recognize the fact that the phrase "to keep you in all your ways" is not referring to whatever path you choose, but to *God's* ways.

There is the difference between trusting the Lord and testing Him by taking unnecessary chances with your life or even endangering your spiritual safety by doing stupid things, expecting God to bail you out. God will keep you in all your ways—but your ways must be *His* ways.

And where do you discover His ways? You go back to that "secret place" spoken of in Psalm 91:1, where you open the Bible, meditate on its teachings, and ask the Holy Spirit to bring those truths home to your heart.

Tuesday

He shall call upon Me, and I will answer him; I will be with him in trouble; I will deliver him and honor him. With long life I will satisfy him, and show him My salvation. (Psalm 91:15-16)

Are you facing an emergency today? Dial 911…Psalm 91:1, that is. This psalm of David speaks of both great adversity and the wonderful help and protection of God. The fact is, God can use difficulties and crises in the life of the Christian. None of us wants adversity in our lives, but God can be glorified through such times. You may have faced a serious, even life-threatening illness and experienced the healing power of God. Or perhaps you're still dealing with a troublesome physical condition, and you haven't experienced that longed-for healing. Either way, we bring glory to His name right in the midst of it all.

Psalm 91 doesn't say you will never die. But it is saying that you won't die before your time. It's saying that until God is done with you, His angels will keep you in all your ways…in your ups and downs, when you're awake and asleep, in the sunshine and the rain, in times of crisis and seasons of peace.

What's your part? It is to dwell in the secret place of the Most High and abide under the shadow of the Almighty. Your objective as a Christian should be to stay as close to the Lord as you possibly can, leaning on Him with quiet faith and confidence. Because this all-powerful, all-knowing God who possesses heaven and Earth, has made a covenant with you, loves you, and offers to protect and provide for you, you should make it your objective to get closer to Him, asking, *How can I walk so closely with Him that I will be in His very shadow?*

You should periodically ask yourself whether you are meeting the criteria of this great psalm, whether you are living up to the conditions that have been set forth. If your answer is "yes," then you have God's word that these promises will be activated in your life.

Wednesday

*"And the Lord, He is the One who goes before you. He will be with you,
He will not leave you nor forsake you; do not fear nor be dismayed."
(Deuteronomy 31:8)*

Years ago, Roy Orbison recorded one of the great rock and roll classics, entitled, "Only the Lonely." A couple of the lines from the song were, "Only the lonely know the way I feel tonight... Only the lonely know the heartaches I've been through." That song resonated with a lot of lonely people who knew what it was like to be isolated, rejected, or abandoned.

Maybe you've been abandoned—perhaps it was by your parents, your spouse, or your children. Or maybe you even feel that you've been abandoned by God Himself. There are many people who feel estranged and alienated from God. Even if they have everything they want in life, they may still face a deep, inner loneliness.

We read in John 5 of a man at the pool of Bethesda who was in a seemingly hopeless situation. He had been abandoned. He was uncared for and unable to help himself. What's more, he'd been in that condition for many long, weary years. He must have been desperately lonely.

In this account, we learn that Jesus changed the man's life forever. It's a story that tells us you and me how to change as well. Before Jesus brought transformation and healing into this man's life, however, He first asked him a rather pointed question: "Do you want to be made well?"

What if Jesus asked you the same question? Is there something that needs healing or changing in your life? Do you want to be made well? Maybe it's an addiction to a certain vice or a lifestyle you are trapped in. Maybe it's something you've tried to shake time and time again. Or maybe it's an old hatred or resentment, nursed along over the months and years and becoming more and more toxic with the passing of time.

Jesus turned the course of this man's life around forever, giving him the ability to live a life free from loneliness and the power of sin. We can live that life, too—the ability to break old habits and to forgive old hurts and resentments. He has all the transforming power we need, but we must "want to be made well."

Thursday

For if you just listen and don't obey, it is like glancing at your face in a mirror. You see yourself, walk away, and forget what you look like. (James 1:23–24 NLT).

I've had the opportunity over the years to sit down with many famous Christian leaders, household names, if you will, in the evangelical world. And I can say, without reservation, that the most spiritual people I have met have always been the most humble. Neither proud nor arrogant, they had a sweetness and a humility about their lives that seemed to leave a fragrance in the room after they left. The fragrance of Jesus Himself.

It was after years of walking with the Lord that the apostle Paul referred to himself, not as the chief of all saints, but rather as the chief of all sinners (see 1 Timothy 1:15). This was a man who had simply been looking into God's mirror, and saw the depravity of his own heart—even as he was still being conformed into the image of Christ. Paul could have spent a lot of time thumping his suspenders and talking about all he had accomplished. Instead, he said, I'm not there yet. I'm not the spiritual man I need or want to be. So I'm going to give it all I've got and press toward that goal (see Philippians 3:12-14).

If you are a true believer, if you are truly a spiritual person, if you are really growing in your faith, then you will be humble and open, always realizing there is so much to learn. This is the mark of a person who really wants to know God.

Paul's advice in Romans 12 rings as true as ever: "As your spiritual teacher I give this piece of advice to each one of you. Don't cherish exaggerated ideas of yourself or your importance, but try to have a sane estimate of your capabilities by the light of the faith that God has given to you all" (Romans 12:3, PHILLIPS).

The self-deceived person, however, the individual who thinks he or she is "spiritual," won't be open to counsel or teaching. Imagining that they "know it all," they're really only revealing how little they truly do know.

Friday

What good is it, dear brothers and sisters, if you say you have faith but don't show it by your actions? Can that kind of faith save anyone? Suppose you see a brother or sister who has no food or clothing, and you say, "Good-bye and have a good day; stay warm and eat well"—but then you don't give that person any food or clothing. What good does that do? So you see, faith by itself isn't enough. Unless it produces good deeds, it is dead and useless. (James 2:14-17, NLT)

The Great Blondin, probably the Evel Knievel of his day, was notorious for his incredible, death-defying acts. On one occasion, he strung a tightrope across the Niagara Falls. As a crowd gathered, he stood before them and said, "How many of you believe that I, the Great Blondin, can walk across this tightrope to the other side?"

They all said, "We believe! We believe!" So he walked across the tightrope and came back again. The people applauded, thrilled by his death-defying feat.

Then he said, "How many of you believe that I, the Great Blondin, can not only walk back across that tightrope, but this time do it while I push a wheelbarrow?"

"We believe!" they yelled louder, wanting to see him do this.

Then he said, "How many of you *really* believe it?"

"Oh, we really believe it!" they shouted back. One man was yelling a little bit louder than all the others, so the Great Blondin pointed to him and said, "Then get in the wheelbarrow." The man quickly disappeared.

That's how a lot of people are today. We'll say, "I believe! I believe!" But how many are truly willing to get into God's wheelbarrow, so to speak? Some people have a pseudo-faith, but not real belief as the Bible would require. It is, therefore, of the greatest importance that we know what true faith is. The Book of James points out that there is such a thing as a phony or dead faith. And any declaration of faith that does not result in a changed life and good works is a false declaration. It is faith alone that justifies. But faith that justifies can never be alone.

Weekend

All your waves and billows have gone over me, and floods of sorrow pour upon me like a thundering cataract. Yet day by day the Lord also pours out his steadfast love upon me, and through the night I sing his songs and pray to God who gives me life. (Psalm 42:7-8, TLB)

In our lives here on earth, we will experience pain, grief, sickness, and the death of loved ones. I know we don't like to think about that reality, but since it's true, we might just as well come to grips with it and stop running from it.

When you're younger, you don't necessarily understand this. As you get older, however, you usually experience the death of your grandparents first. And then, as time passes, your parents will die. As you continue to age, you know that day will eventually come for you, too, and your children will bury you.

Hard as those realities may be to deal with, there are situations that are even more difficult still. And those are the *unexpected* deaths that we encounter in the course of our lives. It might be the death of a sibling, a spouse, or a child.

No one ever wants to bury their children. And suddenly we are made aware of our own mortality. Our world seems to come crashing down around our ears, and we cry aloud to God.

How does God feel about that? When we read the psalms, we learn that there were many times when David and the other psalmists told Him exactly what was going on in their hearts. They cried out to Him, and emptied the contents of their souls in His presence.

In Psalm 42, the writer says, "'O God my Rock…why have you forsaken me? Why must I suffer these attacks from my enemies?' Their taunts pierce me like a fatal wound; again and again they scoff, 'Where is that God of yours?'" (vv. 9-10, TLB)

So the psalmist is saying, "Lord, from where I sit right now, it sure seems to me like You've forsaken me…Like You're not even paying attention to me." And then he corrects himself and says in verse 11 of the same psalm, "But, O my soul, don't be discouraged. Don't be upset. Expect God to act! For I know that I shall again have plenty of reason to praise Him for all that He will do. He is my help! He is my God!"

Monday

Since we have such a huge crowd of men of faith watching us from the grandstands, let us strip off anything that slows us down or holds us back, and especially those sins that wrap themselves so tightly around our feet and trip us up; and let us run with patience the particular race that God has set before us. Keep your eyes on Jesus, our leader and instructor. He was willing to die a shameful death on the cross because of the joy he knew would be his afterwards; and now he sits in the place of honor by the throne of God. (Hebrews 12:1-2, TLB)

Holocaust survivor Corrie ten Boom once said, "Look within and be depressed. Look without and be distressed. Look at Jesus and be at rest."[16] Looking without, she had very good reason to be distressed. She lived in a concentration camp. She saw her sister and father—and many others—die at the hands of the Nazis. Looking within, she felt depressed as she saw the darkness of her own heart. But seeing the example of her godly sister Betsy, who saw the bright side of everything and was always trusting God, she concluded, "Look at Jesus and be at rest."

The Bible says that Abraham "did not waver at the promise of God through unbelief, but was strengthened in faith, giving glory to God, and being fully convinced that what He had promised He was also able to perform" (Romans 4:20-21). The word "waver" used in this verse could also be translated "stagger." It would imply that this unwavering walk of Abraham took place with his eyes fixed on the promise of God.

As we walk with God, people will let us down and disappoint us. Circumstances will be difficult. The enemy will hassle us. This is when we need to remember why we started to walk with God in the first place. It was because of Jesus. So keep your eyes fixed on Him. That will keep you moving forward, because the only way we will make it as Christians is by keeping our eyes on Jesus Christ.

Tuesday

Don't worry about anything; instead, pray about everything. Tell God what you need, and thank him for all he has done. Then you will experience God's peace, which exceeds anything we can understand. His peace will guard your hearts and minds as you live in Christ Jesus. (Philippians 4:6-7, NLT)

One of the first things I remember about the day I put my faith in Christ was the sense of peace filling my heart. It was as though someone had lifted a heavy burden from me. It wasn't until later, when I read the Bible, that I learned about God's promise of peace to every believer. He has given it to us as a gift.

This peace, however, doesn't come from what or who we are, but from what God has done—how He has justified us in response to our faith. A beautiful byproduct of this reality is a deep inner peace that floods our soul.

But we can't have this transforming effect without the beginning cause. If we're fighting with God—resisting His plan and purpose for our lives—then we won't experience this supernatural peace.

I think many people would like to have the desirable results and benefits of the Christian life without having to pay the price. In other words, they would like to know they are forgiven and going to heaven when they die, but they still want to live as they please. They don't want to put their complete faith and trust in Jesus.

That sort of attitude just won't fly. We can't have the pleasing, life-transforming privileges of God's peace without first meeting God's requirements. Colossians 1:20 (NLT) says that through Jesus Christ, "God reconciled everything to himself. He made peace with everything in heaven and on earth by means of Christ's blood on the cross." The only way we will experience the peace of God that passes all human understanding is through the blood of the cross, the blood Jesus shed.

You can't have the peace *of* God until you first have peace *with* God.

Wednesday

For Christ himself is our way of peace. He has made peace between us Jews and you Gentiles by making us all one family, breaking down the wall of contempt that used to separate us. (Ephesians 2:14, TLB)

As a child, I always wanted to go to Disneyland on my birthday. I still remember making a vow in the backseat of the car that one day, saying to myself that when I became an adult, made my own money, and had my own wheels, I would go to Disneyland every single day. And if I couldn't do that, then at least I would go twice a week.

Some years ago, someone gave me an annual pass to Disneyland, which meant that I could go any time I wanted. But do you know how many times I actually went? Let's just say that it wasn't every day. It wasn't even twice a week. There was always some reason for not going.

We can be that way with our access to the presence of God. We can go into His presence 24/7, anytime we want. Yet how often do we actually do that?

This was a radical concept for the people of Jesus' day, specifically the Jews. The Gentiles had no hope whatsoever of entering the temple of the living God. Any attempt to do so was punishable by death. The Jews couldn't go much further. A veil separated the rest of the temple from the Holy of Holies, where only the high priest could enter once a year to meet with God.

Now through Jesus Christ, we have access into that most holy place. For the Jews, the veil has been ripped in two. For the Gentiles, the wall has been knocked down. We can all go into God's presence because of the blood of Jesus Christ that was shed.

It's a marvelous, incredible truth. But how do we benefit from this unspeakable privilege if we never take advantage of it? In fact, we don't get to enjoy this wonderful reality simply by talking about it (or writing about it) or pondering how amazing it is. The benefit comes when we actually enter His presence through the way made for us, bow low before His throne, and find the pleasure of His companionship.

In that moment, we enter into the great reality.

Thursday

Hear my cry, O God; listen to my prayer. From the ends of the earth I call to you, I call as my heart grows faint; lead me to the rock that is higher than I. (Psalm 61:1-2, NIV)

My prayers to the Lord, especially when I am grieving, are wide open and honest. I pour out my heart before God, telling Him all my pain. At the same time, however, I also remind myself of God's truth. That's what prayer is all about.

God wants us to cry out to Him. He invites us to pour out our hearts before Him. David writes: "Trust in him at all times, O people; pour out your hearts to him, for God is our refuge" (Psalm 62:8, NIV).

Sometimes you and I don't do that. We keep the pain bottled up in our hearts, rather than sharing it with our God. We allow trouble and trauma and hardship to cause us to be angry with Him, so that we withdraw from Him, and don't want to talk to Him.

No, my friend, those seasons of deep pain are when you need Him more than ever! Cry out to Him with your doubts. Cry out to Him with your pain. He will patiently, lovingly, hear you. He might set your crooked thinking straight as you seek Him, but He wants you to pour out your pain. He loves you!

As *The Message* paraphrase of Psalm 55:22 puts it: "Pile your troubles on God's shoulders—he'll carry your load, he'll help you out."

As best I knew how, I wanted to keep writing and preaching after Christopher's death. Why? Because I want hurting people who hear or read my words to understand that my thoughts aren't coming from some ivory tower of theory…they have also come from the valley of the shadow of death. And here's what I want my readers and listeners to understand: You can take the hardest things that happen to you in life—the unexpected death of a loved one or even the realization that you are going to die soon—and know this: God *will be with you.*

As Corrie Ten Boom, who survived imprisonment in a concentration camp during WW2 wrote, "There is not pit so deep that God is not deeper still."[17]

Friday

"You are worthy, O Lord, to receive glory and honor and power; for You created all things, and by Your will they exist and were created."
(Revelation 4:11)

Years ago, I remember one of my sons asking me, "Dad, why did God put us here on the Earth?" It was one of those surprise questions that kids will sometimes ask you. Thankfully, I believe I had the right answer that day. I said, "God put us here on the Earth so that we might worship Him and glorify Him and know the God who created us."

Our ultimate purpose in life is not to attain success, fame, or even happiness. It should be to know the God who made us. In fact, the Bible says there are those in heaven singing, *"You are worthy, O Lord, to receive glory and honor and power..."* We were created to worship God. Any lesser purpose falls short, and will never satisfy us.

Everybody worships. Certainly, we don't all worship the true God in heaven. But everyone, no matter who they are, worships someone or something. What do they worship? That all depends. Some worship the true and living God. Others worship a god of their own making. Some people worship people—sports heroes, actors, musicians. Some people worship possessions. Some people even worship themselves. But when you get down to it, every person everywhere worships. And the reason for this is that God created us with an inner drive. We are created with a sense that there is something more to life than what we experience on this Earth.

You can worship a false god—a god of your own making, a god that you have brought out of your own imagination—and ultimately be disappointed. Or you can worship the true God. The true God—the living God, the only God, the God of the Bible—is the One to worship and bow down to. And the eternal Scriptures declare about Jesus:

> "I am placing a stone in Jerusalem, a chosen cornerstone, and anyone who believes in him will never be disappointed" I am placing a cornerstone in Jerusalem, chosen for great honor, and anyone who trusts in him will never be disgraced." (1 Peter 2:6, NLT).

Weekend

But the Holy Spirit produces this kind of fruit in our lives: love, joy, peace, patience, kindness, goodness, faithfulness, gentleness, and self-control. (Galatians 5:22-23, NLT)

An extensive survey conducted in the United States by a leading polling agency distributed questionnaires to people of various ages and occupations, asking, "What are you looking for most in life?" When the results were compiled, the analysts were surprised. Most expected those who were polled to say they wanted to achieve certain materialistic goals. But the top three things that people wanted in life were love, joy, and peace—in that order.

Isn't that amazing…those just happen to be the first three qualities of life mentioned in Paul's description of the fruits of the Spirit. Right off the top– *love, joy, and peace.* In other words, the very things people are looking for today can be found in a relationship with God. Yet some have given up on these things. They say, "Love, joy, and peace? That's a pipe dream of flower children. Give me a break. You're not going to find things like that in the real world."

As a result, people end up settling for much less than what their hearts truly desire. They long for lifelong love, but settle for something much, much less. They dream of living a life of joy, but (with a shrug of the shoulders) end up settling for something temporary, something that falls well short of the mark. They desire a deep, heartfelt peace, but end up settling for a slight decrease in anxiety—if they can find it.

Would that describe how you feel right now? That isn't the way life ought to be—and deep down, we know it. We know there ought to be something more in life—more than we've ever experienced.

In a relationship with God through Jesus Christ, we are promised not only life beyond the grave, but a life that is full and rich and worth living on this Earth. Jesus gives us life with purpose and, of course, life with the hope of heaven.

Monday

And not only that, but we also glory in tribulations, knowing that tribulation produces perseverance. (Romans 5:3)

The apostle Paul didn't merely endure his hardships, he celebrated them. He *gloried* in them. The meaning of the word "tribulation" that Paul used in Romans 5:3 comes from a term that describes a threshing instrument with which a farmer would separate the grain from the husks. It's the idea of being under pressure, such as squeezing olives in a press to extract the oil, squeezing grapes for their juice, or pounding garlic to release its aroma. Through the pounding process, something comes out that wasn't visible or discernible before. In the same way, our lives can be pounded out on the threshing floor of tribulation.

Paul made a choice about his hardships. He said he gloried in tribulation because it produced something he needed. We have a choice as well. We can become bitter, or we can become *better*.

Ready or not, like it or not, tribulation will come into our lives. Scripture is clear on that. Jesus said, "These things I have spoken to you, that in Me you may have peace. In the world you will have tribulation; but be of good cheer, I have overcome the world" (John 16:33). The apostles encouraged the believers in Acts 14 to continue in the faith, saying that through much tribulation they must enter the kingdom of God (see Acts 14:22). And Philippians 1:29 says, "For to you it has been granted on behalf of Christ, not only to believe in Him, but also to suffer for His sake."

It's a choice. Hardships will come, but how you *respond* to them is entirely up to you. The writer to the Hebrews said, "Endure hardship as discipline; God is treating you as sons." He went on to say, "God disciplines us for our good, that we may share in his holiness. No discipline seems pleasant at the time, but painful. Later on, however, it produces a harvest of righteousness and peace for those who have been trained by it" (Hebrews 12:7, 10-11, NIV).

When hard times come, you can either get mad at God, or you can accept His loving discipline and seek to learn what He wants to teach you.

Tuesday

This doesn't mean, of course, that we have only a hope of future joys—we can be full of joy here and now even in our trials and troubles. Taken in the right spirit these very things will give us patient endurance; this in turn will develop a mature character, and a character of this sort produces a steady hope, a hope that will never disappoint us. Already we have some experience of the love of God flooding through our hearts by the Holy Spirit given to us. (Romans 5:3-5, PHILLIPS)

When you want to get in shape, it's actually through the process of tearing your muscles down that you build them up. The first day of your workout isn't so hard. But the next day, you're in some serious pain. Everything hurts. The next time, you feel weak, but you work out anyway. A couple of days later, you're still weak and sore, but you're also a little stronger. You increase the weights a bit, then you do a little more. Pretty soon, you notice that you're getting stronger. It is through the breaking-down process that the building up comes.

In the same way, we need to build up our spiritual muscles. God allows us to go through difficulties. He increases the weights on us. Pretty soon, we're benching a whole lot more than we ever thought possible. We're learning more than we ever thought we would learn. We're doing more than we ever thought we would do. Iron is entering our souls, and we're developing that heroic endurance, perseverance, and strength that only comes through difficulty.

The Bible tells us, "My brethren, count it all joy when you fall into various trials, knowing that the testing of your faith produces patience. But let patience have its perfect work, that you may be perfect and complete, lacking nothing" (James 1:2-4). In the original language, the word used here for "patience" means, "perseverance," "endurance," "steadfastness," or simply "staying power."

If you find yourself experiencing a time of testing and trial, realize that God has a purpose in it. Most likely, He is preparing you and training you today for what He will do in your life tomorrow.

Wednesday

For we are God's [own] handiwork (His workmanship), recreated in Christ Jesus, [born anew] that we may do those good works which God predestined (planned beforehand) for us [taking paths which He prepared ahead of time], that we should walk in them [living the good life which He prearranged and made ready for us to live].
(Ephesians 2:10, AMPLIFIED)

A traveler was visiting a logging area in the Pacific Northwest and was interested to see how logs were chosen that eventually would be used for furniture. As the logs came down the stream, the logger would suddenly reach out and hook one, pull it up, and then set it down. He would sometimes wait for a few minutes before grabbing another. There didn't seem to be any rhyme or reason to his choices.

After a while, the visitor said to him, "I don't understand what you're doing."

"These logs may all look alike to you," said the logger, "but I can recognize that a few of them are quite different. The ones that I let pass came from trees that grew in a valley. They were always protected from the storms. The grain is rather coarse. The logs that I pulled aside are from high up on the mountain, where they were beaten by strong winds from the time they were quite small. That toughens the trees and gives them a fine grain. We save these logs for choice work. They're too good to be used for ordinary lumber."

It was through the trying and testing that the logs were prepared for choice work. The same could be said of us as Christians.

If you were to ask Moses how he became who he was, he would remind you of his trials with Pharaoh and his times of testing in the wilderness. If you were to ask Joseph, he would most likely refer back to his years as a slave, his imprisonment on a false accusation, and his imprisonment in Pharaoh's dungeon. Talk to Peter, and he would probably point back to his denial and how he learned many difficult yet important lessons.

Maybe you find yourself facing something similar in your life today. Don't discount the possibility that God is preparing you for a choice work.

Thursday

Later Jesus appeared again to the disciples beside the Sea of Galilee. This is how it happened. Several of the disciples were there—Simon Peter, Thomas (nicknamed the Twin), Nathanael from Cana in Galilee, the sons of Zebedee, and two other disciples.

Simon Peter said, "I'm going fishing."

"We'll come, too," they all said. So they went out in the boat, but they caught nothing all night. (John 21:1-3, NLT)

It was *déjà vu* time for the disciples. They had been fishing all night on the Sea of Galilee and hadn't caught anything. The Lord had risen, and had already appeared to some of the disciples. But since there were no clear marching orders, they thought they'd go back to what they knew how to do-- fishing.

Early in the morning, while it was probably still dark, they saw a figure standing on the shore. He called out, "Fellows, have you caught any fish?" (v. 5).

Throughout the Bible, God often asked probing questions when He wanted a confession. In the book of Genesis, after Adam and Eve's sin, God came walking in the Garden in the cool of the day, calling out, "Adam, where are you?" (see Genesis 3).

In the same way, Jesus was asking His disciples, "Did you catch anything? Have you been successful? Have things gone the way you had hoped they would go? Are you satisfied?"

Why did Jesus want them to admit their failure? So He could bring them to the place where they needed to be.

When they cast the net on the right side of the boat, as Jesus told them to, their net became so heavy with fish that they couldn't pull it in. The Lord was teaching the disciples an important lesson: Failure often can be the doorway to real success.

We need to come to that point in our lives as well. We need to come and say, "Lord, I'm not satisfied with the way my life is going. I'm tired of doing it my way. I want to do it Your way." If you will come to God like that, He will extend His forgiveness to you. Then He will take your life and transform it in ways you couldn't imagine.

Friday

But in fact, Christ has been raised from the dead. He is the first of a great harvest of all who have died. (1 Corinthians 15:20, NLT)

I read about a person who wrote the following to a newspaper advice columnist: *"Our preacher said on Easter that Jesus just swooned on the cross and that His disciples nursed Him back to health. What do you think?"* The letter was signed, *"Sincerely, Bewildered."*

The columnist replied, *"Dear Bewildered, Beat your preacher with a cat of nine tails with 39 heavy strokes, nail him to a cross, hang him in the sun for six hours, run a spear through his heart, embalm him, put him in an airless tomb for 36 hours, and see what happens."*

What sets the Christian faith apart from all other beliefs and religious systems in this world? It might come down to this: If you go to the tombs of any of the prophets on which world religions have been founded, you will find them occupied. But if you go to the tomb of Jesus Christ, you will find it empty, because He is alive. We serve a living Savior.

This is why the resurrection of Jesus is such an important message—and also why it has been so fiercely opposed throughout history. The devil knows that the resurrection spells his defeat. He also knows that if you believe this great truth that Jesus died on the cross for your sins and rose again from the dead, it can change your life.

Not only can it change your life, but putting your faith in Him also means that you will have a new, resurrected body someday. As believers, we have this great hope that we too will live again. And while we still occupy the world on this side of eternity, we have a infinite source of resurrection power through our vital union with our risen Lord.

The apostle Peter described it with these triumphant words: "Because Jesus was raised from the dead, we've been given a brand-new life and have everything to live for, including a future in heaven—and the future starts now! God is keeping careful watch over us and the future. The Day is coming when you'll have it all— life healed and whole" (1 Peter 1:3-5, THE MESSAGE).

Weekend

When Jesus had raised Himself up and saw no one but the woman, He said to her, "Woman, where are those accusers of yours? Has no one condemned you?" She said, "No one, Lord." And Jesus said to her, "Neither do I condemn you; go and sin no more." (John 8:10-11)

Throughout His earthly ministry, Jesus saved His most scathing words not for the sinners of the day, but for the self-righteous, religious hypocrites. When the religious elite dragged the woman caught in the act of adultery before Him, dumping her at His feet, they pointed out that the law required death by stoning (John 8:5). For His part, Jesus simply stooped down and began to write something in the dust. We don't know what He wrote. But whatever it was, they all left quickly, from the oldest to the youngest.

When Jesus asked the woman where her accusers were and if anyone had condemned her, she told Him, "No one, Lord." So Jesus said, "Neither do I condemn you; go and sin no more."

Does this mean that Jesus approved of the way she lived? Far from it. Jesus was simply getting to the heart of the matter. He knew the real problem was a *heart* issue—a heart captured by sin and estranged from God. If He could win her heart, it would change her lifestyle, too.

Sometimes I wonder if we in the church spend too much time protesting what unbelievers do and not enough time giving them the answer to their problems. Listen, I *expect* the world to be worldly. I *expect* sinners to behave sinfully. I don't expect them to live according to Christian standards.

There is a place to take a stand for righteousness and say what we are against. But the bottom line is that people are empty and need to hear the gospel of Jesus Christ. Let's expend our primary energy getting to the heart of the matter instead of dealing with the symptoms, because the heart of the matter is that people are lost. They need Christ. And we need to take that message to them.

Monday

Immediately Jesus made His disciples get into the boat and go before Him to the other side, while He sent the multitudes away.
(Matthew 14:22)

Although He knew that a storm was coming, Jesus clearly instructed His disciples to get into a boat, and cross over to the other side of the Sea of Galilee (see Matthew 14:22-24). Jesus sent them out on the sea because He knew there was a lesson for them to learn. He knew very well that they would make it safely to the other side, so He allowed His disciples to go through the storm. You might say the storm was a part of the day's curriculum for the disciples.

Life is like that, too. We don't always know when a storm is coming or when a tragedy may drop on our lives out of the blue. We don't know when a hardship may come up in our lives. But God does, and He knows when we are ready to face these things.

Now here is the question: How *will* we face life's storms? It has been said that into every life some rain must fall. To put it biblically, the rain falls on the just and the unjust. Hard times happen to everyone, but as Christians, we have this promise: "And we know that all things work together for good to those who love God, to those who are the called according to His purpose" (Romans 8:28). Whatever we are going through, in His wonderful providence, God will turn it around for our good.

Courageous people are a lot like tea bags. We don't know their strength until they are in hot water. It takes courage to face your trials. It takes courage to say, "I've made a commitment to follow Jesus. I'm not going to give up. I'm going to make it to the other side of this stormy sea because Jesus said I would!"

With the Son of God in your boat, you can never go under. And even when the time comes to cross over to the next life in heaven, you will make that journey safely and arrive quickly on the safest of all shores. How can you know that? Because He *said* you will.

Tuesday

Now in the fourth watch of the night Jesus went to them, walking on the sea. (Matthew 14:25)

In Matthew 14, we read about the disciples being tossed by the wind and waves in their boat on the Sea of Galilee. Then Jesus came, walking on the water, at the fourth watch of the night. The fourth watch was the last part of the night, just before dawn. This means the disciples had been at sea—their hands probably blistered and bloodied from toil at the oars—for at least nine hours in this fierce storm. So we see that Jesus came to them at the last conceivable moment.

This reminds us that God's delays aren't necessarily His denials. Jesus had heard their first cries for help. He knew what He was doing all along. Why did He wait so long before He intervened? Probably because it took a long time for these men to exhaust their resources and completely trust in Him.

Lifeguards will tell you that often the hardest person to save is the one who is panicking. But when an individual is exhausted, when he or she has no energy left, the lifeguard can pull that person back in to safety. In the same way, sometimes God will allow us to get to the end of our rope, to the end of our resources, so we will finally cling to Him.

The disciples were exhausted and afraid. "[Jesus] said to them, 'It is I; do not be afraid.' Then they willingly received Him into the boat, and immediately the boat was at the land where they were going" (John 6:20-21). For many of us, that is what Jesus is waiting for. He is waiting for us to say, "I can't row another second. I can't go another inch in my own strength. Please Lord, help me. Come on board." If you will invite Him, He will step into your storm-tossed boat and take control. He will be there for you…even on the darkest night, just before dawn.

Wednesday

"I have told you all this so that you may have peace in me. Here on earth you will have many trials and sorrows. But take heart, because I have overcome the world." (John 16:33, NLT)

Have you ever been afraid of the future? Maybe you feel as though you're in a rut, or maybe you're discouraged. Perhaps you feel that you will have to face the problems and challenges of life all alone.

If any of these things are true of you, then take heart, because you certainly aren't the first child of God to feel that way (nor will you be the last!). The mighty prophet Elijah once became so discouraged and depleted that he crawled under a bush in the desert and asked God to kill him. God heard His servant's prayer, but answered in another way: He provided Elijah with rest, a meal, a friend, and a fresh assignment. Instead of taking an early exit, Elijah took heart, and continued his ministry.

Jesus had a message for His disciples to give them hope as they faced an uncertain future, so they would not be afraid, but would be courageous.

During the last week of His life on Earth, Jesus knew His departure was at hand. So before He left His disciples, He wanted to encourage them. First, He warned them that they would face hardship and difficulty. But then He told them, "These things I have spoken to you, that in Me you may have peace. In the world you will have tribulation; but be of good cheer, I have overcome the world" (John 16:33).

"Be of good cheer." Take courage! Take heart! It was Christ's call to courage in the lives of His frightened disciples. Jesus wasn't simply saying, "Cheer up. Come on, put a smile on your face!" He was saying more than that. He was saying, "Be brave. Be courageous."

If you are courageous, cheerfulness will follow. Yes we will face trouble and heartaches in this broken world of ours. It's part of life on this side of heaven. But we also have the assurance that He has already overcome the world.

And that makes us overcomers, too.

Thursday

And He said to her, "Daughter, be of good cheer; your faith has made you well. Go in peace." (Luke 8:48)

As Jesus made His way to the home of Jairus, a ruler of the synagogue whose daughter was ill, there was a woman in the crowd who had been sick for twelve years. It almost appears that Jesus was unaware of her in the crowd. But in reality, He had been waiting for her.

This woman had spent all her money trying to find a cure for her disease. She thought, *If I could just touch Him when He passes by, I know I will be healed.* So as Jesus passed by, she reached out and touched the hem of His garment. And suddenly, instantaneously, right there on the spot, she was healed. She knew it...and so did the Lord!

When she touched Him, Jesus stopped and said, "Somebody touched Me, for I perceived power going out from Me" (Luke 8:46). The term Jesus used for "power" here is the Greek word *dunamis*, which speaks of a mighty, miraculous act or work. In fact, it is the same Greek term from which we get our English words, *dynamic*, and *dynamite*. So Jesus was essentially saying, "Someone just tapped into my dynamic, explosive power."

As the crowd parted, the woman fell down before Jesus. He assured her, "Daughter, be of good cheer; your faith has made you well" Go in peace" (Luke 8:48). In this woman's moment of need, the power of Jesus healed her and gave her courage.

The same power that impacted this woman can impact you today. It's the very same dynamic that came from the Holy Spirit to the disciples on the Day of Pentecost, just before they went out to turn their world upside down. And the same power is available to every Christian, to give us courage to live the Christian life and to share our faith.

Jesus specializes in empowering weak people who turn to Him for strength. All this woman did was reach out a hand in faith and touch Him. And that's all we need to do, as well.

Friday

"When you are reviled and persecuted and lied about because you are my followers—wonderful! Be happy about it! Be very glad! for a tremendous reward awaits you up in heaven. And remember, the ancient prophets were persecuted too." (Matthew 5:11-12, TLB)

There are two primary sources of spiritual attack in the life of the Christian: outward and inward. While an inward attack comes in the form of infiltration, an outward attack is persecution. And for many, an outward assault takes them down.

Persecution is one of Satan's primary methods of attack in the life of men and women who seek to follow Christ. Jesus talked about persecution in the parable of the sower, in which the seed symbolizes the Word of God. He explained, "But he who received the seed on stony places, this is he who hears the word and immediately receives it with joy; yet he has no root in himself, but endures only for a while. For when tribulation or persecution arises because of the word, immediately he stumbles" (Matthew 13:20-21).

If you are going to be a true follower of Jesus Christ, then you *will* be persecuted. But Jesus said, "Blessed are you when they revile and persecute you, and say all kinds of evil against you falsely for My sake. Rejoice and be exceedingly glad, for great is your reward in heaven, for so they persecuted the prophets who were before you" (Matthew 5:11-12). In other words, you're in great company!

But if we are being hassled as believers, let's make sure it's for the right reasons. As the Scripture says: "For it is commendable if a man bears up under the pain of unjust suffering because he is conscious of God. But how is it to your credit if you receive a beating for doing wrong and endure it? But if you suffer for doing good and you endure it, this is commendable before God. To this you were called, because Christ suffered for you, leaving you an example, that you should follow in his steps" (1 Peter 2:19-21, NIV).

Let's not be persecuted because we're acting like jerks and deserve it, but rather because we are like Jesus Christ and reflect Him to a lost world. And let's never forget that in Him we have peace and victory over persecution and tribulation.

Weekend

And I am convinced that nothing can ever separate us from God's love. Neither death nor life, neither angels nor demons, neither our fears for today nor our worries about tomorrow—not even the powers of hell can separate us from God's love. No power in the sky above or in the earth below—indeed, nothing in all creation will ever be able to separate us from the love of God that is revealed in Christ Jesus our Lord. (Romans 8:38-39, NLT)

When you go to a place like Disneyland with your children, you know where they are. You don't leave the park and forget them, because you protect what you love.

In the same way, God never forgets those He loves. Writing to first-century believers, Jude addressed his letter, "to all who have been called by God the Father, who loves you and keeps you safe in the care of Jesus Christ (v. 1, NLT)." In the original language, the clear implication is, "You are *continually kept* by Jesus Christ."

Continually kept. What could be more encouraging than that?

Whatever your difficulties may be today, you need to know that you are preserved in Christ, and that He will maintain His investment, which He purchased at such a great cost at the Cross. He will protect you, preserve you, watch over you, and keep you.

But here's something interesting: the Bible also tells us to *keep ourselves* in the love of God (Jude 21). Is this a contradiction? No. It's merely two sides of the same coin. The Bible is teaching that God will keep us, but at the same time, we must keep ourselves in His love. We don't keep ourselves *saved*, but we keep ourselves *safe*.

There are things we must do on a daily basis to keep ourselves in a place where God can actively bless us, and to keep ourselves away from all that is unlike Him, and those things that would drag us down spiritually.

Attacks will certainly come our way. Were it not for the preserving grace of God, none of us would make it. Clearly, we are preserved, protected, and kept by the power of heaven. Let's make sure we walk in that generous protection and covering of our God, putting it on like a garment—or body armor—every morning before our feet hit the floor.

Monday

*They couldn't take their eyes off them—Peter and John standing there so
confident, so sure of themselves! Their fascination deepened when they
realized these two were laymen with no training in Scripture or formal
education. They recognized them as companions of Jesus.*
(Acts 4:13, THE MESSAGE)

We can often tell where people have been just by looking at
them. For instance, if someone walked by wearing a wet
swimming suit and sand-encrusted sandals, we would conclude that
person had just come from the beach. We could see the telltale signs.

The Bible tells us there was something about Peter and John,
something about the way they lived and the things they said, that
were telltale signs to unbelievers that they had been with Jesus. One
day on their way to pray in the temple, they met a crippled man. He
asked them for money, but Peter told him, "Silver and gold I do not
have, but what I do have I give you: In the name of Jesus Christ of
Nazareth, rise up and walk" (Acts 3:6).

It was a dramatic, radical miracle that shocked the city, and the
religious leaders didn't like it one bit. They thought they had already
dealt with this "problem" when they eliminated that man from
Nazareth known as Jesus. But now His followers were popping up
everywhere. So they called Peter and John to appear before them.
Our opening Scripture in today's devotional speaks of how stunned
the Jewish leaders were when they saw the boldness and confidence
of Peter and John. Weren't these guys just common, uneducated
fishermen? But then it clicked: They realized that they had been
with Jesus.

If you were arrested for being a Christian, would there be enough
evidence to convict you? You may put Christian stickers on your car.
Perhaps you have three or four Bibles in your home. Your wardrobe
might include several T-shirts with Christian slogans on them. But
what about your behavior? What about your countenance? Would
there be enough evidence to prove that you have been with Jesus?

Tuesday

But you must not forget this one thing, dear friends: A day is like a thousand years to the Lord, and a thousand years is like a day. The Lord isn't really being slow about his promise, as some people think. No, he is being patient for your sake. He does not want anyone to be destroyed, but wants everyone to repent. But the day of the Lord will come as unexpectedly as a thief. Then the heavens will pass away with a terrible noise, and the very elements themselves will disappear in fire, and the earth and everything on it will be found to deserve judgment.
(2 Peter 3:8-10, NLT)

We live in a culture in which everything happens fast. We don't have to wait for much of anything anymore. So when we're told to wait for the Lord's return, it can be difficult for us. We look around at our world and say, "Lord, come on. Look how bad it's getting! Have You forgotten? When are You coming back?"

But we must understand that God has His own schedule, and He is not bound by ours. Jesus came the first time at the appointed hour, and He will come the second time in the same way. The Bible tells us, "But when the right time came, God sent his Son, born of a woman, subject to the law. God sent him to buy freedom for us who were slaves to the law, so that he could adopt us as his very own children" (Galatians 4:4–5, NLT). God watched this little world of ours, and He knew when the right moment in time had come.

When Jesus arrived on the scene, the people were ready. The Romans ruled the known world, with their vast system of roads, easing transportation. Taxes were high, morale was low, and morals were even lower. It had been 400 years since Israel had heard from God…since a prophet had come…since an angel appeared…since a miracle had been performed. Then John the Baptist burst on the scene, announcing that the Messiah had indeed arrived.

When the time was just right, God sent His Son. And when the time is just right, the Son will return again to this earth.

Wednesday

He has planted eternity in the human heart. (Ecclesiastes 3:11, NLT)

There are four things we should know about every person on earth. No matter how successful or unsuccessful they may be, no matter how famous or obscure, no matter how attractive or unattractive, everyone shares these four traits.

First, there is an essential emptiness in every person who hasn't yet come to Christ. No matter how much money or prestige someone has, everyone has to deal with that emptiness. Scripture says that God made His creation subject to vanity or emptiness, meaning there is a void, a hole if you will, inside every man, woman, and child (see Romans 8:20-21).

Two: people are lonely. We can assume there is a sense of loneliness in every individual. Solomon wrote about an instance of this in his book of Ecclesiastes: "I observed yet another example of meaninglessness under the sun. This is the case of a man who is all alone, without a child or a brother, yet who works hard to gain as much wealth as he can. But then he asks himself, 'Who am I working for? Why am I giving up so much pleasure now?' It is all so meaningless and depressing" (Ecclesiastes 4:7-8, NLT). Albert Einstein once wrote, "It is strange to be known so universally and yet be so lonely."[18]

Three: people have a sense of guilt. They may try to mask it with alcohol or have a psychologist or psychiatrist tell them it's not really there. Even so, they have to deal with their guilt over the things they have done wrong. The head of a mental institution in London said, "I could release half of my patients if I could find a way to relieve them of their sense of guilt."

Four: people are afraid to die. Some may strut around and say, "Not me. I'm not afraid to die." But they are.

So don't be so intimidated by the facades that people hide behind and assume they don't want to hear what you have to say about your faith in Christ. Remember, you used to be one of those people. I used to be one of those people. We responded to the gospel. And so will they.

Thursday

No temptation has come your way that is too hard for flesh and blood to bear. But God can be trusted not to allow you to suffer any temptation beyond your powers of endurance. He will see to it that every temptation has a way out, so that it will never be impossible for you to bear it.
(1 Corinthians 10:13, PHILLIPS)

In the New Testament, we have the account of Jesus saying to Peter, "Simon, Simon! Indeed, Satan has asked for you, that he may sift you as wheat. But I have prayed for you, that your faith should not fail; and when you have returned to Me, strengthen your brethren" (Luke 22:31-32).

Put yourself in Peter's sandals. You're sitting near the Lord when He turns to you, looks you in the eyes, calls you by name, and says, "Satan has been asking excessively that you be taken out of the care and protection of God. The devil has been asking for you by name." I don't know about you, but if Jesus Christ, the Son of God, said that to me, it would be cause for great concern.

Peter was such a big fish that Satan himself went after him. I wonder if the Lord paused for effect: "Satan has been asking for you...by name...But I have good news, Peter. I have prayed for you."

It's a good reminder to us that when the devil comes knocking at our door, we should say, "Lord, would You mind getting that?" We are no match for the devil. But even though he is a powerful foe, he is still a created being, and certainly not as powerful as God. Even so, we don't want to tangle with him—or any of his servants. We want to stand behind God's protection.

In spite of the devil's power and wicked agenda, he must first ask permission when it comes to attacking the children of God, because of the hedge of protection that God has placed around us.

God knows what you are ready for. And He won't give you more than you can handle. We have His word on that!

Friday

If I make you light-bearers, you don't think I'm going to hide you under a bucket, do you? I'm putting you on a light stand. Now that I've put you there on a hilltop, on a light stand—shine!
(Matthew 5:15, THE MESSAGE)

How should I live my life on this earth? What purpose does God have in mind for me, now that I have received His Son Jesus Christ into my heart?

These are questions every believer should ask, because if you have no goals or purpose, you can waste your life. As I have often said, if you aim at nothing, you're bound to hit it.

Many people simply want to prolong their lives, rather than try to find their purpose in life. Certainly medical science is helping us live longer lives. We can add years to our lives, but we can't add life to our years. Should our primary goal be to prolong our lives, or should it be to live life to its fullest?

Jim Elliot was fresh out of college when he felt the call of God to go to the mission field. Tragically, Jim and four other young missionaries lost their lives in the jungles of Ecuador in an attempt to reach others with the gospel. It might seem like a terrible waste of life for such a young man with so much promise. But after his death, this entry was found in one of his journals: "I seek not a long life, but a full one, like you, Lord Jesus."

That's a good goal: To live a full life, a life with meaning and purpose. We don't know how long we will live; that's up to God. But life isn't merely a matter of years. It's a matter of *how* we live. It's not the years that count, but what you do with those years.

Sometimes, heartaches, trials, and tragedies can threaten to squeeze all of the meaning out of life. In our darkest moments, we may even wonder why God leaves us on the planet. But if our heavenly Father has chosen to give us life for another day, we can be sure that He has a purpose in doing so. We need to wait on Him, keep our eyes open to every opportunity, and trust Him daily for the grace to keep us going.

Weekend

[He] made Himself of no reputation, taking the form of a bondservant, and coming in the likeness of men. (Philippians 2:5-7)

Because Jesus was God, we might ask, did He have the full knowledge of God as a little baby in the manger at Bethlehem? Or did this knowledge come to Him over a period of time? When Jesus was born, could He have turned to Mary and said, "I am God Almighty, the Messiah of Israel. I am God in human form. And by the way, Mary, the earth is round. Some people say that it's flat, but I'm telling you it's round. I made it Myself."

Jesus didn't do that. Instead, He squealed and giggled and made noises like any other baby. And He had a human mind. The Bible says of Jesus, "And the Child grew and became strong in spirit, filled with wisdom; and the grace of God was upon Him" (Luke 2:40). When Jesus was twelve, Mary and Joseph found Him in the temple after the Feast of the Passover, "sitting in the midst of the teachers, both listening to them and asking them questions" (verse 46).

Then in Luke 2:52, we read that "Jesus increased in wisdom and stature, and in favor with God and men." This would appear to be saying that Jesus went through a learning process like anyone else. Yet at the same time, He didn't have the limitations that sin brings on one's life.

Jesus walked the earth in a human body and died like a man, in the sense that His body ceased to function just like ours do when we die. And though He was God, He emptied himself of the privileges of deity and walked among us as a man.

And because He was willing to become a Man, He has become our great High Priest, who "understands our weaknesses since he had the same temptations we do, though he never once gave way to them and sinned. So let us come boldly to the very throne of God and stay there to receive his mercy and to find grace to help us in our times of need" (Hebrews 4:15-16, TLB).

Monday

As for God, His way is perfect; the word of the Lord is proven; He is a shield to all who trust in Him. (Psalm 18:30)

In spite of breathtaking advances in science and technology, we can only shake our heads in amazement as the human condition on our planet seems to grow worse and worse by the day. And in these anxious and critical days in which we are living, people wonder what this world is coming to. Jesus spoke of a day when we would see "men's hearts failing them from fear and the expectation of those things which are coming on the earth" (Luke 21:26).

Many, in desperation, will grasp at straws. We see evidence of this in our bookstores today. When someone comes up with some new belief system, others will quickly buy into it. In fact, I'm absolutely amazed at the things people will believe—*without ever seriously considering the claims of Christ or the teaching of Scripture.* They will reject Christianity and the Bible wholesale, without giving it even a cursory glance. They will believe in just about anything—no matter how wild and implausible—except the right things, the things that would help and heal and save them.

Even so, there's a deep sense of desperation out there these days, a sense of uncertainty and even fear. People all around are searching for answers to questions like, "Why are we here?" "What is the meaning of life?" and "What's going to happen next?" Some will put their faith in political leaders if they make the right promises and repeat the right mantras. Others will reach out to psychics, fortune-tellers, and astrology—or the latest prediction by tabloid prophets—trying to find some kind of meaning.

Yet all the while, there is Someone who knows exactly what the future holds. And He tells us all about it in His book, the Bible. The Bible is the one book that predicts the future with absolute accuracy. Within the pages of the book many people seem to love to hate, we find the true God, the true faith, the true prophets, and the true belief.

We who know the Truth must continue to speak the Truth— with compassion, tact, wisdom, and much grace.

Tuesday

I even found great pleasure in hard work, a reward for all my labors. But as I looked at everything I had worked so hard to accomplish, it was all so meaningless--like chasing the wind. There was nothing really worthwhile anywhere. (Ecclesiastes 2:10-11, NLT)

Did you know that success can be a form of failure…and that failure can lead to true success? Some argue, of course, that success is the most important thing in life. We hear that on all sides, don't we? But is it? That all depends on whose definition of "success" you choose.

Some people actually achieve their ambitious goals, but what did it cost them? Did they "win by intimidation"? Did they succeed by using deception and betrayal? Did they climb the ladder by abandoning their principles and sacrificing integrity? Did they claw their way to the top by neglecting family and friends? Ultimately, did they succeed by forgetting about, and in some cases, outright abandoning, God?" If so, they may be successful by certain definitions, but ultimately, they're pitiful failures.

We can do worse than fail.

We can succeed and become puffed up about our success. We can succeed and worship the accomplishment rather the One who helped us to reach it. We can succeed and forget whose hand it is that gives and withholds.

And what about failure? Humiliating and disappointing as it might be, failure can be good…if we truly learn from our mistakes. And even when we do something that is wrong, if we learn from it, we're in a sense "failing forward."

By failing forward, I mean that after we've made a serious error in judgment and done something sinful or foolish—and then tasted the bitter results of our actions—we say to ourselves, "I really don't want to do that again." So (if we are wise) we put safeguards around our lives and take precautionary steps to never fall into that same trap again. If that is the case, then we have learned something from our failures.

If it takes humiliation and loss to help us wake up to the reality of our need for God, we will someday see our failure as "the best thing that could have happened to me."

Wednesday

Though he was God, he did not think of equality with God as something to cling to. Instead, he gave up his divine privileges; he took the humble position of a slave and was born as a human being. When he appeared in human form, he humbled himself in obedience to God and died a criminal's death on a cross. Therefore, God elevated him to the place of highest honor and gave him the name above all other names, that at the name of Jesus every knee should bow, in heaven and on earth and under the earth, and every tongue confess that Jesus Christ is Lord, to the glory of God the Father. (Philippians 2:5-11, NLT)

What do we consider success? If we were to classify a successful person, what would be the earmarks? Power? Wealth? Popularity? Respect?

If that's our criteria, then apparently Jesus was a failure. Was He popular? Not for long. The fickle multitudes sang His praises for awhile, but turned on Him a short time later. So in a sense, He wasn't popular. In fact, after one of His sermons, all of His followers deserted Him, except for the twelve disciples.

Was He politically powerful? No. He was a political failure. All levels of government first rejected Him and then conspired to kill Him.

Did Jesus have lots of friends? Not really. He had a lot of fair-weather friends, and people who claimed to be friends, but when it came to the end, only a handful stuck with Him.

Did He have money and possessions? Not at all. He said, "The Son of Man has nowhere to lay His head" (Matthew 8:20; Luke 9:58). He had one garment that we know of, for which the soldiers gambled at the foot of the cross.

Was Jesus respected by His peers? It you consider the religious leaders His peers, then the answer would be "no." They rejected His work and ridiculed His teaching.

But despite His "failure" by these standards, Jesus Christ was the greatest success that anyone could have ever been. Why? Because He came with a purpose: to die for the sins of the world. And He accomplished that task.

Was the cross a failure—dying such a lowly, humiliating death before the mocking eyes of His enemies? No. By giving His life on that cross, He purchased eternal success for billions of people... including you and me.

Thursday

And He was withdrawn from them about a stone's throw, and He knelt down and prayed, saying, "Father, if it is Your will, take this cup away from Me; nevertheless not My will, but Yours, be done."
(Luke 22:41-42)

I'm so glad that God will overrule my prayers at times, because I have prayed for things fervently, believing they were the will of God, and they were flat-out wrong. I am so thankful that God said "no" to those prayers.

Yet I have actually heard some people say, "Never pray, 'Not my will, but Yours be done.' That is a lack of faith." Some have even said, "What you should really pray is, 'Not Your will, but mine be done.'"

Let's just say that I don't want to be standing too close to those people when lightning strikes, because they have things turned around.

Never be afraid to pray, "Not my will, but Yours be done." By saying that, you are simply saying, "Lord, I don't know all the facts. I don't know everything there is to know. My knowledge is limited. My experience is limited. So if what I am praying is outside of Your will for any reason, please graciously overrule it." You won't always understand how you should pray. What it comes down to is telling God that you want His will more than your own.

I know this is hard at times. Sometimes you don't understand why God doesn't give you what you ask for. When you're young and single, you may see a handsome guy or beautiful girl and just *know* that person is the one for you. But as the lyrics to a country song say, "Sometimes I thank God for unanswered prayers."

As time passes, you will look back with 20/20 hindsight, and you will say, "Thank God He did not answer my prayers," or "Thank God He answered my prayers," whichever the case may be.

Finally…remember the words of Jesus: "Your heavenly Father already knows all your needs. Seek the Kingdom of God above all else, and live righteously, and he will give you everything you need" (Matthew 6:32-33, NLT).

Friday

*Show me, O Lord, my life's end and the number of my days; let me know
how fleeting is my life. (Psalm 39:4, NIV)*

L et's say that your phone rings tomorrow morning, and it's a call from the manager of your bank. He tells you, "I received a very unusual call the other day. Someone who loves you very much and is quite wealthy has given you a large sum of money. This anonymous donor will be depositing 86,400 cents into your account every single day."

"How's that again?" you ask.

"Every single day, this person will deposit 86,400 cents into your account."

Is that much money? you wonder at first. Then you get out your calculator and figure out that it amounts to $864 every day. *That's pretty good*, you're thinking.

"But there is one condition," the banker continues. "You have to spend it every single day. You can't save it up. You can't add it to the next day's balance. Every day, you must spend that money. What is not spent will be taken away. This person will do this each and every day, but the condition is that you must spend the money."

So you go back to your calculator and figure out that $864 times 7 equals $6,048 per week. That amount, multiplied by 52, comes to $314,496 per year. That's a pretty good deal. And that is also a fantasy.

So let's deal with reality. Someone who really does love you very much deposits into your bank of time 86,400 seconds every single day. That someone is God. And the condition is that you must spend it. You can't save up time today and apply it toward tomorrow— there's no such thing as a 27-hour day. Each and every day, you have the opportunity to invest your precious commodity of time.

I like the way Paul wrote about this in (Ephesians 5:15-17, NIV):

"Be very careful, then, how you live—not as unwise but as wise, making the most of every opportunity, because the days are evil. Therefore do not be foolish, but understand what the Lord's will is."

Weekend

He will not let you stumble; the one who watches over you will not slumber. Indeed, he who watches over Israel never slumbers or sleeps. (Psalm 121:3-4, NLT)

If I had a say about how any given day would go, I would never write in, "crisis." I would never write, "Get sick" here, or "Have my tire go flat" there, or "Have this unexpected disaster take place." I would just write in all the good stuff in life. I would plan for everything to go my way. There would be no traffic on the freeways. It would always be green lights and blue skies.

But guess what? We're *not* in charge of our lives. God is.

I love what the prophet once admitted to the Lord: "O Lord, I know the way of man is not in himself; it is not in man who walks to direct his own steps" (Jeremiah 10:23).

The fact is, God will allow so-called "bad things" to happen to us in the course of our days. But as time goes by, you will find that the significant things you learn in life didn't really come from the good times and the mountain-top experiences. They came from those times of crisis in which you were more dependent on God. Many of the most difficult days will, in retrospect, turn out to be unbelievably valuable, because it is through those so-called "bad times" that you will learn some of life's most important lessons.

The things we experience are not random events that float in and out of our lives. They are rather specific events that have been chosen by God and are timely and purposeful. This means the good things as well as the bad things. It means the wonderful, happy times of life as well as the dark, difficult days.

When you put your faith in Jesus Christ, you come under His protective care. God is fully aware of everything that happens to you, and thankfully, He is never asleep on the job. He pays careful attention to the smallest details of your life and is in complete in control of all circumstances that surround you. He knows what's happening in your life right now—knows it better than you do. And His presence and provision will be all you need to make it through.

Monday

"Nor is there salvation in any other, for there is no other name under heaven given among men by which we must be saved." (Acts 4:12)

I'm so grateful that the way to God has been made known to us. God has not said to humanity, "Find your own path. If you're really diligent, then you'll eventually chase it down. You may have to climb mountains in Tibet or walk barefoot over hot coals in Bali. You may have to explore the teachings of eastern mysticism. You may even have to call the psychic hotline. But you'll get to Me… eventually…maybe…with a little luck."

Thankfully, God has clearly told us how we can be forgiven of our sins. Only one lifeline has been dropped from heaven, and that is Jesus Christ and knowing Him. There is only one correct answer to the question "What must I do to be saved?" and the answer is coming to God through Jesus Christ. He said, "I am the way, the truth, and the life. No one comes to the Father except through Me" (John 14:6).

Did any other religious leaders die for our sins, and more importantly, rise again from the dead? No, they didn't. They're all still in their tombs today. But Jesus is alive. As the resurrected Christ told His friend, John: "Do not be afraid; I am the First and the Last. I am He who lives, and was dead, and behold, I am alive forevermore" (Revelation 1:17-18).

He was uniquely qualified to bridge the gap between God and humanity, because He was the only person to ever walk this earth who was both fully God and fully man. When He died on the cross for the sins of humanity, He became the bridge between a flawless, perfect, and holy God and flawed, imperfect, and unholy people like us.

Repenting of your sins and putting your faith in Jesus Christ as your Savior and Lord is a decision that only you can make for yourself. He is ready and willing to come into your life, forgive you, and be your Savior, your Lord, your God, and your Friend.

Tuesday

"If you don't go all the way with me, through thick and thin, you don't deserve me. If your first concern is to look after yourself, you'll never find yourself. But if you forget about yourself and look to me, you'll find both yourself and me. (Matthew 10:38-39, THE MESSAGE)

If you were visiting first-century Jerusalem and happened to see a contingent of Roman soldiers come down the street with a man bearing his cross, you would think, *That poor guy is going to die today.* It was a shameful thing to be crucified. It was a long, tortuous, and painful death reserved for the most hardened criminals. The Romans would utilize this horrible form of torture to make an example of people. It was common knowledge that any man bearing his cross was going to die.

So when Jesus said, "If anyone desires to come after Me, let him deny himself, and take up his cross daily," it meant dying to yourself. Some people will misunderstand this. They will say, "Well, we all have a cross to bear. My cross to bear is my career," or "My cross to bear is this physical impairment," or "My cross to bear is this difficult circumstance." But that's not really using the phrase properly. The cross is the same for every man and woman; it doesn't vary from person to person. *Bearing the cross simply means dying to self.*

This means exchanging your life for the life of God, your plans for His plans, and your goals for His goals. Jesus said, "If you grasp and cling to life on your terms, you'll lose it, but if you let that life go, you'll get life on God's terms" (Luke 17:33, THE MESSAGE).

Samuel Rutherford said, "His cross is the sweetest burden that I ever bare. It is such a burden as wings are to a bird, or sails are to a ship, to carry me forward to my harbor."19 Rutherford discovered what we can know as well: When you really die to yourself, you will find yourself.

Wednesday

"I tell you, her sins—and they are many—have been forgiven, so she has shown me much love. But a person who is forgiven little shows only little love." Then Jesus said to the woman, "Your sins are forgiven."
(Luke 7:47-48, NLT)

It's often those who realize just how much they deserve hell who become the most passionate followers of Jesus. Think of Saul of Tarsus, later to become the apostle Paul. Here was a man who went out of his way to hunt down Christians, arrest them, and have them executed. Here was a man who presided over the execution of an innocent young man named Stephen—stoned to death by an angry mob for simply declaring the Lord Jesus.

But after Saul met the living Jesus on the Damascus Road, he dedicated himself to God with the same fervor he had dedicated himself to the devil. In his letter to the Corinthians, he wrote: "For I am the least of the apostles and do not even deserve to be called an apostle, because I persecuted the church of God. But by the grace of God I am what I am, and his grace to me was not without effect. No, I worked harder than all of them—yet not I, but the grace of God that was with me" (1 Corinthians 15:9-10, NIV).

I wish more Christians would serve the Lord with as much as energy as they once served the devil. Granted, there are some believers today who were once into a life of crime. Some were drug addicts or prostitutes, but were transformed by Christ and are serving Him. But there are others who lived a relatively moral life.

The bottom line is that we were all sinners. All separated from God. All without hope. All on our way to hell. When Jesus died on the cross, He shed His blood for our sins. And when we put our faith in Him as our Savior and Lord, we were forgiven. The forgiveness that God extends to the most hardened criminal is just as significant as the forgiveness He extends to the most moral person. All of us need Jesus. But it's often those who have come from the lowest pit who want to do the most for the Lord.

Maybe we all need to think more about all that He has done for us.

Thursday

I eagerly expect and hope that I will in no way be ashamed, but will have sufficient courage so that now as always Christ will be exalted in my body, whether by life or by death. For to me, to live is Christ and to die is gain. (Philippians 1:20-21, NIV)

With everything going on in our world today, we could be really fearful about our lives: *I don't know if I should do such and such—an accident might happen…I'd better not get on that plane, because it might crash…I'd better not get in that car—I might not make it home…I'd better not do this…I'd better not do that.* We could find ourselves living in a constant state of paranoia.

Is there an alternative? Yes! We could commit our ways to God each day and say, "If this is my last day on Earth, Lord, then I'm ready to meet You. If it isn't, then I will serve You one more day." As Paul said, "For me to live is Christ, and to die is gain." Another translation renders those words: "For living to me means simply 'Christ,' and if I die I should merely gain more of him" (PHILLIPS). What a great outlook to have.

But that doesn't mean we should be foolish and unnecessarily test God, being careless with our lives—driving without a seatbelt or taking a wilderness hike without proper equipment or simply ignoring safety precautions. There is a distinct difference between trusting the Lord and testing the Lord.

It does mean, however, that we should accept each day as a gift from God Almighty and live it to its fullest, totally committed to Him. We should live each day as if it were our last.

Let's just say, for instance, that this day was your last. If you were to think back on this day, would you be ashamed of how you lived it? Or would you say, "I think I lived it well. I did what I should have done. I have no real embarrassment to speak of. It was a well-lived day."

Good. That's how you should live each and every day.

Friday

His mother said to the servants, "Whatever He says to you, do it."
(John 2:5)

When David was called by God to be king, he was out watching sheep, just being faithful. The day David killed Goliath, he didn't wake up that morning and hear God say, "David, today you are going to the valley of Elah. There will be a giant Philistine named Goliath, and you will kill him with a stone." No, at his dad's request, David was taking some cheese sandwiches to his brothers out on the front line...just being faithful on an errand for his dad.

What was Gideon doing when God called him? He was hiding from his enemies. He was terrified. But God saw his potential, and the next thing Gideon knew, he was leading troops into battle.

And what was Elisha doing when Elijah called him to carry on the work? He was out plowing in the field. Moses was watching a bunch of sheep in the desert when God called him to deliver the Israelites. Then there was Daniel, who was so faithful to the Lord that his enemies couldn't find one thing wrong with him. They had to make up lies about him so that he would be sentenced to death. And how about that teenage girl in Nazareth who had a visit from one of God's most powerful angels, with a message about a Child, who would be called the Son of the Most High?

My point is this: They were faithfully doing what God had set before them. They weren't running around, looking for big, important things to accomplish. They didn't have public relations consultants or agents. They were simply doing the little things, waiting on God.

Sometimes, we have great ideas of what God will do. But we have to wait on Him. What are your dreams right now? Maybe you want to do something for God, but you think it will never happen. Then again...maybe it will. Maybe it will even surpass your wildest dreams. Just be faithful to do what God has set before you right now.

Your future is safe in His hands.

Weekend

What I am saying, dear brothers and sisters, is that our physical bodies cannot inherit the Kingdom of God. These dying bodies cannot inherit what will last forever. But let me reveal to you a wonderful secret. We will not all die, but we will all be transformed!
(1 Corinthians 15:50-51, NLT)

When he reached the age of seventy, historian Will Durant said, "To live forever would be the greatest curse imaginable."

Will we live forever? The answer is "yes" and "no." Will our bodies live forever? No. Will our bodies cease to exist at one point? Absolutely. But the soul is immortal. Each one of us has a soul. It is the soul that gives each of us uniqueness and personality…and that part of us *will* live forever.

Today, many people are searching for immortality, that elusive fountain of youth. Sometimes, it's hard for us to accept the fact that life is passing and death is approaching. One day, you will wake up and realize you have more life behind you than you have in front of you. But the question we should be asking is not, "Can I find immortality?" Rather, it should be, "Where will I spend my immortality?"

If you have put your faith in Jesus Christ and have asked Him to forgive you of your sin, the Bible teaches that you will go immediately into the presence of God in heaven when you die. That is God's promise to you.

But God not only promises life beyond the grave. *He also promises life during life*, not just an existence, but a life that's worth living. Jesus said, "My purpose is to give them a rich and satisfying life" (John 10:10, NLT).

In Romans 5:17, the apostle Paul declares: "For if, by the trespass of the one man, death reigned through that one man, how much more will those who receive God's abundant provision of grace and of the gift of righteousness reign in life through the one man, Jesus Christ" (NIV).

Reign in life! No matter what our circumstances, we are sons and daughters of the great King. He will watch over us through our days on earth, and take us home to be with Him when this brief life is over. That's the hope and promise for all Christians. And that's why the believer does not have to be afraid to die…or afraid to live.

Monday

Whoever has no rule over his own spirit is like a city broken down, without walls. (Proverbs 25:28)

In this day of instant information, we can get our news so fast that we don't have to wait for the evening news anymore. We don't have to wait for the newspaper. We can go out on the Internet and get our news in real time.

I think this makes it hard for us to slow down and listen, especially to God. Many of us are like Martha in Luke's Gospel, running around in our little self-made circles of activity, instead of calmly sitting at His feet and listening like Mary did. (see Luke 10:39-41)

The book of James tells us: "My dear brothers, take note of this: Everyone should be quick to listen, slow to speak and slow to become angry, for man's anger does not bring about the righteous life that God desires" James 1:19-20 (NIV).

We ought to post that verse where we can see it every day. How different our lives would be if we heeded its admonition.

James tells us we should be quick to listen, but we also should be *slow to speak*. How many times have you blurted out something, only to regret it the moment it left your lips? Jesus said, "But I say to you that for every idle word men may speak, they will give account of it in the day of judgment. For by your words you will be justified, and by your words you will be condemned" (Matthew 12:36-37).

We should be slow to anger. With our spoken words. With our e-mails and texts and however else we choose to communicate. How easy it is to rationalize our outbursts of rage (especially when we're driving). But Proverbs 29:11, (NLT) says, "Fools vent their anger, but the wise quietly hold it back."

How much better our lives and our witness would be if we were quick to hear, slow to speak, and slow to become angry. According to the book of Proverbs, people who exercise self-control are the real heroes in life!

Better a patient man than a warrior,
a man who controls his temper than one who takes a city.
Proverbs 16:32 (NIV)

Tuesday

Do not marvel, my brethren, if the world hates you. (1 John 3:13)

I heard a story about some fish suppliers who were having problems shipping codfish from the East Coast. By the time the fish reached the West coast, they were spoiled. They froze them, but by the time the fish arrived, they were mushy. So the seafood company decided to send them alive…but the fish arrived dead. On their third try, they once more shipped the fish alive, but with one difference. They included a catfish in each tank. The catfish, you see, is the natural enemy of the codfish. By the time the codfish arrived, they were alive and well, because they had spent their trip fleeing the catfish.

Could it be that God in His wisdom has put a catfish in your tank to keep you alive and well spiritually? Maybe there's a person at work who always has eight hardball questions for you every Monday morning regarding spiritual things. Maybe it's that neighbor who constantly gives you a hard time about your faith in Jesus. Maybe it's a spouse or family member who doesn't believe. And you begin to wonder, "Why is this happening to me?"

It's just that catfish in your life…keeping you spiritually alert and on your toes. It's God's provision to protect you from a weak, mushy faith.

Shortly before He went to the cross, Jesus told the disciples, "If you were of the world, the world would love its own. Yet because you are not of the world, but I chose you out of the world, therefore the world hates you" (John 15:19).

God will allow persecution in the life of the believer. If you're experiencing persecution—whether subtle or out front and in the open—here are two things to remember: First, persecution confirms that you are a child of God. Be glad in that. And second, persecution causes you to cling closer to Jesus.

When you endure persecution for your faith, remember that this world is not your home.

And as far as I know, there are no catfish in heaven.

Wednesday

"And these are the ones by the wayside where the word is sown. When they hear, Satan comes immediately and takes away the word that was sown in their hearts." (Mark 4:15)

Temptation comes to everyone, but the enemy focuses many of his attacks on those who are young in the faith—and those who are making a difference in the kingdom.

Right after we make a decision to follow Jesus Christ, the devil shows up, tempting us to doubt our own salvation. He whispers in our ears, "You think Christ really came into your life? Are you crazy?" This is a tactic the enemy keeps recycling again and again. (And why not? He'll use it as long as it works!)

The Bible warns us that when we are young in the faith, we are especially vulnerable. We see in the parable of the sower that young believers are immediately attacked. Jesus said, "And these are the ones by the wayside where the word is sown. When they hear, Satan comes immediately and takes away the word that was sown in their hearts" (Mark 4:15). The evil one is there to pounce upon those who are young in the faith.

Temptation also comes to those who are making a difference in the kingdom of God. First of all, Satan doesn't want you to come to Christ. But once you have made that commitment, his next strategy is to immobilize you, to get you to compromise yourself and be ineffective. He doesn't want you to be a threat to his kingdom.

If you want to make a difference, if you want to reach people who don't know the Lord, then don't expect a standing ovation in hell. The enemy won't take it lightly. He will attack you. He'll come at you from the front, from the rear, and from those blind spots just out of your peripheral vision. You had better expect it and brace yourself for it. And while you're at it, pray for other believers, whether new in the faith or are already making a difference.

Thursday

But we Christians have no veil over our faces; we can be mirrors that brightly reflect the glory of the Lord. And as the Spirit of the Lord works within us, we become more and more like him.
(2 Corinthians 3:18, TLB)

When two people have been married a while, they start becoming like each other. This has happened with my wife and me. We know each other so well that I can start a sentence, and she can finish it. She knows what I'm thinking even when I'm not saying it. I'm just amazed at her intuition. But I can usually read her as well. Having been married for more than three decades now, we've spent a long time together.

This is even more the case when we have been spending time with Jesus Christ. We become like Him, "a chip off of the ol' Rock," we might say. This is God's ultimate plan for every Christian—to make us like Jesus.

We see this in the life of Peter. He was burned by the enemy's fire when he denied the Lord. But when touched with the Spirit's fire at Pentecost, he became the new-and-improved Peter. The same thing that happened to him can happen to you. The same power is available to every believer. That's because when someone has been with Jesus—and by that I mean when they spend time in the Lord's presence and spend time growing spiritually—they will become more like Him.

Before you ever made your appearance on earth, God chose you. God knew there would come a day when you would put your faith in Him, and He chose you before you chose Him. And what is His goal for you? His goal is that you might become like Jesus.

Many of us know and can quote Romans 8:28—the verse that starts "All things work together for good…." But the verse that follows, Romans 8:29, is every bit as important. Here are the two verses together: *"And we know that in all things God works for the good of those who love him, who have been called according to his purpose. For those God foreknew he also predestined to be conformed to the likeness of his Son, that he might be the firstborn among many brothers"* (NIV).

We are being shaped and conformed—sometimes through our hardships and trials—to be more and more like God's Son.

Friday

Happy is the man who doesn't give in and do wrong when he is tempted, for afterwards he will get as his reward the crown of life that God has promised those who love him. (James 1:12-13, TLB)

Have you ever had the bottom drop out of your life? Things had been going along reasonably well. The birds were singing. The sun was shining. Then without warning, the storm clouds began to gather…and it started to rain on your parade. A calamity hit. A tragedy struck, and suddenly you felt lower than you had ever felt before. What was it all about?

Or have you ever had one of those times where you were walking with God, trying to do all the things that should build you up in your Christian faith, when, out of nowhere, you were hit with a heavy-duty, intense temptation? Sometimes it happens at the most unbelievable times…like when you're in prayer or in church. And you ask yourself, *Why is this happening to me? Why me? Why now? Why this?*

What is the purpose of trials and temptations in the life of the Christian? Is there anything we can do to move them along a little more quickly?

Of course, none of us enjoy trials. None of us enjoy being tested and tempted, but there are some valuable lessons that come through these times God allows in our lives.

One of the worst aspects of enduring hardships and difficult seasons in our lives is that inevitable feeling that our lives are spinning out of control. And that tends to add the element of fear to our struggle and frustration. That's why I like this passage in James so much, where the apostle says: "My brethren, count it all joy when you fall into various trials, knowing that the testing of your faith produces patience. But let patience have its perfect work, that you may be perfect and complete, lacking nothing" (James 1:2-4).

We can be patient, and even joyful, knowing that our lives are not out of control…they're in His control. No matter how hot it make get for us, the hand on the thermostat is that of our Lord and Savior, who loves us more than we could begin to understand.

Weekend

Therefore submit to God. Resist the devil and he will flee from you. (James 4:7)

When the Bible tells us to "submit to God," and to "resist the devil" (James 4:7), it doesn't mean we're to go out and attack the devil. The devil will do the attacking. The word "resist" is essentially a defensive word meaning "to withstand an attack."

Nor does the Bible say to "converse with the devil and he will flee from us" or to "consider all of the temptations the devil offers, then resist him, and he will flee from us." Once you start messing with sin and with the devil, it's only a matter of time before you get hooked. It's like the free samples you're offered when you walk though the store or the mall. You're given just enough to whet your appetite, but not enough to satisfy it.

The devil has been at this for a long time. He's no idiot, and when he tries to tempt you away from God's path, he won't present his full agenda. Instead, he will say, "Take just a little nibble. Just have a taste for the fun of it. It won't hurt you. Just this one little time." And you know the rest of that story. This is why the Bible tells us to resist the devil. Keep as much distance from him as possible. Flee from temptation—and don't leave a forwarding address.

So where do we find the resolve and strength to resist? We need to submit to God as we resist the devil. "Submit" is a word used to describe a soldier under the authority of a commander and speaks of a willing, conscious submission to God's authority. It means to completely surrender yourself to the Word and will of God. That is your best defense.

And after you have successfully resisted the evil one, don't relax your guard. It's true that the devil may flee when resisted, but he'll be back! Satan and his demons will simply regroup and attack you from yet another angle. The lesson? For the rest of our lives, we must stay alert and vigilant, fully submitted to the will of God.

Monday

And now I have a word for you who brashly announce, "Today—at the latest, tomorrow—we're off to such and such a city for the year. We're going to start a business and make a lot of money." You don't know the first thing about tomorrow. You're nothing but a wisp of fog, catching a brief bit of sun before disappearing. Instead, make it a habit to say, "If the Master wills it and we're still alive, we'll do this or that."

As it is, you are full of your grandiose selves. All such vaunting self-importance is evil. (James 4:13-16, THE MESSAGE*)*

The Bible doesn't condemn the person who makes plans for the future. Rather, it criticizes the person who makes those plans with no thought whatsoever for the will of God. That is a dangerous thing to do. God will not share His glory with another.

There's nothing wrong with making plans. Paul told the believers in Ephesus that he would return for renewed ministry among them, "God willing" (Acts 18:21). He wrote to the Corinthians that he planned another visit "if the Lord wills" (1 Corinthians 4:19). On other occasions, Paul spoke of his plans to do certain things and how the Lord changed his plans. We have our plans. We have our purposes. We have our agendas. But we also have to leave room for the Lord to redirect us.

Jesus taught us to pray, "Your will be done" (Luke 11:2). Our prayers will be effective and successful when we align our will with the will of God and pray accordingly. Prayer isn't getting our will in heaven; it's getting God's will on earth. It's not moving God our way; it's moving ourselves His way. We need to remember that His will may be different from ours. And we must be willing to accept that.

The God who knows you inside out also knows what lies ahead for you in life. We can always fall back on the simple promise of Jeremiah 29:11 (NIV): "'For I know the plans I have for you,' declares the Lord, 'plans to prosper you and not to harm you, plans to give you hope and a future.'"

God's plans for you are better than any plans you have for yourself. So don't be afraid of God's will, even if it's different from yours.

Tuesday

Dear friends, now we are children of God, and what we will be has not yet been made known. But we know that when he appears, we shall be like him, for we shall see him as he is. Everyone who has this hope in him purifies himself, just as he is pure. (1 John 3:2-3, NIV)

Most Christians would readily agree with the simple truth that Jesus Christ is coming back again. But here's the question: If we believe that, how should it affect the way we live? We should be interested in taking the great truths of the Christian life and applying them to the way that we live. James 5:8 (NLT) tells us, "You, too, must be patient. Take courage, for the coming of the Lord is near."

It's important to remember that God didn't give us the prophecies of Scripture to entertain or tantalize us. Rather, these truths were given to us for a number of reasons. In the first place, understanding that our Lord may come back at any moment ought to motivate us toward personal godliness and bold evangelism. It's a reality that should motivate us to live a holy life, and it should have a purifying effect on us, keeping us on our toes, spiritually.

It's interesting that when God points out what is wrong with a nation spiritually, He doesn't point His finger at the government; *He points His finger at the church.* God says that when a nation is sick, it's because there is a problem with His people. But He also tells us how to fix it: "If My people who are called by My name will humble themselves, and pray and seek My face, and turn from their wicked ways, then I will hear from heaven, and will forgive their sin and heal their land" (2 Chronicles 7:14).

It all comes down to this: How does the knowledge that Jesus Christ will come back soon affect your daily life? Don't worry about the rest of the world. Don't even worry about your Christian friends. How does this truth affect *you*?

Wednesday

Therefore be patient, brethren, until the coming of the Lord. See how the farmer waits for the precious fruit of the earth, waiting patiently for it until it receives the early and latter rain. (James 5:7)

The early rains in Israel would usually come in late October or early November. The farmer anxiously awaited these, because they would soften the hard-baked soil for plowing. The latter rains would come in late April or May. These were essential to the maturing of the crops. If the farmer were to rush out and harvest his crops before their time, he would destroy them. So he had to wait.

As James wrote, patience is also an important factor in awaiting the Lord's return. No crop appears overnight. Like farmers, we need to be patient and recognize that it takes time for growth to happen in our lives. The word "patience," however, doesn't speak of a passive resignation, but of *expectancy*. This isn't a casual, nonchalant approach. Rather, it's an excited expectancy, a readiness.

When you think of this kind of waiting, don't picture someone watching the clock or playing Solitaire. Think of a good *waiter*, who keeps eagerly checking in on you and making sure everything's okay. We are to "wait" on the Lord like *that*.

The psalmist wrote: "I wait for the Lord, my soul waits, and in his word I put my hope. My soul waits for the Lord more than watchmen wait for the morning..." (Psalm 130:5-6, NIV). And how would you wait for the morning, if you were a night watchman out on the city walls? You would strain your eyes looking for the first hint of gray in the east. After a long night's work, you would long for the morning.

Do you see the longing, yearning, and desire in this "waiting"? Some believers don't live this way, choosing instead to sit back and passively bide their time. But the Bible tells us we should be actively preparing as we await the return of Christ: "And do this, knowing the time, that now it is high time to awake out of sleep; for now our salvation is nearer than when we first believed. The night is far spent, the day is at hand" (Romans 13:11-12).

Let's be sure we are living in a holy manner as we patiently—and eagerly—wait for Christ's return.

Thursday

So they sat down with him on the ground seven days and seven nights, and no one spoke a word to him, for they saw that his grief was very great. (Job 2:13)

Job certainly stands out as a shining example of someone who was patient in adversity. He went through incredible difficulties. You probably remember his story: It started out in heaven, with God telling Satan about the faithfulness of the man Job. We can almost imagine God beaming and pulling on His suspenders as He spoke of His servant. But then He allowed hardship to fall on Job.

Hardship? Maybe *catastrophe* would be a better word. If it's true that into every life a little rain must fall, then Job was hit by a tsunami. In one day, he lost his flocks, his servants, all his children, and his health.

Then Job's friends came to visit, and they could hardly recognize their friend, because he was in such sad shape. Wisely, they simply sat with him on the ground; for a long time, no one spoke a word.

One of the best things you can do for people who are hurting is to just be there for them. Sometimes people shy away from someone who has experienced a heartbreak or tragedy, because they think, "I wouldn't know what to say."

Then don't say anything! Just *be there* for awhile. The Bible says we should "weep with those who weep" (Romans 12:15). You don't have to give them a sermon. You don't need to have all the answers. You don't have a degree in counseling or seminary. You just need to be a friend and show up.

I've been a pastor for many years, and I still don't have all the answers—or even most of them! Sometimes the best thing I can do for a person who is hurting, for someone who has lost a loved one, for the one who is facing a horrible sickness, is to be there and pray for him or her. By simply being there, you can be of great comfort to a friend in need.

Whatever other mistakes Job's friends might have made later, for seven days they kept their silence and held the grieving man's hand. That much, at least, was the right thing to do.

Friday

We can be full of joy here and now even in our trials and troubles. Taken in the right spirit these very things will give us patient endurance; this in turn will develop a mature character, and a character of this sort produces a steady hope, a hope that will never disappoint us. Already we have some experience of the love of God flooding through our hearts by the Holy Spirit given to us. (Romans 5:3-5, PHILLIPS)

One of the first things that comes to mind when we go through difficulties is, *What have I done to deserve such a thing?* But it's important for us to know that God has important life lessons He wants to teach us during seasons of difficulty and trials. I definitely want to learn what He is seeking to teach me, so that He doesn't have to repeat the lesson later on!

Remember in school when the teacher would announce, "Class, get out your pens and paper. Today I'm going to give you a pop quiz"? What a sinking feeling that was for those who hadn't studied!

God gives pop quizzes, too, times when He will allow certain tests to enter our lives. We find a good example of this in a little exam Jesus gave His disciples one day. The multitudes came wanting to hear Him, but they were in a remote area and were all hungry. John 6:5-6 tells us, "Then Jesus lifted up His eyes, and seeing a great multitude coming toward Him, He said to Philip, 'Where shall we buy bread, that these may eat?' But this He said to test him, for He Himself knew what He would do."

Jesus wanted to see if His disciples were learning anything. He wanted them to reply, "Lord, You are the Creator of the universe. You have a plan. We trust You."

God will test you because He wants you to grow up. He wants you to mature. He wants you to develop a walk with Him that isn't based on your fluctuating emotions, but rather on your commitment to Him as you learn to walk by faith…and find Him faithful.

When a crisis comes into your life, it's exam time. It will become clear to you just how much faith you really have.

Weekend

My brethren, count it all joy when you fall into various trials, knowing that the testing of your faith produces patience. But let patience have its perfect work, that you may be perfect and complete, lacking nothing. (James 1:2-4)

It would be nice if we could see the trials in our lives as options, as electives. It would be convenient if we could say, "I'm going to skip the trials course."

But the fact is, we don't have that option. Trials will come into the life of every believer. Notice that James says, "Count it all joy *when* you fall into various trials." The phrase, "various trials," could also be translated, "many-colored trials," or "trials of many kinds." In other words, no two trials or experiences are necessarily alike.

You will be tested. The question is, will you pass or fail?

We must remember that God never tests us without a reason. God's ultimate purpose is to conform us to the image of Jesus Christ. God wants to produce a family likeness in us. This means that some difficulties and testings will show us immediate results, while others will produce long term ones.

There are times when I can emerge from a trial, look back, and say, "I learned this when I went through that experience." But there will be other times when I come through a difficulty, and all I will be able to do is shake my head and say, "What was *that* all about?" I may not be able to tell you (at that moment) what I have learned.

But what has happened, maybe unnoticed by me, is that I have become a little bit more like Jesus. He has worked in my life to mold me and shape me into His own image. It may be hard or impossible to point to definitive results in our lives after a time of pressure, setbacks, or testing. Even so, we *can* know that God is in control. And we *can* know that His ultimate purpose is to conform us to the image of His own dear Son.

Monday

Oh come, let us worship and bow down; let us kneel before the Lord our Maker. For He is our God, and we are the people of His pasture, and the sheep of His hand. (Psalm 95:6-7)

Worship can turn the most miserable circumstances into a wonderful time. But our reason for worshiping should not be because we happen to be in a good mood or "just feel like it." Nor should we refrain from worship because we're *not* in a good mood or "don't feel like it."

We should worship because God is worthy. No matter what we are going through, no matter what our circumstances, God merits our worship. And He is pleased when we worship Him with a proper heart.

Let me share a little secret with you: Your problems may not go away because you've invested time in worship before the Lord. At the same time, however, those same problems may not seem as overwhelming to you, because your perspective has changed. You see, before you begin to worship, your problems can seem very big. But as you worship God and think about His glory, His power, His splendor, and His love, you come away with the realization that God is great and mighty, and your problems are actually tiny. You see Him—and your situation—in proper perspective.

The Book of Acts tells the story of Paul and Silas, who were beaten and imprisoned for preaching the gospel. The Bible tells us that at midnight, they worshiped God (see Acts 16:25). As they sang and worshiped, an earthquake came and the whole prison fell apart. It's wonderful when you can be lifted above your circumstances as Paul and Silas were. I'm not talking about mind over matter; I'm talking about faith over circumstances, about honoring the true God who is still on the throne, no matter what you may be facing or enduring.

God may deliver you immediately from your situation, as He did with Paul and Silas. Sometimes God will step in and abruptly change your circumstances. At other times, however, He chooses not to. But whatever our circumstances may be, our God is worthy of our worship.

Tuesday

For no other foundation can anyone lay than that which is laid, which is Jesus Christ. (1 Corinthians 3:11)

Each year, millions of people watch the Academy Awards, tuning in to see what the celebrities are wearing and who will win the Oscars.

Now when it comes to that future day of rewards in heaven called the Judgment Seat of Christ, it's not going to be quite like the Academy Awards. We think the names of certain people will be called out, great men and women of the faith that we have heard of, and that they will get all of the awards. But it depends on what their motives were. It depends on why they did what they did. We don't really know who will receive what.

But I do know this: God will judge us on the quality of what we did rather than on the quantity. He will look at the motive. That is what matters.

Paul said of this judgment, "Now if anyone builds on this foundation with gold, silver, precious stones, wood, hay, straw, each one's work will become clear; for the Day will declare it, because it will be revealed by fire; and the fire will test each one's work, of what sort it is. If anyone's work which he has built on it endures, he will receive a reward" (1 Corinthians 3:12-14).

The wood, hay, or straw that burns quickly doesn't refer to gross sin as much as it speaks to putting more importance on the passing things of this life than on the things of God.

Jesus told a story about a rich man who became consumed with building extra storage for all his many goods. On the night he died, however, God called him a fool, saying, "Who will get what you have prepared for yourself?" Then Jesus added, "This is how it will be with anyone who stores up things for himself but is not rich toward God" (Luke 12:20, 21, NIV).

Are you "rich" toward God? Rich in the most important things?

If you have built your life on the right foundation, if you have done the works of God with the right motive for His glory, then you will receive an eternal reward.

Wednesday

That same day, Sunday, two of Jesus' followers were walking to the village of Emmaus, seven miles out of Jerusalem. As they walked along they were talking of Jesus' death, when suddenly Jesus himself came along and joined them and began walking beside them. But they didn't recognize him, for God kept them from it.

"You seem to be in a deep discussion about something," he said. "What are you so concerned about?" They stopped short, sadness written across their faces…. (Luke 24:13-17, TLB*)*

Sometimes as a Christian I find that I need some timely reminders. In other words, I forget things that I ought to remember…and sometimes remember things I ought to forget.

In Luke 24, we find the story of two men who had forgotten some things they should have remembered. At one time, they had been passionate followers of Christ, but their dreams had been destroyed as they watched their Lord die on a Roman cross. Even as He hung there, they kept hoping for a last-minute miracle. But no miracle came. They felt discouraged and let down. So they decided to leave town.

The fact is, Jesus had clearly told His disciples that He would be crucified, and after three days, would rise again. He spoke of it often. But these two had forgotten that promise. Now, in their crushing disappointment, they just wanted to put as much distance between them and the cross as possible.

That's always a mistake. Any step away from the cross of Jesus Christ is a step in the wrong direction. A time of pain or loss or failure is not the time to run away from the cross. On the contrary, it's a time to run and fall on our knees before the cross as fast as we can.

Maybe something has happened in your life and you feel as though God has let you down. Perhaps as you read these words you're wrestling with a major disappointment or some tragedy in your life. For His part, however, God has neither failed nor forgotten you. In fact, He's waiting for you with open arms. Now is the time to run back to the cross. Now is the time to remember His Word and the promises it holds for you.

Thursday

"Can anyone hide in secret places so that I cannot see him?" declares the Lord. "Do not I fill heaven and earth?" declares the Lord.
(Jeremiah 23:24, NIV)

When my son Christopher was a little boy, he would sometimes try to hide something from me in one of his hands. He would say, "Dad, guess which hand it's in," as he held his small fists out in front of me.

"Buddy," I would say, "you should put your hands *behind* you," because I could easily see his secret sticking out of his hand. He thought he had concealed the prize, but it was really as obvious as could be.

That's how we are with God sometimes: *God, I'll bet You can't find out about this sin. I'll bet You don't know this about me.* But God sees it as clearly as I saw what was going on with my son. He sees right through us. When God looks at us, we are transparent to Him. We have no secrets from God.

John's Gospel tells us, "Now when He was in Jerusalem at the Passover, during the feast, many believed in His name when they saw the signs which He did. But Jesus did not commit Himself to them, because He knew all men, and had no need that anyone should testify of man, for He knew what was in man" (John 2:23-25). He knows what is in you, and He knows what is in me. It's as plain as day to Him.

The book of Proverbs reminds us of a truth we try to put from our minds sometimes: "For a man's ways are in full view of the Lord, and he examines all his paths" (Proverbs 5:21, NIV).

It all comes down to the sincerity of our hearts. God wants you to be honest. He wants you to tell the truth. He knows everything about you—whether you're sincere, playing a religious game, or just fooling around. We might even fool ourselves in some of these matters, but we will never deceive Him.

By the same token, if you hunger for God to reveal Himself to you…if you long for His presence in your life…if you want more than anything else for Him to use you, then He sees that, too. And He will reveal Himself to you in surprising and life-changing ways.

Friday

Notice how God is both kind and severe. He is very hard on those who disobey, but very good to you if you continue to love and trust him.
(Romans 11:22, TLB)

"If God is so good, why does He allow evil?"

This always tops the list of questions about God, along with, "Why does God allow war or tragedy or injustice?" These very questions, however, spring from a flawed premise: that we can determine what is good or not good about God. By asking these questions, we are in effect passing judgment on God. (Which is definitely above our pay grade as fragile, finite human beings.)

Let's just take the basic question that presumes that if God is all-powerful, then He isn't loving. Or, maybe God is loving, but He isn't all-powerful. These assumptions place all responsibility for evil on God.

Yes, certainly God *could* have made a world with no suffering, a world with no pain, a world in which we are all robots. But that's not what He, the Creator, wanted. He wanted us to make the choice ourselves whether to love Him, so He gave us free will.

When we look at many of the problems in our world today, we can place the blame not on God, but on man. God has given us clear standards to follow. He has given us basic moral laws with which to govern a society. But what does humanity do? It says we don't need God. And when we inevitably reap what we sow, we say that God blew it. But we really brought it on ourselves.

In spite of it all, we know that God answers prayer. Sometimes God can use our problems to bring us to Him. God can even use suffering in our lives.

The great hope we have as Christians is that one day, we will be in heaven with Him. So whatever suffering or trials you may be facing right now, know that if you're a Christian, God has something good—something better than you could ever imagine or dream—beyond this life for you.

Weekend

The eyes of the Lord are in every place, keeping watch on the evil and the good. (Proverbs 15:3)

A little boy was always getting into trouble in his Sunday School class. Finally, in exasperation, his teacher said to him, "I want you to know that God is *watching* you all the time. Even when I can't keep my eyes on you, God has His eyes on you. He's watching you. So you'd better straighten up."

The boy was terrified by the thought of God watching him all the time, like some great "eye in the sky." After Sunday School, he told his parents, "The teacher said that God is watching me all the time." They could see that the thought terrified their son rather than bringing comfort to his heart. So his parents put it into proper context for him. They said, "Yes, it's true that God is always watching you. But there's a reason for that. The truth is, He loves you so much that He just can't take His eyes off you."

Many times when we think of God watching us, what comes to mind are the seemingly omnipresent surveillance cameras we have in public places today. I knew someone who worked in a department store, and he showed me how these work. They are hidden in places where we tend to never look, and can pretty much watch everyone. Most people don't even realize that in many public places, cameras are basically tracking them wherever they go.

So when we consider the fact that God is watching us, we might think, *That's terrifying.* But it all depends. If we are rebelling against the Lord, then the thought of His constant surveillance could be more than a little frightening.

But if our hearts are right with Him, then…what an incredible comfort! He never loses track of us, never misplaces our file, never takes His loving attention from us for even one moment. God is watching us, but He loves us so much that He can't take His eyes off us. We may lose sight of God, but He never loses sight of us.

Monday

He who dwells in the secret place of the Most High shall abide under the shadow of the Almighty. I will say of the LORD, "He is my refuge and my fortress; my God, in Him I will trust." (Psalm 91:1-2)

To show us different facets of His nature, God gives us different names for Himself. The words used in Psalm 91:1-2 include *'Elyôwn, Shaddai, Jehovah,* and *'Elōhîm.*

First, we have "the Most High:" *"He who dwells in the shelter of the Most High..."* The Hebrew word used here for Most High, *'Elyôwn,* speaks of possession. It is the idea of owning something. It simply reminds us that God owns and possesses everything, and that includes you and me.

Then there is the word "Almighty:" *"He who dwells in the secret place of the Most High shall abide in the shadow of the Almighty..."* That is the word *Shaddai.* The thought here is of provision. It's wonderful to know that God owns everything. But it is also wonderful to know that He wants to provide for us. Not only is He a living God, but He also is a giving God.

Then we have "the LORD:" *"I will say of the LORD..."* That phrase "the LORD" is *Jehovah,* or *Yahweh,* a unique name God called Himself before His own people, the Jews. It speaks of covenant and His promise to them.

Finally, there is "My God:" *"My God, in whom I trust."* That is the Hebrew word *'Elōhîm,* which tells us there is one God who is triune, or three in one: the Father, Son, and Holy Spirit. It also reminds us of the power of God.

So when we put it all together, we see that the all-knowing, all-powerful God who possesses heaven and earth, who has entered into a special covenant with us, wants to provide for our needs. And this is only scratching the surface of Who He is. We'll have eternity to learn and experience more and more and more about Him, and never, ever "learn it all." For now, however, God has graciously invited us to know Him better and walk with Him on *this* side of heaven. You can begin right now, as you pray to your heavenly Father.

Tuesday

Do you not know that those who run in a race all run, but one receives the prize? Run in such a way that you may obtain it.
(1 Corinthians 9:24)

There are some events in the Olympics that don't interest me at all. When it comes to track and field, however, I really sit up and take notice. I love to watch the runners—whether it's relay races, long distant runs, or the short sprints. (Probably because I ran track in high school.)

During a recent Olympics, I was watching one of the long distance events. One of the runners started off back in the pack. Gradually, he moved up toward the middle. With about four laps to go, he suddenly broke ahead and took the lead. I thought, *Is he going to make it? Could he possibly win?* But it wasn't to be. In those last laps he fell back again. The next thing I knew, he was in second place, third place, fourth place, fifth place. He didn't even win a medal.

I know what it's like to be in the last lap of a race. You're giving it your all, but your legs feel like rubber—as if you have no control over them. They feel like they are burning inside, and it's so difficult to just keep running, let alone reach for a burst of speed.

The apostle Paul often used athletic terms to describe what it is to be a Christian. In today's opening passage, He wrote about running in such a way as to receive the prize. He told the Ephesians that he had finished his race with joy.

Let's not quit running our race. Let's run to win a prize. Let's finish with joy.

In a normal race, we know where the finish line is. We know how many miles or laps we have to run to finish the contest. But when it comes to life, you and I don't really know when we will round that last bend or run that last step. Even though we think we have a long ways to go, we might be right at the tape. What an encouragement to live each day for Jesus as though it were our last.

Run well today. Reach for the prize.

Wednesday

"So don't worry at all about having enough food and clothing. Why be like the heathen? For they take pride in all these things and are deeply concerned about them. But your heavenly Father already knows perfectly well that you need them, and he will give them to you if you give him first place in your life and live as he wants you to."
(Matthew 6:31-33, TLB)

When Jesus told us not to worry about food and clothing, His emphasis was on the word "worry." He didn't say, "Don't think about it." Nor did He imply, "Don't plan ahead for your needs." He said, "Don't worry."

The fact of the matter is that the Bible criticizes the lazy person who lives off the generosity of others and neglects or refuses to work for a living. The New Testament bluntly asserts that if you don't work, you shouldn't eat (2 Thessalonians 3:10). Go get a job. Provide for yourself. The Bible even encourages us to plan for the future and learn from the example of the ant, that tiny creature which is always planning ahead (Proverbs 6:6-8).

But there's an important balance here. The Bible is saying to us, "Yes, do an honest day's work and be financially responsible, but *don't be obsessed with these things.*" Jesus said that's how nonbelievers are.

"Therefore do not worry, saying, 'What shall we eat?' or 'What shall we drink?' or 'What shall we wear?' For after all these things the Gentiles seek. For your heavenly Father knows that you need all these things. But seek first the kingdom of God and His righteousness, and all these things shall be added to you. (Matthew 6:31-33)

Isn't that the emphasis of so many people today—what to eat, what to wear? There are whole cable TV channels devoted to "what to eat" and "what to wear." As a result, the lives of many in our culture tend to revolve around materialistic goals. Jesus, however, insisted that these will never satisfy the deepest needs of your heart.

Don't make food, clothing, shelter, and *things* the primary purpose and focus of your life. Rather, seek God first and foremost in your life, and everything that you need will be provided for you. God will take care of you. He cares about you. And He will supply all of your needs.

Thursday

"Fear not, for I am with you; be not dismayed, for I am your God. I will strengthen you, yes, I will help you, I will uphold you with My righteous right hand." (Isaiah 41:10)

Have you ever had someone forget an occasion that was important to you? Maybe your spouse forgot your anniversary or your birthday. Or maybe your children forgot you at Christmas. Even when people forget you, you need to know that God never forgets you. He marks every birthday. He remembers every prayer. He knows your calendar—and all of those things that aren't on your calendar—backwards and forwards. You are always on His mind. Romans 8:31 says, "What then shall we say to these things? If God is for us, who can be against us?"

God is thinking about you right now. He isn't thinking about you merely as a member of the human race or as a part of your church. You're not just one little dot among billions of dots on His radar. He is thinking about you as an individual—your struggles, your needs, your desires and longings. The psalmist wrote, "Your thoughts toward us cannot be recounted to You in order; if I would declare and speak of them, they are more than can be numbered" (Psalm 40:5).

God's thoughts toward you are continual and uncountable. God Almighty, the one who holds the heavens in the span of His hand, the One who spoke creation into being, is thinking about you this very instant.

Not only is God the Father thinking about you, but God the Son is interceding for you. Hebrews 7:25 says, "Therefore He is also able to save to the uttermost those who come to God through Him, since He always lives to make intercession for them."

God the Father is thinking about you, God the Son is interceding for you, and God the Holy Spirit is helping you as well: "Now He who searches the hearts knows what the mind of the Spirit is, because He makes intercession for the saints according to the will of God" (Romans 8:27).

God is for you. God is thinking about you. God is on your side!

Friday

As parents feel for their children, God feels for those who fear him. He knows us inside and out, keeps in mind that we're made of mud.
(Psalm 103:13-14, THE MESSAGE)

When we look back on the first-century believers and the apostles in particular, we tend to see them on pedestals. It's as though they walked around carrying pedestals under their arms, and when they were preparing to say something, they would climb up on them, and speak in beautiful King James English. We see them as perfect people in stained glass, with radiant light shining through them.

But in the final analysis, they were just people, and put their sandals on one foot at a time. The biblical accounts of their lives makes no effort to glamorize (or canonize) these men and women. If we had had the opportunity to check these people out back then, the last thing we would have thought was, *I think these men and women will change their world.* These were common, salt-of-the-earth-types. They had calloused hands and few social graces. They were largely uneducated, with a limited knowledge of the world. They had undefined leadership and no money. Frankly, I don't think we would have bet too much on their future.

But something happens to a person when he or she witnesses someone rising from the dead. That has a way of changing your perspective. It dramatically impacted these followers of Jesus.

One of the things I love about the Bible is that it's a thoroughly honest book, presenting us with those whom God used, warts and all, shortcomings and all. We read of Abraham and his struggles with cowardice, Moses with his violent temper, David with his lust issues, Noah with his prejudices, Peter with his impetuous tongue, and Thomas with his skepticism.

That's one of the reasons I'm so appreciative of the Bible. It gives hope to people like me…people who fail…people who fall short. We think, *If God can use someone like that, maybe there's hope for me.* That's precisely the point. God recorded all this for us so we can see that He can work in us and through us in spite of our weakness.

Weekend

Then Jesus went about all the cities and villages, teaching in their synagogues, preaching the gospel of the kingdom, and healing every sickness and every disease among the people. But when He saw the multitudes, He was moved with compassion for them, because they were weary and scattered, like sheep having no shepherd. (Matthew 9:35-36)

Everywhere Jesus went, He was very much in demand. There was always a crowd around Him, and understandably so. Here was the long-awaited Messiah, the God of Israel in human flesh, walking through their streets, and everyone wanted something from Him. There would be those who always wanted a touch, like the woman who had spent all of her money on doctors, trying to be cured, but to no avail. When she touched the hem of His garment, she was immediately restored and healed. There is the story of the Syro-Phoenician woman who brought her demon-possessed child to Jesus, and the account of Jairus, the synagogue leader, who came and asked Jesus to touch his desperately sick daughter.

Everyone needed something, but Jesus knew they needed more than just a healing, more than a touch, and more than a word. He knew the deepest need was in their soul. We see this demonstrated time and again. In John 4 we read how He went out of His way to meet someone in a little town where Jacob's well was located, even though this particular woman had no idea she had an appointment with God. She went to that well at that time of day because she was a social outcast.

Sometimes when people do things that are wrong, our first response is to get angry with them. Not only do we hate the sin, but we end up hating the sinner, too. Yet God wants us to see that while we can hate the sin, there is still a sinner who is loved by God. Maybe no one has ever told him or her that there's another way to live. May God give us eyes to see this world as He sees it.

Monday

Therefore by Him let us continually offer the sacrifice of praise to God, that is, the fruit of our lips, giving thanks to His name. (Hebrews 13:15)

A popular contemporary worship song speaks of blessing the Lord "on the road marked with suffering."

That's certainly the right thing to do. But no one said it would be easy! It's easier to give thanks at the healthy birth of a baby than it is at the death of a loved one. It's easier to offer up praise to God at a wedding than in a hospital ER. It's one thing to give thanks when the bills are paid and your health is good and the future is bright. But then when there is a sudden or even tragic turn in our lives, and we find ourselves overwhelmed…the thanks and praise don't come quite as readily, do they?

Psalm 106:1 tells us: "Praise the Lord! Oh, give thanks to the Lord, for He is good! For His mercy endures forever." The psalmist *doesn't* say, "Give thanks unto the Lord when you feel good. Give thanks unto the Lord when you wake up in the morning with a happy heart."

Sometimes I feel good, and frankly, there are other days when I don't feel very good at all. But regardless of my circumstances or emotions, I am to give thanks to the Lord for His goodness and His mercy that endure forever. As Paul said, I am to "Rejoice in the Lord always. I will say it again: Rejoice!" (Philippians 4:4, NIV).

The patriarch Job basically lost everything he had—including his family, health, and possessions—in one day. Anything that could have gone wrong went wrong. Even so, in Job 1:21, he said, "Naked I came from my mother's womb, and naked shall I return there. The LORD gave, and the LORD has taken away; blessed be the name of the LORD."

What we need to understand is that thanks should be offered to God no matter what our situation. I think Job's words of thanks on that day, through his tears, represented "a sacrifice of praise." He didn't feel like praising God, but he did…because it was right. And notice that the Hebrews passage speaks of the "fruit of our lips." That means verbalize your praise.

You don't have to make a show of it, but if you offer thanks to the Lord in the dark times, others will notice…including people, angels, demons, and God Himself.

Tuesday

My lips will shout for joy when I sing praise to you—I, whom you have redeemed. My tongue will tell of your righteous acts all day long. (Psalm 71:23-24, NIV)

You were created to give glory to God. That is the highest use of your vocal chords, lips, mouth, and the formation of your words. God wants to hear us give Him praise.

Let's say you're a husband who loves his wife. Does she know that you do?

"Well…yes."

Do you tell her that?

"Well, no. But she knows."

Does she? How does she know?

"Because I *think* it often."

You might consider verbalizing it—opening your mouth and actually saying, "Honey, I want you to know that I love you." It would mean a lot to her.

Now God, in contrast to your wife, is a mind reader. He knows what you're thinking. But as we have seen, He actually wants you to give a sacrifice of praise by the fruit of your lips. We need to give God what He deserves, and that is glory. Psalm 29:2 says, "Give unto the LORD the glory due His name; worship the LORD in the beauty of holiness."

But far too often we're like those ten lepers in the gospel of Luke who had called out loudly to Jesus for intervention and healing. He graciously heard their prayer and healed all of them of the dreaded disease of leprosy. But as you know, only one out of ten returned to give thanks, and "with a loud voice glorified God" (Luke 17:15). Jesus said in response, "Didn't I heal ten of you? Where are the other nine?"

We're often quick to cry out for help during times of crisis, but we can also be very slow to offer God thanks after He intervenes in our troubles. Essentially we say, "Thanks God. See You next crisis." By the way, that phrase "loud voice"—referring to the thankful man who had been healed—is formed from two Greek words from which we get our English word *megaphone*. He was loud with His praise to God. Why? Because he knew that this One called Jesus had instantly cleansed him and given him a brand new life.

It sounds like our story, too, doesn't it? Let's give Him our whole-hearted praise.

Wednesday

A man's steps are directed by the LORD. How then can anyone understand his own way? ...In his heart a man plans his course, but the LORD determines his steps. (Proverbs 20:24; 16:9, NIV)

God is in control of all circumstances that surround my life. Sometimes we may feel we understand these circumstances, but at other times we don't have a clue why certain things happen as they do, and we are mystified. We make our plans. But God will always have His way.

There's nothing wrong with making a plan for tomorrow or for next month or next year. But we must always plan with this proviso: the Lord may change our plans, and take us in a completely different direction. It is His prerogative to do so; He, not you, is in control of your life.

Jeremiah 10:23 says: "O LORD, I know the way of man is not in himself; it is not in man who walks to direct his own steps." And in the book of Proverbs, the writer asks the question: The Lord directs our steps, so why try to understand everything along the way? (Proverbs 20:24, NLT)

We sometimes call this guiding of our steps "divine providence."

Does that mean, then, that bad things will never happen to good or even godly people? No...but it does mean that even when bad things happen, God can bring good out of bad, as Romans 8:28 assures us.

All of God's good promises, however, won't be fully realized until we get to heaven. There are some things we can look at in life and say, "That was a really terrible experience, but now as I look back in retrospect, I can see the good that has come from it." But then there are other things we will experience in life that we will never see good come out of—or at least, "good" as we understand it. It won't be until we get to the other side and see the Lord face to face that we will understand these things.

Even so, we entrust our lives to His good hands and His great wisdom, and praise Him for directing us step by step.

Thursday

For our present troubles are small and won't last very long. Yet they produce for us a glory that vastly outweighs them and will last forever! So we don't look at the troubles we can see now; rather, we fix our gaze on things that cannot be seen. For the things we see now will soon be gone, but the things we cannot see will last forever.
(2 Corinthians 4:17-18, NLT)

God loves me and is always looking out for my eternal benefit. This is true, even when my present circumstances are very difficult, or even tragic. I would suggest to you that what we sometimes perceive as "good" could potentially be "bad," and what we sometimes perceive as "bad" could potentially be "good."

Let me illustrate. We think that having perfect health and plenty of money and influence is good—and it can be! I'm not suggesting otherwise. But I am suggesting that what's good for one person may not always be good for another. Just look at some of the people who have won millions in the lottery, and what happens to their lives. Winning may have been something they have longed for and dreamed of, but then when it really happened, they found themselves in a nightmare. Lives and families have literally been torn apart through the immediate accumulation of vast amounts of wealth. Rather than bringing happiness, it can slam the door on happiness for years, or even a lifetime. So what some people would imagine as "the greatest thing that could happen to me" could in reality be a terrible curse.

On the other hand, others might be blessed with affluence, influence, and material possessions, and seem to handle it all in a wise and balanced way. God is the one who determines these things. By the same token, sometimes what I think of today as "bad" might ultimately produce a great good in my life. Why? Because it changes me to be more like Jesus. Anything that refines the image of Jesus in me is a good that lasts forever. Anything, however, that causes me to forget God and trust more in myself is a *disaster*—no matter how desirable it may seem at first glance.

Friday

Next Paul and Silas traveled through the area of Phrygia and Galatia, because the Holy Spirit had told them not to go into the province of Asia at that time. Then coming to the borders of Mysia, they headed for the province of Bithynia, but again the Spirit of Jesus did not let them go there. So instead, they went on through Mysia to the seaport of Troas.
(Acts 16:6-8, NLT)

Sometimes the Lord will step in and say "no" to even the most loving and carefully considered of our plans. There are many ways, of course, that God can stop or redirect us. Sometimes it's through the warning of a respected friend. Sometimes it might be through a lack of peace in our lives; all of the circumstances might look just fine, but something inside us doesn't feel quite right. We have a lack of peace about it.

We're told in the book of Colossians that we should let the peace of God settle with finality all matters that arise in our mind (see Colossians 3:15). If we're starting to do something or go somewhere and sense a lack of God's blessing on that plan, we need to learn to stop, and seek His peace and His desire for our lives.

God can also redirect us through simple circumstances. The car won't start. A particular door won't open. A check won't clear. A flight is delayed. An illness comes. Has it happened to you? You had plans in a certain direction, and God stepped in and said, "No. That's not what I had in mind for you at this time. I have another plan." You may have wanted to go into the ministry, and instead God called you into business. Or perhaps you had prepared yourself for a career in business, and God called you into ministry! You have wanted to be married, but God called you to be single. Or perhaps you were sure you'd be single, but then He dropped someone into your life "out of the blue." You may have wanted a large family, but you had a small family—or no children at all.

Sometimes things turn out differently from what we had imagined or planned. Ultimately, however, our lives belong to Him, not to ourselves. And His plans, even when they seem difficult, are the very best plans for this life and the next.

Weekend

Let all bitterness, wrath, anger, clamor, and evil speaking be put away from you, with all malice. And be kind to one another, tenderhearted, forgiving one another, even as God in Christ forgave you.
(Ephesians 4:31–32)

Have you ever been angry with someone—and held onto that anger for a long time?

Many people, in the depths of their heart, have anger and hatred to such a degree that their true desire would be for the one they hate to be dead. But that is clearly forbidden in Scripture. We read in 1 John 3:15, "Whoever hates his brother is a murderer, and you know that no murderer has eternal life abiding in him." The word used here for "hates" means "to habitually despise." It implies not just a transient emotion of the affections, but a deep-rooted loathing. The Bible isn't saying here that it's a sin to be angry sometimes. But the idea in 1 John 3:15 is that of a long-term, seething anger, driven by continuing resentment.

Some people hold grudges. They operate by the phrase, "I don't get mad, I get even." Maybe someone has wronged you. Maybe they have taken advantage of you or slandered you, and you've thought, "I hate them. I wish they would just drop dead." But there is no place for thinking like this on the part of the believer.

In Romans 12 we read: "Do not repay anyone evil for evil. Be careful to do what is right in the eyes of everybody. If it is possible, as far as it depends on you, live at peace with everyone. Do not take revenge, my friends, but leave room for God's wrath, for it is written: 'It is mine to avenge; I will repay,' says the Lord" (vv. 17-19, NIV).

The Bible instructs us to let our hatred and resentments go, forgiving the one who has offended us, whether or she deserves it or not.

As children of God, we have been forgiven a debt so wide, so high, so deep, that we can't begin to conceive of it. If we would stop to consider all that God has done for us, we might find ourselves more willing to extend forgiveness to others.

Monday

Now no chastening seems to be joyful for the present, but painful; nevertheless, afterward it yields the peaceable fruit of righteousness to those who have been trained by it. (Hebrews 12:11)

Have you ever had the bottom drop out of life? Suddenly and without warning, one problem after another comes tumbling into your life. And then, when it seems completely hopeless, like there's no way out, everything improves.

Why does God allow calamities into our lives as Christians? Why does God permit tragedies and heartbreaks in the life of the believer? Why do we experience trials? James addresses these questions in the first chapter of his letter. But the first thing he tells us is, "My brethren, count it all joy when you fall into various trials" (v. 2). What kind of counsel is that for someone who is suffering? And what does it mean? Is it like saying to someone who is going through really hard times, "Don't worry. Be happy!"? Is that what James is saying? Yes and no. He encourages us to rejoice. But there is a reason for what he is saying.

James isn't suggesting that we should be experiencing some all-encompassing emotion of joy or happiness in our times of hardship. Nor is he demanding that we must necessarily "enjoy" our trials in life. James isn't saying that trials themselves are a joy, because usually they aren't. And yet James says, "Count it all joy." In other words, the apostle is saying, "Make a deliberate and careful decision to experience joy in your troubles and trials." It is not easy, but it is possible.

You see, there are lessons to be learned during times of trial. And there are lessons that can only be learned through times of trials. Just remember, they won't last forever. As Peter told a group of suffering believers, they had reason to greatly rejoice in their faith, "Even though now for a little while, if necessary, you have been distressed by various trials" (1 Peter 1:6, NASB).

In the big picture of things, our suffering, heavy as it may be, is only for "a little while," or "a season." The old commentator Matthew Henry reminds us that "Life itself is but for a little while, and the sorrows of it cannot survive it."[20]

Tuesday

Isaac pleaded with Jehovah to give Rebekah a child, for even after many years of marriage she had no children. Then at last she became pregnant. And it seemed as though children were fighting each other inside her! "I can't endure this," she exclaimed. So she asked the Lord about it.

And he told her…. (Genesis 25:21-22, 23, TLB)

In the book of Genesis, Isaac's pregnant wife Rebekah found herself experiencing more than the average of baby movement within her womb. Something didn't seem right, and it troubled her so much she almost felt at the end of her rope. That's when Rebekah did a very wise thing; she went to the Lord in prayer, and asked Him what was going on. And He told her!

One of the first things that we ask when the bottom drops out and trials overwhelm us is "Why Lord? Why are You allowing this to happen? What have I done to deserve this?"

Maybe you've lost your job, become ill, or lost a loved one, and you're in anguish over what has happened. The heartache just seems to go on and on, and you wonder why. James 1:5 says, "If any of you lacks wisdom, let him ask of God, who gives to all liberally and without reproach, and it will be given to him." Or, as another translation puts it, "If you need wisdom ask our generous God, and he will give it to you. He will not rebuke you for asking" (NLT).

When find yourself enduring these times of protracted pain, there is nothing wrong with saying, "Lord, what are You trying to teach me? Lord, is there a lesson to be learned here? Because if there is, then I want to learn it. I want to get through this as quickly as possible. If this is going to go on for awhile and there's nothing I can do to change that, fine. But if there is something I need to learn that will cause this to come to an end, then tell me now, Lord."

It's important for us to know that God does have lessons He wants us to learn in times of trial. And many times, God allows our tests to see how well we've learned the material.

Wednesday

I walked by the field of a lazy person, the vineyard of one with no common sense. I saw that it was overgrown with nettles. It was covered with weeds, and its walls were broken down. Then, as I looked and thought about it, I learned this lesson: A little extra sleep, a little more slumber, a little folding of the hands to rest—then poverty will pounce on you like a bandit; scarcity will attack you like an armed robber.
(Proverbs 24:30-34, NLT)

History tells us that during World War II, Hitler had an interesting strategy for attacking the various European nations: he always did it on a weekend. Hitler knew the various parliaments would not be in session, making it more difficult to react swiftly to an invasion.

In the same way, the devil will wait for an opportune moment, that decisive time to attack. It may be when our guard is down, when we're not expecting it. It may even come when we think we are the strongest, when we tell ourselves, "I'm doing pretty well spiritually. I think I'm really growing. Everything is going great."

Here's an irony for you: Often weaker believers are less vulnerable than stronger ones, because weaker believers recognize their frailty and vulnerability. The Bible says, "Let him who thinks he stands take heed lest he fall" (I Corinthians 10:12).

Perhaps recently you have experienced a great blessing in your life. That blessing may involve your family, your career, your ministry, or your personal walk with God. But the enemy wants to rob you of it. Remember, when Jesus was baptized in the Jordan River, the Holy Spirit came upon Him in the form of a dove, and a voice was heard from heaven from the Father saying, "You are My beloved Son; in You I am well pleased" (Luke 3:22). The Bible says that after this, Jesus was tempted by the devil in the wilderness (see Luke 4:1-14).

It's not a sin to be tempted. Even Jesus was tempted. The sin takes place only when we give in to that temptation, when we open the door to it, indulge it and entertain it. That is why we should be alert to temptation and the subtle attacks of our enemy. We must flee temptation…and never leave a forwarding address.

Thursday

But Jesus told him, "Anyone who puts a hand to the plow and then looks back is not fit for the Kingdom of God." (Luke 9:62, NLT)

I find it interesting how we can look at the past through rose-colored glasses. Remember the children of Israel? They had been delivered from the tyranny and bondage of Egypt, where they had been slaves for years. They cried out to God for deliverance, and the Lord answered their prayers through a man named Moses.

As they were making their way through the wilderness, God supernaturally fed them with an incredible substance called manna. It was like bread from heaven. The Israelites had it daily for breakfast, lunch, and dinner. Both sweet and highly nutritious, the Bible called it "the bread of angels" (Psalm 78:25, NIV). But after awhile, they got a little tired of it. They said, "We're sick of manna. We remember the good old days back in Egypt, where we used to eat garlic, leeks, and onions. [Their breath must have really been gross, by the way.] Those were the good old days. … If we could only go back."

They spoke of the good old days, but they basically ate table scraps in Egypt, because they were slaves. Their lives were miserable—almost unbearable. Yet in their imaginations, they had magnified those scraps of food to some sumptuous feast they had each and every day. They weren't looking at the past accurately. In the same way, the devil may remind you of the old days: "Remember the good old days? Remember the fun you used to have? Remember that old flame? If only you could reignite that." And suddenly you begin to think about it.

Don't build up the past in your mind. Remember it for what it was. Don't allow the enemy to pull you down by fantasizing about it. Protect your mind, and don't look back.

Yes, the Lord wants us to always remember His mighty works of the past and all He has done for us. There are certain things we should never forget. At the same time, however, the emphasis on the Christian life is always forward—pressing toward the mark, reaching for the prize, and setting our eyes on the heaven that awaits us, just over the horizon.

Friday

Now that we know what we have—Jesus, this great High Priest with ready access to God—let's not let it slip through our fingers. We don't have a priest who is out of touch with our reality. He's been through weakness and testing, experienced it all—all but the sin. So let's walk right up to him and get what he is so ready to give. Take the mercy, accept the help. (Hebrews 4:14-16, THE MESSAGE)

When Jesus was tempted in the wilderness, He responded to every enticement of the enemy by beginning with the words, *"It is written..."* When the devil suggested that Jesus turn a stone into bread to satisfy His raging hunger, He replied, "It is written, 'Man shall not live by bread alone, but by every word of God'" (Luke 4:4).

When the devil promised to give Him all the world's kingdoms if Jesus worshipped him (and notice that the Lord never refuted the devil's authority to do this), Jesus responded, "Get behind Me, Satan! For it is written, 'You shall worship the Lord your God, and Him only you shall serve'" (Luke 4:8).

Then the devil pulled a fast one. He quoted Scripture, too. The devil knows Scripture and knows it pretty well. Of course, he pulls it out of context and twists it, but he can quote it. So he said, "If You are the Son of God, throw Yourself down from here. For it is written: 'He shall give His angels charge over you, to keep you,' and, 'In their hands they shall bear you up, lest you dash your foot against a stone'" (Luke 4:10–11).

Jesus brought that passage back into context and responded, "It has been said, 'You shall not tempt the Lord your God'" (Luke 4:12). Christ faced temptation as a human being. He didn't use His executive privilege as God to get out of the situation. When the devil attacked, He quoted Scripture. And He occupied ground that we, too, can occupy.

So when temptation comes our way, it's important that we know the Word of God. God has given us the weapons for winning the spiritual battle.

Weekend

"Therefore you shall lay up these words of mine in your heart and in your soul, and bind them as a sign on your hand, and they shall be as frontlets between your eyes. You shall teach them to your children, speaking of them when you sit in your house, when you walk by the way, when you lie down, and when you rise up." (Deuteronomy 11:18-19)

I have often quoted that old saying about the Bible: "Sin will keep you from this book, and this book will keep you from sin." If you obey God's Word, it will keep you from sin. But sin will also keep you from God's Word.

It's worth bearing in mind that the adversary will do everything in his power to keep you from reading and memorizing Scripture. Back in the Garden of Eden with Eve, our first mother, Satan first questioned the Word of God, then distorted it, and finally added to it. And he has been attacking Scripture ever since.

In Ephesians 6, we're told as believers to take up the whole armor of God. But have you ever noticed in that passage that there's only one weapon listed that is both defensive *and* offensive? God has given us the Sword of the Spirit, which is the Word of God. That's what Jesus used in the wilderness against Satan, and that's what we need to use, too.

The psalmist had this to day about the strengthening power of God's Word: "How can a young man keep his way pure? By living according to your word. I seek you with all my heart; do not let me stray from your commands. I have hidden your word in my heart that I might not sin against you" (Psalm 119:9-11, NIV).

What shape is your sword in today? Is it polished from daily use and sharpened on the anvil of experience? Or is it rusty from lack of preparation or dulled by disobedience?

Take time for the Word of God. Make it a top priority to not only read the Bible, but to memorize it. It will prepare your heart for what you will face throughout the day.

Monday

He canceled the record of the charges against us and took it away by nailing it to the cross. In this way, he disarmed the spiritual rulers and authorities. He shamed them publicly by his victory over them on the cross. (Colossians 2:14–15 nlt)

When I was little, I remember walking down the street in my neighborhood with some little cap guns that looked like six shooters, complete with holsters. I was feeling pretty good as I made my way down the street, firing those things off. But then I encountered some kids on the corner who grabbed my guns, pushed me, and told me to go away. I went home crying. Then I found my brother, who was five years older than me, and said, "Let's go back there. I want to get those guns."

We went back to the same street, where I found the kids with my cap guns. Suddenly I had courage like never before. With my brother behind me, I successfully retrieved my cap guns. By myself, I wasn't very intimidating. But with my big brother standing behind me, arms folded and a fierce glare on his face, I was suddenly a force to be reckoned with.

It reminds me of our encounters with Satan and his demons. Instead of facing the enemy in our own strength, instead of going out and trying to do this or that for God, we need to stay as close to Christ as possible. In Scripture, He is known as both our Brother and our Friend. We can stand in Christ, and in His protection, because He dealt a decisive blow against Satan and his minions at the cross of Calvary.

So in spiritual battles, when temptation comes, we as Christians are not fighting *for* victory. We are fighting *from* it. As Ephesians 6:10 urges, "Finally, my brethren, be strong in the Lord and in the power of His might."

In other words, we are resting in the work that Christ has done for us. Therefore, we should never want to stray from Him, because if we are caught alone, we will be weak and vulnerable. But thankfully, He is with us. The question is, are we with Him?

Tuesday

Can the dead live again? If so, this would give me hope through all my years of struggle, and I would eagerly await the release of death. (Job 14:14, NLT)

In one of the oldest books of the Bible, the Book of Job, the question is asked, "If mortals die, can they live again?" That is something everyone should ask in life: "What's going to happen to me when I die? What is there beyond this place called Earth?"

In the Old Testament—in contrast to the New Testament—there isn't a lot of clear teaching about what happens after an individual dies. But every now and then, like a piercing beam of sunlight through a sudden parting of the clouds, we're given a glimpse of what comes next. We see it, for instance, in David's words after his infant son died: "I will go to him, but he will not return to me" (2 Samuel 12:23, NIV).

Before I became a Christian, I thought about death and a possible afterlife quite often. Admittedly, it was sort of a heavy subject for a teenager to be contemplating, but I did find myself thinking about death on a semi-regular basis. It isn't that I was obsessed with death or that I wanted to die. My belief at the time was that once people stopped living, they simply ceased to exist. I wasn't sure at all that there was a place called heaven. I was definitely hoping there wasn't a place called hell. My conclusion was that when you're gone, you're gone. It's all over with.

We all know that death is coming, but what happens beyond the grave? According to the Bible, there is life beyond the grave. And because of what Jesus Christ did on the cross, and because He rose from the dead three days later, we as Christians have the hope that when we die, we will immediately go into the presence of God into a wonderful place called heaven.

That is why the resurrection of Jesus from the dead is one of the most important biblical truths there is. The resurrection of Christ from the dead, next to the crucifixion itself, is the most significant event in church history. It's not a peripheral issue. It is foundational. It is bedrock. It is the very bottom line of life itself.

Wednesday

But if it is preached that Christ has been raised from the dead, how can some of you say that there is no resurrection of the dead? If there is no resurrection of the dead, then not even Christ has been raised. And if Christ has not been raised, our preaching is useless and so is your faith.
(1 Corinthians 15:12-14, NIV)

Not only does the Bible tell us we will live beyond the grave, but it also tells us there is hope beyond this life. The resurrection of Jesus from the dead proves there is life beyond the grave for the believer. The Bible says, "He has set a day when the entire human race will be judged and everything set right. And he has already appointed the judge, confirming him before everyone by raising him from the dead" (Acts 17:31, THE MESSAGE).

No doubt this is why the devil has tried to discredit the Resurrection over the centuries. This is why, ever since the first century, the evil one has been spreading his rumors about what happened to the body of Christ. And one of the oldest rumors of all—dating back to hours after the resurrection—was that His body was stolen by the disciples.

But claiming that the body of Jesus was stolen actually proves the resurrection of the Lord. His friends couldn't have taken it, because they had already left the scene, convinced He was dead. The apostles had no reason to counterfeit a Resurrection they didn't even believe in themselves.

As we look at church history, we know that with the exception of John (who survived an execution attempt and was banished to the island of Patmos), all the apostles were martyred for what they believed. Don't you think at least one of them—under torture and the threat of death—would have suddenly exposed such a lie, if it were a lie? But they didn't, because none of them could deny what they knew very well was true: Christ *was* risen, Christ *is* risen, and He is alive.

That fact—the point on which all of life turns—is true today. And always will be. He is "alive forevermore."

Thursday

It was early on Sunday morning when Jesus came back to life, and the first person who saw him was Mary Magdalene—the woman from whom he had cast out seven demons. She found the disciples wet-eyed with grief and exclaimed that she had seen Jesus, and he was alive! But they didn't believe her! (Mark 16:9-10, TLB)

Of all the people Jesus could have first appeared to after His resurrection, He appeared to Mary Magdalene. It's interesting to think about, because among the Jews of that day, the testimony of a woman was not held in high regard. In fact, some of the rabbis falsely taught that it was better for the words of the Law to be burned than to be delivered by a woman. Yet Jesus chose a woman to be the first herald of His resurrection.

It's also worth noting that women were the last at the cross and the first at the tomb. Mary had courage that many of the men did not have when Jesus was crucified. She stood by Him through it all. In fact, the Bible tells us that after He was crucified, Mary "observed where He was laid" (Mark 15:47). She watched as they took His crucified body from the cross and wrapped it and placed it in a tomb that belonged to Joseph of Arimathea. And while the guards were deciding to post a soldier by that tomb, she spent an entire night there all alone, before the guards were there…before the disciples were there.

And her love was rewarded. God said, "And you will seek Me and find Me, when you search for Me with all your heart" (Jeremiah 29:13). In the Psalms, it says, "The secret of the Lord is with those who fear Him, and He will show them His covenant" (Psalm 25:14).

God rewards the person who is diligent. And for those who will take time in their day to seek the Lord, for those who will take time to read His Word, for those who will take time to wait upon Him, He will reveal His truths to them.

Friday

Jesus said to her, "Do not cling to Me, for I have not yet ascended to My Father; but go to My brethren and say to them, 'I am ascending to My Father and your Father, and to My God and your God.'" (John 20:17)

On the morning of the Resurrection, Jesus didn't allow Mary to touch Him. He was essentially saying, "It's not going to be the way it used to be. You can't hold on to Me in the old way. It's a new covenant."

Then He made a radical statement: "Go to My brethren and say to them, 'I am ascending to My Father and your Father, and to My God and your God'" (John 20:17). In other words, "He's *your* Father now, too."

If you came from a fatherless home, God can be the Father you never had. Jesus opened up a new relationship for us through His death on the cross and His resurrection from the dead. We don't have to go through a high priest and animal sacrifices to seek atonement for sin, as God's people did in days gone by. Why? Because Jesus became the final sacrifice for our sins. And He has given us free access to God the Father, whom we can approach with confidence and joy—in times of need, or any time at all.

Listen to the way the writer to the Hebrews described this great wonder:

> "But Jesus the Son of God is our great High Priest who has gone to heaven itself to help us; therefore let us never stop trusting him. This High Priest of ours understands our weaknesses, since he had the same temptations we do, though he never once gave way to them and sinned. So let us come boldly to the very throne of God and stay there to receive his mercy and to find grace to help us in our times of need" (Hebrews 4:14-16, TLB).

Do you know God as your Father? Or does He seem like some distant force? If that is the case, I have good news for you: God is not some mere force or distant power somewhere in the universe. He is personal, He is caring, and He loves you. And that is why He sent His Son to die on the cross in our place.

Weekend

Then Jesus told them, "A prophet is honored everywhere except in his own hometown and among his relatives and his own family." And because of their unbelief, he couldn't do any miracles among them except to place his hands on a few sick people and heal them. And he was amazed at their unbelief. (Mark 6:4-6, NLT)

There is no question that faith is a key element in effective prayer. On one occasion, Jesus could not do many miracles in a certain place because of the unbelief of the people there. That place was Nazareth, which happened to be His hometown. He had done miracles in other places, but not in Nazareth. The great works of God that might have taken place among them never happened, and it was because of their unbelief.

Our faith does play a part in the work of God. Sadly, there has been a distortion of this truth by false teachers who say that we "make things happen," and that faith is a type of force we need to use to achieve our desires or purposes. In an effort to counter this extreme teaching, however, we may swing too far the other way and end up with no faith (and no miracles) at all.

There is a place for having faith and believing the promises in God's Word. When people ask me to pray for them to be healed, I do. But I always add words like these: "Lord, if You have another purpose that we don't know about, then not our will, but Yours, be done." I think we need as much faith as we can muster when we come before God with our requests. But I appreciate the honesty of the man who said, "Lord, I believe; help my unbelief!" (Mark 9:24). I believe God will honor that.

I believe there is great wisdom in praying like this: "Lord, this seems to be Your will from my understanding of Scripture. …I believe, Lord, but help my unbelief. And if You have another plan, then just overrule it." That is a proper way to bring something before the throne of God.

Monday

Why, you do not even know what will happen tomorrow. What is your life? You are a mist that appears for a little while and then vanishes.
(James 4:14, NIV)

There was a time in my life when I could remember every week and month and year. Now I remember decades more easily than I remember individual years. Time seems to go by so quickly.

When Billy Graham was asked what had been his greatest surprise in life, he answered, "The brevity of it." That's so true. Time marches on—and it also seems to *pick up speed* as you grow older.

Scripture certainly echoes this idea of the shortness of human life. Job said, "Now my days are swifter than a runner; they flee away, they see no good" (Job 9:25). And David expressed his heart like this: "Lord, help me to realize how brief my time on earth will be. Help me to know that I am here for but a moment more. My life is no longer than my hand! My whole lifetime is but a moment to you. Proud man! Frail as breath! A shadow! And all his busy rushing ends in nothing. He heaps up riches for someone else to spend. And so, Lord, my only hope is in you" (Psalm 39:4-7, TLB).

When James wrote, "What is your life?," he wasn't posing a philosophical question as much as describing a reality we all need to face. A better way to translate the phrase might be, "What sort of life do you have?"

It's also important to note that he was speaking to Christians who were involved in the world of commerce, those who seemed to be taking credit where credit was not due. They were boasting of their ability to make money and be successful, and in the process, they were forgetting all about God. It's always dangerous for us to take credit for what God has given us the ability to do. God warns that He will not share His glory with another. So let's be careful to not forget God in our lives.

Tuesday

Just a moment, now, you who say, "We are going to such-and-such a city today or tomorrow. We shall stay there a year doing business and make a profit"! ... Your remarks should be prefaced with, "If it is the Lord's will, we shall be alive and will do so-and-so." As it is, you get a certain pride in yourself in planning your future with such confidence. That sort of pride is all wrong. (James 4:13, 15-16, PHILLIPS)

The Book of Acts tells the story of Philip and how the Lord was blessing him in Samaria as he preached the gospel. Everything was going well. People were coming to faith. Miracles were taking place. It seemed like a wonderful breakthrough for the gospel.

Then, seemingly out of the blue, God told him to go to the desert. And not only did God tell him to go to the desert, but He told him to go to Gaza, to a rarely used road winding through the wilderness. And not only did He tell him to go to this lonely desert highway, but He told him to go at the hottest time of the day. Essentially God said, "Go out to the middle of the desert to a deserted road in the middle of the afternoon, and I will show you what to do next."

Sometimes the will of God doesn't make much earthly sense to us. We may plan to do a certain thing, but God may intervene. He might have another plan. The idea is that we should remember God in our plans, and we should also remember He may change our plans.

Often in his writings, the apostle Paul would refer to the will of God for his life. He told the believers at Ephesus he would return to them for renewed ministry if God willed. And he wrote to the Corinthians that he planned to visit them if the Lord willed. That's important for us to factor into our plans as well. We should always remember, "If the Lord wills."

Sometimes the Lord will lead us differently than we would like to go. But what we must come to recognize is that the will of God is perfect, and we should never be afraid of it.

Wednesday

You also be patient. Establish your hearts, for the coming of the Lord is at hand. (James 5:8)

A number of years ago, we held a Harvest Crusade in Colorado. When we arrived, it was around seventy degrees, the sun was shining, and all looked well for our crusade to begin on the following evening. As we watched the news that night, however, we learned that a cold front was moving in.

Did it ever! The next morning, there was snow on the ground. That's how quickly the weather can change in a place like Colorado. One moment the sun is shining and you're walking around in shorts and shirt sleeves, and the next thing you know there's a howling blizzard outside.

That's how life can be as well. Everything might be looking great, when suddenly, a storm cloud appears. And as we all know, storms can do some heartbreaking damage. That's why the Bible tells us, "Establish your hearts…" (James 5:8). Another way to translate this verse is, "Strengthen and make firm your inner life."

The same word is used to describe Jesus' attitudes and actions when He headed for Jerusalem, knowing what awaited Him there: "Now it came to pass, when the time had come for Him to be received up, that He *steadfastly set* His face to go to Jerusalem" (Luke 9:51).

The Greek word means "to set fast, to turn resolutely in a certain direction." Jesus, being God, had full knowledge of all that was about to unfold, and yet He resolutely set out for Jerusalem. In the same way, James tells us to firmly establish our hearts as we await the return of Jesus Christ.

God wants us to be rooted and grounded, stable and secure in the truths of His Word—and yet many Christians are not. They have never taken the time or effort to develop habits of personal Bible study, prayer, or even regular church attendance. But God is saying we need to get rooted, because our faith will be challenged. We will face hardship. Storms can descend quickly when they come—and often when we least expect them.

David frequently described the Lord as a Shelter and a Refuge. When the enemy army invades or the sky turns black with an approaching storm, you run for refuge. That makes perfect sense. But God offers us something more; God offers us the opportunity to live out our lives inside a refuge that is His personal presence. Then when the storm comes, you're already there, safe and secure.

Thursday

Is anyone among you suffering? Let him pray. Is anyone cheerful?
Let him sing psalms. (James 5:13)

Finding ourselves in trying circumstances, we may be tempted to strike out at the person who helped bring those circumstances upon us. We may even become angry at God for allowing a particular disappointment, hardship, or situation in our lives, and end up wallowing in self-pity.

In times of affliction, suffering, or trouble, however, God tells us exactly what we should do: *pray.* Why? For one thing, God might hear our prayer and decide to change or remove our problem. That's not to say that God will always take away our afflictions, suffering, or troubles. But then again, sometimes He will! James reminds us that "you do not have because you do not ask God" (James 4:2, NIV).

By simply bringing our circumstances before the Lord and acknowledging our need and dependence upon Him, we can see God intervene in the situation we are presently facing. Prayer can also give us the grace we need to endure trouble and be brought much closer to God. Through prayer, we can ask God to open our eyes to opportunities to serve Him or perhaps a greater understanding of our situation.

James 5:13 tells us, "Is anyone among you suffering? Let him pray." The word "suffering" used here could also be translated "in trouble" or "in distress." Is anyone among you in trouble? Are you distressed? Then you should pray.

So when the bottom drops out, when you feel you're just hanging by a thread, when circumstances have become incredibly difficult, or when they have grown worse by the minute, what should you do? You should pray. Jesus told us that we should always pray and not give up (Luke 18:1). Always? Yes, always. When you're sick, and when you're well. When you're wrestling with sin, and when you're resting in Him. When you're in tight circumstances or a place of ease and rest. When you're in need, or when you have all you need. The time to pray is now...and always.

Friday

O God, listen to me! Hear my prayer! For wherever I am, though far away at the ends of the earth, I will cry to you for help. When my heart is faint and overwhelmed, lead me to the mighty, towering Rock of safety. For you are my refuge, a high tower where my enemies can never reach me. I shall live forever in your tabernacle; oh, to be safe beneath the shelter of your wings! (Psalm 61:1-4, TLB)

I have come to realize that when I am seeking to walk in the will of God and when I am engaging in the things of God, then I can expect opposition from the enemy of God, the devil. Our first reaction to opposition or trouble in our lives might be to link it with some sin or disobedience. In fact, it may be quite the opposite. Afflictions, troubles, and hardships may also come to us because we are *obedient* to God, and seeking to serve Him.

Remember Job and all of the hardship that came upon him because he was a perfect and an upright man, a man who feared God and turned away from evil?

Then there was Nehemiah, who went out to rebuild the walls of Jerusalem that had been torn down and lay in ruins. God had directed him to do this, but as soon as he undertook this great work for the Lord, a man named Sanballat opposed him and threatened him. What did Nehemiah do? Did he get a restraining order against Sanballat? Did he immediately stop what he was doing and run and hide? No. Instead, Nehemiah did what James says we should do when we are afflicted or in trouble. He prayed. He said, "Hear, O our God, for we are despised; turn their reproach on their own heads, for they have provoked You to anger before the builders" (Nehemiah 4:4–5). Nehemiah cried out to God and brought his problems to Him.

As 1 Peter 5:7 reminds us, "Casting all your care upon Him, for He cares for you." So when trouble comes, pray. Bring your troubles, your problems, your cares, and your anxieties to God. And receive His reassurance and peace in return.

Weekend

The Lord will command His lovingkindness in the daytime, and in the night His song shall be with me—a prayer to the God of my life. (Psalm 42:8)

The great British preacher C. H. Spurgeon said, "Any fool can sing in the day... It is easy to sing when we can read the notes by daylight; but the skillful singer is he who can sing when there is not a ray of light to read by... Songs in the night come only from God; they are not the power of man."[21]

When Paul and Silas were imprisoned for preaching the gospel in Philippi, it was a hot and horrible environment. Prisons back then were far more primitive than they are today. Archaeologists have discovered what they believe was the actual prison where Paul and Silas were imprisoned as recorded in Acts 16. It was nothing more than a dark hole, without ventilation.

But instead of cursing God and questioning how a God of love could do this to them, Paul and Silas realized it was time to pray. The Bible tells us, "But at midnight Paul and Silas were praying and singing hymns to God, and the prisoners were listening to them" (Acts 16:25). Songs—not groans—came from their mouths. And instead of cursing men, they were blessing God. No wonder the other prisoners were listening, hardly believing their ears.

When we are in pain, the midnight hour is never the easiest time to hold a worship service. There are times when we don't feel like singing to the Lord or praising Him. But Hebrews 13:15 (AMPLIFIED) reminds us, "Through Him, therefore, let us constantly and at all times offer up to God a sacrifice of praise, which is the fruit of lips that thankfully acknowledge and confess and glorify His name."

Are you facing a hardship today? God can give you songs in the night.

You will be singing with the psalmist, "In the night I remember your name, O LORD... At midnight I rise to give you thanks for your righteous laws" (Psalm 119: 55, 62, NIV)

Monday

Let all that I am praise the Lord; with my whole heart, I will praise his holy name. Let all that I am praise the Lord; may I never forget the good things he does for me.

He forgives all my sins and heals all my diseases. He redeems me from death and crowns me with love and tender mercies.
(Psalm 103:1-4, NLT)

I believe that God heals today. We already know He has miraculously built into the human body a natural process in which it heals over time. But I believe God can quicken the healing process. I also believe that He can do a miracle, even after we have been told "there's no hope." I have seen so many of these miracles myself. God promises His healing touch, and tells us that by His stripes we are healed. So we should ask God to heal us when we are facing sickness.

In James 5:14, we are given the scriptural pattern for healing: "Is anyone among you sick? Let him call for the elders of the church, and let them pray over him, anointing him with oil in the name of the Lord."

It's interesting to me that the Bible *does not say,* "Is anyone among you sick? Then go find a faith healer." I'm not suggesting that miracles didn't take place in the early church, because indeed they did. Nor am I saying that healing was done apart from faith, because faith was certainly an element in many of those miracles. My point is that miracles were never the *focus* of the apostles. The early church didn't follow signs and wonders; signs and wonders followed them. That is an important distinction.

To this very day and hour, we can go to God and ask Him to heal. I thank God that healing is available to us today as His sons and daughters. But we make a mistake when we focus on phenomenon. Instead, we should focus on the proclamation of God's Word and leave the miracles, the healings, and the rest up to God to do as He sovereignly chooses.

Tuesday

The prayer of a righteous man is powerful and effective.

Elijah was a man just like us. He prayed earnestly that it would not rain, and it did not rain on the land for three and a half years. Again he prayed, and the heavens gave rain, and the earth produced its crops. (James 5:16-18, NIV)

When we read the words of James 5:16, which says, "The prayer of a righteous man is powerful and effective," we might think, *That counts me out. I am not a righteous person.* In a technical sense, this is true of all of us. None of us are flawless. But in another sense, those of us who have put our faith in Christ are righteous, because He has deposited His righteousness into our account. And without a doubt, His credit is good in the bank of heaven.

The Bible says, "But of Him you are in Christ Jesus, who became for us wisdom from God—and righteousness and sanctification and redemption" (1 Corinthians 1:30). Christ Himself has become our righteousness. And the prayer of a righteous man or woman is powerful and effective. Or as the old King James version had it, "availeth much."

James then cites the example of Elijah, a greatly admired righteous man. When we think of Elijah, we often remember him going toe to toe with powerful kings, outrunning chariots, raising the dead, calling fire down from heaven, and stopping the rain with his prayers. He seemed almost superhuman. What we forget is that after his great contest with the prophets of Baal on Mount Carmel, he became very human indeed. When he heard that he'd incurred the deadly wrath of Queen Jezebel, he ran for his life! He became so exhausted and depressed after his long run that he crawled under a bush in the desert and asked the Lord to kill him.

In other words, he really was a human being just like us, with the same vulnerabilities. So if Elijah could still muster up the faith to believe God for great things, surely we can do the same.

Wednesday

*"'You shall love the Lord your God with all your heart, with all your
soul, and with all your mind.' This is the first and great commandment.
And the second is like it: 'You shall love your neighbor as yourself.'"*
(Matthew 22:37–39)

Conventional wisdom says that if you want to be happy, then you
have to "look out for number one." Come what may, at the end
of the day, you have to make sure your own needs and desires get met
first. In other words, you have to do whatever it takes to succeed. It
doesn't matter who you step on or who you hurt in the process. After
all…if you don't look out for your own interests, who will?

That's certainly what our world says.

But how does that philosophy work out as an operating principle?
Does it bring the happiness and fulfillment men and women long
for and seek? No, it really doesn't. Many of us know from experience
that a self-first-at-all-costs lifestyle invariably leads to lonely, unhappy
dead-ends. We may have little bursts of happiness along the way, but it
never lasts, and it leaves emptiness in its wake.

Here is God's formula for a meaningful life. And it's about as
counter-cultural as it can be:

> "Is there any encouragement from belonging to Christ?
> Any comfort from his love? Any fellowship together in
> the Spirit? Are your hearts tender and compassionate?
> Then make me truly happy by agreeing wholeheartedly
> with each other, loving one another, and working
> together with one mind and purpose. Don't be selfish;
> don't try to impress others. Be humble, thinking of
> others as better than yourselves. Don't look out only for
> your own interests, but take an interest in others, too.
> You must have the same attitude that Christ Jesus had"
> (Philippians 2:1-4, NLT).

Our culture teaches, "Look out for yourself. Think of yourself."
But the Bible says, "Don't think only about your own affairs."

The Bible teaches that we really don't need any help looking out
for number one. We do it naturally. It's part of our fallen human
nature. But walking through life with the attitude of Christ Jesus?
That's not natural at all…it's supernatural. And we need the very
power of God to accomplish it.

Thursday

For we know that when this earthly tent we live in is taken down (that is, when we die and leave this earthly body), we will have a house in heaven, an eternal body made for us by God himself and not by human hands. We grow weary in our present bodies, and we long to put on our heavenly bodies like new clothing. (2 Corinthians 5:1-2, NLT)

When my son Jonathan turned eleven, I remember asking him, "What age are you really looking forward to?"

"Sixteen," he replied. "I want to be sixteen."

That's so typical. When you're young, sixteen is where it's at. Then you hit sixteen, and you say, "Eighteen—that's the age to be!" Then you hit eighteen, and you want to be twenty-one, because you can do so much when you're twenty-one. Then you hit twenty-one, and you say, "No one takes me seriously yet. They think I'm still a kid. Wait'll I hit my thirties. Those are the earning years." You hit your thirties and say, "If I could just be in my forties, then I will have arrived." Then you hit forty, and you say, "I wish I were a teenager again. I wish I could have that carefree life I used to have." That's when the so-called midlife crisis kicks in for a lot of people.

Next come the fifties, and then the sixties...the golden years. You look back, and you have many memories and regrets.

One could almost look back on life and come to the same conclusion that Benjamin Disraeli, former Prime Minister of England came to: "Youth is a blunder; manhood a struggle; old age a regret."[22] That's a pretty accurate assessment of life apart from Jesus Christ.

But when Jesus Christ is at the center of your life, you don't have to feel that way. You can live a life that is rich and full on this earth—in spite of old age or limitations or infirmities. And then...beyond the grave, the best is yet to come! Just around the corner from this life is an eternal life so wonderful we can't even put words to it.

What am I looking forward to? I'm looking forward to each day that God lets me live here on earth. And beyond that, I'm looking forward to that moment in time where I cross over from this world to the next.

Friday

If all we get out of Christ is a little inspiration for a few short years, we're a pretty sorry lot. But the truth is that Christ has been raised up, the first in a long legacy of those who are going to leave the cemeteries.
(1 Corinthians 15:20, THE MESSAGE*)*

A minister conducting a funeral service wanted to speak a few glowing remarks about the deceased. He had the right idea… it just didn't come out quite the way he intended. Pointing at the coffin, he boldly proclaimed, "What we have here is only the shell." Then he added, *"But the nut has gone!"*

That's not exactly what he'd intended to say! But then again, it's not a bad description of what happens to us when we die. That which lives forever gets separated from that which will return to the dust.

Where has the nut gone? To a new shell! In fact, our new God-given resurrection bodies will last forever! And we will need those new bodies, in order to live in the new environment called heaven. Of course, we wouldn't think of sending astronauts into space dressed like they were going to the beach. They must have special suits, designed to allow them to breathe and function in a different reality. By the same token, our earthly bodies suit us fine for life on earth. But in heaven, we will need new bodies.

Consider this: If we were to see God in the bodies we occupy right now, we would vaporize on the spot. Why? Because we're not perfect people, and our present bodies are limited by the effects of sin. The very fact that we age, get sick, and will one day die (if the Lord doesn't come back for us first) means that we have bodies tainted by sin. We need new bodies, made in the image of Jesus Himself, and created to last for all eternity.

Yes, you will leave the shell you have occupied for as long as you can remember, but the "nut," the real you, will go into the presence of the Lord.

Weekend

"But when you do a kindness to someone, do it secretly—don't tell your left hand what your right hand is doing. And your Father, who knows all secrets, will reward you." (Matthew 6:3-4, TLB)

Maybe you achieved great things in academics as a student. As a young boy or girl, you won the spelling bees and collected A's on your report cards. Maybe you were given some special honor, such as a scholarship to attend a great college, because of your special abilities. Or perhaps you were a big sports star, excelling in sports with plenty of trophies and ribbons to prove it.

Me? I always ended up with one of those "honorable mention" ribbons. When you don't finish in the top four or five places, they still give you a consolation prize, just for showing up and trying. As I remember, the ribbons were usually purple, and I had a room filled with them. Try as I might, it was the best I could do.

In heaven, however, there will be many unique and wondrous rewards for those who have been faithful to God over the years—and it will have nothing to do with our earthly IQ or athletic abilities. In fact, even the smallest, seemingly most insignificant gesture on behalf of God's kingdom will not be overlooked by our heavenly Father. What will these rewards be? It's still a mystery—but a fascinating one. The New Testament speaks of glorious crowns, but we have no idea what that really means. In the book of Revelation, the Lord Jesus speaks of rewarding faithful servants using mysterious words like "new name," "white stone," and "hidden manna."

Those terms may not mean much to us right now...but one day they will be incredibly significant to us.

Jesus said that our service to God, even though it may not be observed, noted, or honored here on earth, will be noted without fail by our heavenly Father. One day in our future, when we stand before the Judgment Seat of Christ, the Lord will reward us openly.

There will be no purple ribbons or "also-ran" trophies in that day. The Father will delight to honor us in unique ways beyond our present finite understanding...because we have honored His Son.

Monday

For we must all appear before the judgment seat of Christ, that each one may receive the things done in the body, according to what he has done, whether good or bad. (2 Corinthians 5:10)

The Bible tells us that we must all appear before the Judgment Seat of Christ. This word "appear" can be translated, "to make manifest." This suggests that the purpose of the Judgment Seat of Christ is a public manifestation, or demonstration, of an individual's essential character and motives.

This judgment, then, isn't about whether we will get to heaven, because it takes place in heaven. Rather, it is about the rewards believers will receive. Jesus said, "And behold, I am coming quickly, and My reward is with Me, to give to every one according to his work" (Revelation 22:12). God has a reward for those who have faithfully served Him.

What will be judged, according to 2 Corinthians 5:10, is what we have done, whether good or bad. The word used for "bad" in this verse is not speaking of something ethically or morally evil, because Christ paid the price for our sins at the cross of Calvary.

Rather, the word used for "bad" speaks of evil of another kind. Another way to translate it would be "good-for-nothingness," or "worthlessness." The idea of good or bad is not of someone who has done something outwardly and blatantly wrong. The idea is of someone who has simply wasted days, months, or years of his or her life. It is someone who has thrown away his or her time, energy, and life in general, or frittered it away on empty, non-essential activities and preoccupations.

How do we respond to this future date with destiny? It's time to wake up and live! Here is how Paul put it to the believers in Rome: "And do this, understanding the present time. The hour has come for you to wake up from your slumber, because our salvation is nearer now than when we first believed. The night is nearly over; the day is almost here. So let us put aside the deeds of darkness and put on the armor of light" (Romans 13:11-12, NIV).

What are you doing with your life for Christ's sake? I know what He has done for you. What are you doing for Him? Are you wasting your life on empty activities?

Tuesday

Fix your thoughts on what is true and honorable and right and pure and lovely and admirable. Think about things that are excellent and worthy of praise. (Philippians 4:8 NLT)

If you want peace in your heart, then the Bible says you need to get your thoughts in order. As Isaiah 26:3 tells us, "You will keep him in perfect peace, whose mind is stayed on You, because he trusts in You." You need to keep your mind stayed on God. In the original language, that term "stayed" means to lean upon or take hold of.

Think of yourself on the rooftop of a house, with floodwaters swirling right up to the eaves. A helicopter hovers overhead, and drops a rope to you, just as the house is about to crumble in the raging waters. You take hold of that rope and grip it with all your might! Your hands are "stayed on" the rescue rope.

What we think about ultimately affects what we do. Therefore, we want to nip in the bud any thoughts that would be impure or spiritually destructive. The Bible says, "For as he thinks in his heart, so is he" (Proverbs 23:7). Maintaining personal peace involves both the heart and the mind.

When the devil approached Eve in the Garden, notice that he didn't come and say, "Hi, I'm Lucifer. I fell from heaven. Listen, Eve, I hate your guts. I hate Adam. I hate the descendants that are going to come. In fact, I have been thinking about getting you thrown out of the Garden of Eden and wreak havoc on your life."

He's not going to do that, is he? No, he is a more subtle enemy than that. He came to Eve in a more casual, deceptive way. We learn from 2 Corinthians 11:3 that he attacked her mind, because Paul wrote, "But I fear, lest somehow, as the serpent deceived Eve by his craftiness, so your minds may be corrupted from the simplicity that is in Christ."

What do you allow to fill your mind? My point is that we need to have a right mind. If we don't, then it is only a matter of time until we fall into sin. If we allow garbage into our minds, then ultimately, it will work its way into our lives.

Wednesday

"God blesses those who are persecuted for doing right, for the Kingdom of Heaven is theirs. God blesses you when people mock you and persecute you and lie about you and say all sorts of evil things against you because you are my followers. Be happy about it! Be very glad! For a great reward awaits you in heaven. And remember, the ancient prophets were persecuted in the same way (Matthew 5:10-12, NLT)

Your decision to follow Jesus may have led you to leave a number of associations, activities, or habits behind you. You may have lost friends, or even family, in the process of becoming His servant. You may have resisted many temptations or endured hardships that no one else knows about because of your faith. If so, God promises you a special reward in heaven.

No matter what we must endure, however, there are many who have suffered far worse: those who throughout church history who have laid down their lives. I'm speaking here of men and women who were put to death for their faith in Christ—refusing to deny their Lord, even at the cost of their lives. They have a unique, matchless reward waiting for them in heaven.

James 1:12 says, "Blessed is the man who endures temptation; for when he has been approved, he will receive the crown of life which the Lord has promised to those who love Him." If you have suffered the loss of a friendship for the Lord's sake, or had to take ridicule and persecution, know that God will certainly reward you (see Matthew 5:11–12). Whatever you have given up along the way, He will make it up to you—a million times over.

Sometimes we may think about certain activities that we've surrendered, and say to ourselves: *I know it's wrong, but it looks kind of fun. I kind of wish I could do it.* But we know we shouldn't. So we resist. As time passes, you will look back at the fallout, the repercussions of those choices, and say, "I am so glad I avoided those things." And ultimately, in that final day, God will give you a reward.

Thursday

"But lay up for yourselves treasures in heaven, where neither moth nor rust destroys and where thieves do not break in and steal."
(Matthew 6:20)

People employ different strategies in the game of Monopoly. Some buy every piece of property on the board, hoping to quickly put their opponents out of business. Others save up, hoping they will land on Boardwalk and Park Place, and put hotels on them. You can make a lot of money when you play Monopoly, but that money isn't going to do a thing for you in the real world, because when the game is over, so are your winnings. It all goes back in the box.

In the same way, when we get to heaven, all that we have on this earth will have no value at all unless we have invested it wisely. That's why it's important to think about what we're spending our money on. It has been said that you can't take it with you, but you can send it on ahead. How? By investing in the work of the kingdom of God. In doing so, you are laying up for yourself treasures in heaven.

Money is neither good nor evil. Money is neutral. The Bible doesn't say that money is the root of all evil. Rather, it says, "The *love* of money is a root of all kinds of evil" (1 Timothy 6:10, emphasis mine). So it isn't money itself that is the problem; it is the love of it. If money is the most important thing to you, then it can be the root of all kinds of evil in your life. But if you can get it into the proper perspective, it can be a force for good to help and touch people.

Here is how Paul expressed it to Timothy:

> "Command those who are rich in this present world not to be arrogant nor to put their hope in wealth, which is so uncertain, but to put their hope in God, who richly provides us with everything for our enjoyment. Command them to do good, to be rich in good deeds, and to be generous and willing to share. In this way they will lay up treasure for themselves as a firm foundation for the coming age, so that they may take hold of the life that is truly life" (1 Timothy 6:17-19, NIV).

Friday

Now David said, "Is there still anyone who is left of the house of Saul, that I may show him kindness for Jonathan's sake?" (2 Samuel 9:1)

Mephibosheth was only five years old when his father Jonathan and his grandfather Saul were killed on the battlefield. Imagine, if you will, life as he had known it up to this point. The privilege and potential of his present could not have prepared him for the hard life he would face in the future. There was life in the palace as a young prince, with people waiting on him hand and foot, and being raised by his good and godly father, Jonathan. Life was good for this young boy.

But there were dark clouds gathering in his world. In one moment, through no fault of his own, his entire life would change forever. Jonathan knew things were going to change. With that in mind, he persuaded his friend David to make an agreement to look out for his descendants. He made David promise to show kindness to his family forever. David made that promise. And he kept it.

When news hit the palace that Saul and Jonathan had been killed on the battlefield, the nurse who was caring for Mephibosheth grabbed up the young prince in a frenzy, only to drop him on the ground. As a result of his fall, the boy would be crippled for life.

Perhaps you went through hardships in your childhood. Maybe something traumatic happened to you along the way. People who were supposed to love you and protect you ended up shaming you or harming you. You were dropped…like Mephibosheth. And the falls you have taken since that time have seemingly changed your destiny or limited your potential. And now you wonder if anything good can come out of your life.

Mephibosheth was dropped in life, but God intervened. In fact, God specializes in taking people who have been dropped in life and picking them back up again. That's what David did for Mephibosheth. And that is just what God will do for you.

Weekend

"Nevertheless, when the Son of Man comes, will He really find faith on the earth?" (Luke 18:8)

I *hate* being sick.

Sometimes I wonder, however, if certain people really like their sickness—such as hypochondriacs, who are forever talking about their illnesses and maladies. They love to go on and on about all their aches and pains, their allergies and intolerances. They almost seem to enjoy it, in a perverse sort of way.

But as for me, I hate feeling weak, and can't stand being cooped up. I don't want to be lying on my back somewhere, I want to be up and doing. (Yes, that does make me a lousy patient.) As soon as I feel my energy coming back—even a little—I'm up off the bed or couch, dragging myself around, and trying to get busy again. Unfortunately, I often end up prolonging my sickness because I refuse to rest and basically can't sit still.

When you've been sick and first start to get a little better, you're still wobbly on your feet. You're not as bad as you once were, but you know very well you're not as good as you need to be. It's an uncomfortable, vulnerable, in-between stage.

That describes the condition of the church of Philadelphia that Jesus speaks to in Revelation 3. This church was getting back to its roots, returning to its foundation, and rediscovering those things that had once made it strong. But it wasn't as powerful as it once was. It had just a little strength.

What kind of spiritual condition will the church be in when Christ returns? Jesus said, "When the Son of Man comes, will He really find faith on the earth?" (Luke 18:8). It was more of a statement than a question. He was saying that there won't be the level of faith there ought to be. And as we look at the church today, we can clearly see that the further the modern church has strayed from the New Testament model, the weaker and more ineffective it has become.

If the church wants to return to the battle and once again do mighty works in Jesus' name, it needs much strength, not just a little. And that can only come when we turn from those things that have distracted us and sapped our strength, and follow the Lord with all our hearts.

Monday

"I am coming soon. Hold on to what you have, so that no one will take your crown. Him who overcomes I will make a pillar in the temple of my God. Never again will he leave it." (Revelation 3:11-12, NIV)

As the days in which we live grow more difficult, as hostility increases and the world becomes more and more secular, casting aside even the trappings of Christianity that it formerly practiced, we as Christians living in the last days must be careful not to give up and go along with these worldly attitudes and pursuits.

When Jesus said, *"Hold on to what you have, so that no one will take your crown,"* He was not referring to losing our salvation. In the Bible, the concept of a crown is something that is given to a believer for his or her faithfulness. Various crowns are promised to believers, depending on how they lived. Paul said, "Finally, there is laid up for me the crown of righteousness, which the Lord, the righteous Judge, will give to me on that Day, and not to me only but also to all who have loved His appearing" (2 Timothy 4:8). If you look forward with great anticipation to the return of Christ, then you will have a crown of righteousness waiting for you.

The crown Jesus spoke of in Revelation 3 represents the opportunities God has given to us. There is a reward promised to every believer who faithfully serves the Lord. *Don't lose that opportunity.* Don't squander it, because by missing it, you will forfeit the crown that Jesus has for you.

If you don't faithfully serve the Lord with the right motives and do what God has set before you, you will still get to heaven, but there won't be a crown waiting for you. But if you take hold of those opportunities God has given to you, then He will give you that crown.

The apostle John put it like this: *"Watch out that you do not lose what you have worked for, but that you may be rewarded fully"* (2 John 8, NIV).

Tuesday

Now the serpent was more crafty than any of the wild animals the Lord God had made. He said to the woman, "Did God really say, 'You must not eat from any tree in the garden'?" (Genesis 3:1, NIV)

I find it interesting that the devil didn't deny that God had spoken to Eve. Rather than challenging the fact that God had spoken, he twisted God's words to say something the Creator had never intended. In so doing, of course, he was questioning God's fairness and love for Eve: *Why would God make trees with fruit, and then forbid you to eat the fruit? Does that make sense? If God really loved you, He would let you eat of this tree, too. Why is He holding out on you? It's not fair. God must not love you to keep something this important from you.*

Maybe you've felt that way before—or possibly feel that way now. Maybe you feel as though God is holding something back from you that you think you really need *right now*. Just remember, if God says "no", then He does so for your own good.

We wrestle with that thought, don't we? It's a little difficult for us to process sometimes. But consider the way you would deal with young children. You wouldn't let them live entirely on sugar, watch cartoons all day, stay up all night, or play tag on the freeway, even though they think they need to do these things. Instead, you set certain limits, because you know what's good for them (and much better than they know themselves).

God does the same with us. In His wisdom and far-seeing love, He says "no" to certain things. But if God says "no", then it is the right thing—and the *best* thing for us. Psalm 84:11 says, "No good thing will He withhold from those who walk uprightly." In other words, God isn't in the business of withholding good and helpful things from His children. If He does tell me to avoid something, then it's because He knows it would harm me. If He says, "Don't do this. It's not good," then we must take His word for it.

Wednesday

I know how to live on almost nothing or with everything. I have learned the secret of living in every situation, whether it is with a full stomach or empty, with plenty or little. For I can do everything with the help of Christ who gives me strength. (Philippians 4:12-13, NLT)

Have you ever been sorely mistreated through no fault of your own? Perhaps you were the victim of an orchestrated campaign of slander and lies. Maybe you were falsely accused of things that, ironically, you had gone to great lengths to avoid. Maybe you have been a victim of another kind of injustice. It may seem that God has somehow forgotten you.

Most of us live by a code of ethics, and within this code, we believe that if people do what is right, they should be rewarded. By the same token, if people do what is wrong, they should ultimately face some sort of punishment. It's true that much of life works this way…but sometimes it doesn't. And then we want to know why.

I don't have any easy answers to this dilemma. But in the Book in Genesis, we see how one man named Joseph dealt with this very issue. He suffered not for doing wrong, but for doing right. He experienced mistreatment, misunderstanding, and even downright hostility.

If anyone had a good reason to question God, it was Joseph. If anyone could have claimed victim status and moaned that the world was out to get him, it was Joseph. If anyone could have felt that God had possibly forgotten him, it was Joseph. Yet amazingly, as far as we know, he never did any of those things.

To his brothers who had so violently mistreated him in his younger days, he could say, "You intended to harm me, but God intended it all for good. He brought me to this position so I could save the lives of many people" (Genesis 50:20, NLT).

The single greatest characteristic of Joseph's life was his unwavering faithfulness to God in all circumstances. No matter what came his way, Joseph trusted God. He is an amazing example for all of us to emulate.

Thursday

Not that I was ever in need, for I have learned how to be content with whatever I have. I know how to live on almost nothing or with everything. I have learned the secret of living in every situation, whether it is with a full stomach or empty, with plenty or little. For I can do everything through Christ, who gives me strength.
(Philippians 4:11-14, NLT)

Have you learned the secret of contentment? Many of us are content when things are going our way. When life unfolds day by day the way we want it to, we can be content with that, for the most part. But when life deals us a hard blow, when the bottom drops out, and when we face a conflict, suddenly we are no longer content.

Maybe find yourself in a situation like that right now. Maybe you've been the victim of untrue, unfair accusations. Maybe someone you love has abandoned you. Maybe you have helped someone out who was really in a miserable situation, only to have that person turn on you. Maybe someone made promises to you that they didn't keep. Maybe something like this has happened to you and you feel abandoned.

Even though it may seem everyone else has deserted you, God has not. God never forgets about His children. Sometimes God will allow us to experience hardship because He is teaching us to walk by faith, not by sight and not by feeling, just as He did with Joseph in the Book of Genesis. In that case, the Lord wanted to whip young Joseph into shape, because he had some formidable tasks ahead—like running a world empire. There would be no time for pity parties. You could say that Joseph was in "wait" training.

Maybe you are in "wait" training too. You wonder why the Lord doesn't seem to be doing anything for you, and why certain doors that you expected to open remained closed and locked. Just hang in there. There are some lessons that God may want to teach you. The Bible says, "Godliness with contentment is great gain" (1 Timothy 6:6).

But here's the secret: You will never be able to draw such contentment from your life situation or circumstances. True contentment grows out of your relationship with the living God.

Friday

But He knows the way that I take; when He has tested me, I shall come forth as gold. (Job 23:10)

God specializes in placing us in situations where the only way out is through Him. That way, we can't "thank our lucky stars" or compliment ourselves on our own cleverness or resourcefulness. Rather, we must say, "Only God could have done this." The Lord wants to receive the glory for what He does. And He clearly says in Scripture that He will not give His glory to another (see Isaiah 42:8).

It reminds us of a man who knew something about suffering, whose very name, in fact, is synonymous with the word. I am speaking, of course, of Job. Here was suffered the loss of his children, his home, and virtually everything he owned, *including his health.* And it all happened in a matter of days.

Did Job have a lot of questions for God? Yes, he did—and they are the same questions that many of us have as well. At one point he cried out, "Oh, that I knew where to find God—that I could go to his throne and talk with him there. I would tell him all about my side of this argument, and listen to his reply, and understand what he wants" (Job 23:3-5, TLB).

Job honestly admitted where he was struggling. Then he added what would become a classic statement of faith: *"But He knows the way that I take; when He has tested me, I shall come forth as gold"* (Job 23:10). Job was saying, "I really don't understand what's happening in my life right now, and for the life of me, I can't figure out why God would allow these things to happen. How will I survive this broken heart? How will I move into a future that looks so dark and grim? I don't know those things, either. But there's one thing I do know: When He has finished testing me, I will come forth as gold."

That was God's objective for Job. And it's His objective for you, too.

Weekend

But Job replied, "You talk like a foolish woman. Should we accept only good things from the hand of God and never anything bad?" So in all this, Job said nothing wrong. (Job 2:10, NLT)

Sudden reversals in our lives can be difficult to take. They can leave us despondent, and perhaps feeling that God has abandoned us.

When our fortunes suddenly change for the better, however, we have a tendency to become arrogant. Instead of thinking God has abandoned us, we sometimes abandon God. Prosperity often can be a harder test to pass than adversity. After all, when you're experiencing adversity, you're dependent upon God for all your needs. You need food, clothing, good health, and life itself. But when you find yourself walking on the sunny side of the street, soaking up some prosperity, when good things in your life seem to be percolating, you can forget about the Lord. Or worse—you can even begin to take personal credit for what you have accomplished.

Let's imagine, for example, that you're working very hard in a business, and barely making it. Then, all of a sudden, everything comes together. You start making sales left and right, and find yourself at the top of the heap. But instead of giving the glory to God, you say to yourself, *I'm pretty good, aren't I?* Or let's say you're in school, and all of a sudden, you find yourself doing better than the other students. You're acing your tests and getting A's on your papers, and you think, "I'm a little smarter than the rest of this bunch." Or maybe you're achieving in some other area of life. Don't forget: It was God who brought that success to you, and who can just as easily take it away.

When the people of Israel were about to cross the Jordan and enter the promised land, Moses reminded them: "When the LORD your God brings you into…a land with large, flourishing cities you did not build, houses filled with all kinds of good things you did not provide, wells you did not dig, and vineyards and olive groves you did not plant—then when you eat and are satisfied, be careful that you do not forget the Lord…" (Deuteronomy 10-12, NIV).

The question is, will you remember God in prosperity as well as adversity?

Monday

*But I do not want you to be ignorant, brethren, concerning those who
have fallen asleep, lest you sorrow as others who have no hope.*
(1 Thessalonians 4:13)

Have you ever had a significant reunion with a member of your
family? Maybe it was someone you thought you would never
see again or someone you had been separated from for many years.

But then again, maybe there is someone who was taken from
you quickly and unexpectedly. There are things you wish you had
said to that person, and maybe a few regrets along the way. There's
something for all of us to learn in this. If there is anyone in your life
you need to say something to, *say it now*, while you can. Tell that
person you love him or her. Let that person know what he or she
means to you. Do something to communicate with them, because
you never know when their time may come. Then again, you never
know when your time may come, either.

The good news is there will be a family reunion for every child of
God, a day when we will see those believers who have died and are
in heaven.

When his young child died, David said, "I shall go to him, but
he shall not return to me" (2 Samuel 12:23). That's the hope of every
Christian. Our friends and loved ones cannot come to us, but we
will go to them someday.

You can join them one day in the great reunion when the Lord
comes for His church, as described in 1 Thessalonians 4:

> "I can tell you this directly from the Lord: We who are
> still living when the Lord returns will not rise to meet
> him ahead of those who have died. For the Lord himself
> will come down from heaven with a commanding shout,
> with the voice of the archangel, and with the trumpet
> call of God. First, all the Christians who have died will
> rise from their graves. Then, together with them, we who
> are still alive and remain on the earth will be caught up
> in the clouds to meet the Lord in the air. Then we will
> be with the Lord forever. So comfort and encourage each
> other with these words" (vv. 15-18, NLT).

Talk about the ultimate family reunion!

Tuesday

Bless the Lord, O my soul, And forget not all His benefits: Who forgives all your iniquities… For as the heavens are high above the earth, so great is His mercy toward those who fear Him; as far as the east is from the west, so far has He removed our transgressions from us.
(Psalm 103:2-3, 11-12)

Many times, sins we have committed years ago come back to haunt us. You would think that, with the passing of the years, those former sins wouldn't bother us so much. But sometimes they bother us even more, because we have witnessed the repercussions of them.

Sometimes I will see evidence of this in our services at the church where I pastor. During our invitations to receive Christ, some of the same people will come forward week after week, seeking forgiveness and salvation. The counselors explain to them that they don't need to keep doing this, because those who have received Christ into their lives are forgiven, and now possess salvation. Nevertheless, many who have received God's complete and total forgiveness can't seem to forgive themselves.

We dishonor Jesus Christ when we come to Him again and again, asking forgiveness for sins He has not only forgiven, but also forgotten. We don't need to get saved again and again. Yes, we do need to go God for regular cleansing from sin, because the Bible tells us, "If we confess our sins, He is faithful and just to forgive us our sins and to cleanse us from all unrighteousness" (1 John 1:9). I am speaking of a person who doubts his or her salvation and repeatedly wants to be born again. We only need to be born again once—not twice, not three times, and not four times. In the book of Jeremiah, God declares: "For I will forgive their iniquity, and their sin I will remember no more" (Jeremiah 31:34).

Often we confess our sins to God and then continue to drag them up and spread them out, forgetting that God has already made an end of them. But it doesn't please the Lord when we choose to remember what He has chosen to forget.

Wednesday

And we know that all things work together for good to those who love
God, to those who are the called according to His purpose.
(Romans 8:28)

Without a doubt, Romans 8:28 is one of the greatest verses in the Bible. It's a passage that many believers down through the millennia have claimed as their own, especially during times of stress and hardship. And so it should be.

But let's make sure we meet the criteria of the text: "And we know that all things work together for good *to those who love God, to those who are the called according to His purpose*" (emphasis mine). Do you love God? Are you the called according to His purpose? Speaking plainly, Romans 8:28 does not apply to you if you don't love God or care nothing about His purposes.

There are times in our lives when things seem to be falling apart, when they don't make any sense. Some people will say, "It is the fickle finger of fate." Or, "*Que sera, sera.* Whatever will be will be. The future's not ours to see…"

It's true; the future isn't ours to see. But the Christian can be confident that God is in control and has a master plan for his or her life. We can know that we serve a sovereign God who is good. As I have often said, we may not know what the future holds, but we know who holds the future.

The word used here for "good" doesn't necessarily mean that the event in and of itself is good, but that its *long-term effect* will be useful and helpful. Another translation says, "everything that happens fits into a pattern for good" (PHILLIPS). In other words, in times to come—or maybe beyond time in eternity—we will see that God has worked all of the events of our lives into a pattern for our ultimate good.

It's hard for us to imagine certain things—particularly hurtful things—working for good. But don't misunderstand; the Bible isn't saying here that tragedy is good. Rather, it is saying that God can take a horrible thing and make good come as a result of it.

He's that kind of God.

Thursday

Before I was afflicted I went astray, but now I keep your word. ...It was good for me that I have been afflicted, that I might learn Your statutes.
(Psalm 119:67, 71)

Did you know that everything you have experienced up to this point in life can be used for good? Yes, you may have experienced hardships, and what seems like more than your share of "bad things." Even so, we have an all-powerful, sovereign God who can work out all the events of our lives, threading them together into a pattern for good.

That includes the experiences of your childhood, whether good or bad. That includes your parents, whoever they may be. That includes your education, your present employment, or your lack of it. He will work all things together for good.

I went through a great deal of hardship as a child. I came from a home that was broken many, many times over, a home of alcoholism. I wouldn't wish my childhood on anyone. But God used it to make me the person that I am.

In the same way, God has used what you have gone through to make you the person that you are. In yesterday's devotional, we read the promise of Romans 8:28: "All things work together for good to those who love God, to those who are the called according to His purpose." The phrase, "work together" also could be translated, "working together." In other words, it isn't over yet. The process is ongoing, and you may be right in the middle of that active process right now. Good? You don't see it yet—and sometimes you can barely imagine it. But you are a work in progress. So be patient. You have God's word on it: God is ultimately working all things for good—not just the good things, but *all* things.

I love the assurance of Philippians 2:12-13, where Paul says "work out your own salvation with fear and trembling; for it is God who works in you both to will and to do for *His* good pleasure."

God is working...in your life. And His purposes for you are good.

Friday

You shall tread upon the lion and the cobra, the young lion and the serpent you shall trample underfoot. (Psalm 91:13)

A lion is a fearsome creature, and if you ever saw one up close, you'd remember it. I've had a few opportunities to see lions—once in the wild in Africa and another time in a zoo in Ethiopia, where its roar made my hair stand on end.

The Bible uses the image of a lion to issue a stern warning about the attacks of Satan: it tells us, "Be self-controlled and alert. Your enemy the devil prowls around like a roaring lion looking for someone to devour. Resist him, steadfast in the faith, knowing that the same sufferings are experienced by your brotherhood in the world" (1 Peter 5:8).

Like a lion, sometimes the devil will confront us boldly in obvious ways, frightening ways.

But the Bible also compares the devil to a snake, reminding us that the evil one may sneak up on us in a subtle way, as he did with Eve in the Garden: "Now the serpent was more cunning than any beast of the field which the Lord God had made. And he said to the woman, 'Has God indeed said, "You shall not eat of every tree of the garden"?'" (Genesis 3:1).

If we could have our way, there wouldn't be any lions or snakes. There wouldn't be obstacles in our walk with Christ. But we find this promise in Psalm 91: "You shall tread upon the lion and the cobra, the young lion and the serpent you shall trample underfoot" (v. 13). God is essentially saying, "I will protect you from the enemy, no matter how he comes to you. I will protect you from the obstacles and the opponents that are out there."

He will protect us when Satan comes snarling out of the woods like a roaring lion, and he will protect us when the evil one slithers in through an open window in the night.

Our part is to simply set up camp in the secret place of the Most High, abiding under the shadow of the Almighty. And if we do, then we have God's Word on it that these promises will be realized in our lives.

Weekend

O God, you are my God; I earnestly search for you. My soul thirsts for you; my whole body longs for you in this parched and weary land where there is no water. I have seen you in the sanctuary and gazed upon your power and your glory. Your unfailing love is better than life itself; how I praise you!. (Psalm 63:1-3, NLT)

When I travel, I take my laptop with me, to work on my messages. But often I must work off the battery, so whenever I have the opportunity, I will plug in to the nearest electrical outlet. Why? Because my battery runs down and needs a recharge.

Sometimes that's the way it is for us as believers. We come to church and get plugged in spiritually. Then we try to run off that energy all week long. We don't realize we need the power of Christ at *all* times, in every situation, every conversation, every circumstance in which we find ourselves. In other words, we need a constant power source. We need to be plugged in all the time.

In Psalm 63, David was praying, "Lord, I want to walk with you all the time. Yes, I have seen your glory in the sanctuary, but I want that all week long."

I can't help but think of the prophet Elijah, who became physically, emotionally, and spiritually depleted in his warfare with the enemies of God. An angel of the Lord found him curled up under a bush in the desert, wanting to die. The angel provided him with some bread, let him rest, and then woke him up for another heavenly meal. The angel said, "Get up and eat, for the journey is too much for you" (2 Kings 19:7). We too, become run down and spiritually depleted. And God has a wonderful meal waiting for us every day in the Word of God, served by the Holy Spirit Himself.

Elijah needed to plug in again, and so do we. We need to make time for God and His Word in our day. Sometimes, that means just grabbing it where we can. Read some Scripture verses when you get up in the morning. Listen to some worship or a Bible study on your way to work or school. Take the moments where you can find them to plug in and stay tapped into all that God has for you.

Monday

Following after the Holy Spirit leads to life and peace, but following after the old nature leads to death because the old sinful nature within us is against God. (Romans 8:6-7, TLB)

God has a variety of means at His disposal to show us when we have wandered out of His will. One of those methods is by giving us His incomparable peace when we're walking in His will, and then removing it when we've gone off the path. The Bible tells us, "Let the peace that comes from Christ rule in your hearts" (Colossians 3:15, NLT). Another translation says, "And let the peace (soul harmony which comes) from Christ rule (act as umpire continually) in your hearts [deciding and settling with finality all questions that arise in your minds...]" (AMPLIFIED).

Umpires aren't always the most popular people at baseball games, because not everyone agrees with the calls they make. But you couldn't have a game without an umpire—it would soon disintegrate into arguments and mass confusion. The umpire is there to say, "Safe!" and "Out!" The peace of God can act as a spiritual umpire. Perhaps you can think of certain situations, such as a party you went to, a relationship you were involved in, or a place you were going, and suddenly you sensed a lack of peace in your heart—almost like a spiritual agitation deep inside. That might have been God saying, "No, don't go there. Don't do that. That's not My will for you now."

Another way the Lord sometimes directs us is by closing a door. By that I mean when circumstances in our lives just don't work. Maybe you set out on a big trip, only to get three flat tires. You were trying to do a certain thing when something went wrong, rendering your plan impossible.

Sometimes God can even redirect us through sickness. It has stopped me on a few occasions. However it is the Lord may direct you, remember that it may be in a different way than you wanted to go. But God has His will, and His timing...and believe me, you want both of them!

Tuesday

For the kingdom of God is not eating and drinking, but righteousness and peace and joy in the Holy Spirit. (Romans 14:17)

Today if you were to sum up your life, what truths would you want to emphasize to your family and friends?

In Acts 20, we find the final words of Paul to the elders of the church he had started in Ephesus. Here in this chapter, he was delivering his final charge to them. As he looked back on his life, he said, "But none of these things move me; nor do I count my life dear to myself, so that I may finish my race with joy, and the ministry which I received from the Lord Jesus, to testify to the gospel of the grace of God" (v. 24).

There is one word from this verse I want to bring to your attention: *joy*. Paul was saying, "I'm looking back on my life and on what I have accomplished here, and I'm looking forward into an uncertain future, not knowing what will happen next. But listen friends, if I could sum it all up in one word, it would be the word joy."

The word Paul used here could be translated, "exceedingly happy." Really? Exceedingly happy? He could say that after all the hardships, setbacks, adversity, physical pain, weariness, and opposition he had faced? He could say that even though he had a physical ailment that caused daily discomfort and distress? Yes, he was telling the Ephesians, right in the midst of it all, there is joy.

The fact of the matter is, a holy life is truly the happiest of lives. The life lived for God, walking with God, and drawing on the power and presence of God is the most glad-hearted life of all. Jesus said, "I have come that they may have life, and that they may have it more abundantly" (John 10:10). When you look up the word "abundantly" in the original language, you get the idea of over-the-top, *super* abundance—to the point of excess. And Jesus wasn't only speaking of the life to come beyond the grave, but a joyful abundance right here on earth as well. Right in the middle of everything. Even in the midst of trials and sorrows and serious challenges. And that is just one of the miracles of life in Jesus Christ.

Wednesday

When my spirit grows faint within me, it is you who know my way...
I cry to you, O Lord; I say, "You are my refuge, my portion in the land of
the living. (Psalm 142:3, 5, NIV)

A re you afraid of an uncertain future right now? Are you discouraged, feeling like you have failed in various areas of your life? If you have invited Jesus to be your Savior and Lord, then He is with you. And He will complete the work He has begun in your life. The Bible says, *"And I am certain that God, who began the good work within you, will continue his work until it is finally finished on that day when Christ Jesus returns" (Philippians 1:6, NLT).*

There are many reasons I'm glad that I am not God, one of them being that I'm the kind of the person who starts projects and forgets them. I will be cleaning my desk and almost have it finished when I say, "I'll do this a little bit later. I want to do something else right now."

Aren't you glad that God isn't that way? He would be working with me, suddenly lose interest, and say, "I'm just a little tired of Greg right now. I think I'll move on to someone else. I don't feel like finishing Greg right now. Maybe I'll come back later." How terrible that would be, if He left me hanging.

But He won't.

God *will* complete the work He has begun in our lives. He will complete the work of making us more and more like Jesus. It's not over, even if you have failed, even if you've made a mistake. You can still learn from that mistake and, with God's supernatural help, get out of the situation you're in, and move on. *Even if you're in the hospital. Even if you're in prison.* God knows where you are at this very moment, and knows what you are experiencing. He is saying to you, "Be of good courage," because He is with you. He knows there is a brighter tomorrow for you.

Thursday

But in that coming day, no weapon turned against you will succeed. You will silence every voice raised up to accuse you. These benefits are enjoyed by the servants of the Lord; their vindication will come from me.
(Isaiah 54:17, NLT)

Sometimes when we end up in a certain situation, we say, "Why did God allow this to happen to me?" Then later on, as a few years have passed by, we are able to look back on certain circumstances and see why God did what He did—or why He *didn't* do what we thought He ought to do at the time.

When Paul was thrown into prison in Jerusalem in Acts 23, he was ignorant of what was happening in the outside world. Nevertheless, God knew what was ahead for Paul, and that was all that mattered. And the Lord Jesus Himself came to Paul at night, with special encouragement for his soul. Here's what the text says:

"The following night the Lord stood near Paul and said, 'Take courage!' As you have testified about me in Jerusalem, so you must also testify in Rome" (Acts 23:11, NIV).

The Lord came to Paul in his hour of need, because He knew he would need this special touch. Oblivious to what was going on around him, the apostle was unaware of the fact that, as he sat in that prison cell, forty Jews were conspiring to ambush and kill him. Although he couldn't have known it at the time, prison was probably one of the best and safest places he could have been.

To be honest, I'm glad I don't always know what's going on around me—both in the supernatural as well as the natural realm. We may not know all the plans against us that may be underway. But we do know this: the Lord is with us. Even if people are plotting against you as a child of God, you don't have to be afraid. God was there with Paul in his prison cell, and He is there with you, too… wherever you are.

Friday

Many people say, "Who will show us better times?" Let your face smile on us, Lord. You have given me greater joy than those who have abundant harvests of grain and wine. In peace I will lie down and sleep, for you alone, O Lord, will keep me safe. (Psalm 4:6-8, NLT)

Only humanity has a longing for meaning in life. I can assure you that my dog doesn't sit around pondering the reason for his existence. He won't be looking back on his life and saying, "You know, I tried it all as a dog. I chased cats. I drank toilet water. I tried bones. But deep inside of me, there was a void…" Dogs don't think that way. They mainly think, Food…sleep.

Dogs, you see, aren't made in the image of God. But you and I have been created in His image. We are living souls, designed to know God and live above this mundane existence that we call life. From the time of our birth, we have been on a quest, and the answer to all of our questions is found in a relationship with Him. God can give us pleasure that far surpasses the puny, fleeting pleasures this world offers. And the good news is, there's no hangover in the morning! There is no guilt that accompanies it. As Psalm 16:11 says, "In Your presence is fullness of joy; at Your right hand are pleasures forevermore." There is pleasure in knowing God, not in chasing after happiness.

I have discovered that I will never find happiness by chasing it. But what you will find is that as you chase God, if you will, as you pursue God and walk with Him, then one day you will realize you have become a happy person. Happiness doesn't come through actively seeking it, but rather by getting your life into proper balance. Happiness and joy are the byproducts of that balance.

It's like the Lord Jesus said. If you seek God and His plan first, everything else in life—including happiness and peace—will fall into place.

Weekend

Be on guard. Stand firm in the faith. Be courageous. Be strong. And do everything with love. (1 Corinthians 16:13-14, NLT)

There will come times in all of our lives when we will be tested in our faith, and when everything that we believe and hold dear will be challenged. There will be times when temptation comes in like a flood, threatening to sweep us off our feet.

We might ask ourselves, *Will I be able to stand strong spiritually when this happens?* In one sense, that's entirely up to you. God certainly wants you to stand, and will give you all the resources you need so that you have the power to stand…but He will not *force* you to stand. You will have heaven-sent power to resist and a ready escape route if you have it in your heart to flee the temptation. But you have to resist. You have to take the escape route. You have to cry out to Him for help and strength. And then you have to do the right thing. In other words, there are some things only you can do.

Only God can forgive sin. But only you can fall into sin. Only God can give you the power to change your life. But you need to be willing to have your life changed. You need to cooperate with Him. He won't force you to resist what is evil, you have to be willing to resist it on your own, then take hold of the resources that He gives you.

So whether you stand or fall in the face of temptation is really your choice and decision.

The fact is, the stand you make against sin today will determine what kind of stand you make tomorrow.

When you're building a house, the most important time is not when you lay carpet or paint; it's when you lay the foundation. If you don't do that well, then all of your decorative additions will be for nothing. You have to get the foundation right.

Therefore, you determine today what kind of situation you will be in tomorrow. At this very moment, you are laying the foundation stones.

Monday

What then shall we say to these things? If God is for us, who can be against us? He who did not spare His own Son, but delivered Him up for us all, how shall He not with Him also freely give us all things?
(Romans 8:31–32)

O nce we commit our lives to Jesus Christ, things change. Most things will change for the better. The emptiness and guilt will fade away. A sense of certainty will replace that lack of purpose in life. Best of all, there is a hope of heaven beyond the grave.

While it's true that one set of problems will cease to exist, it's also true that an entirely new set of problems will begin. That's not being negative or gloom-and-doom, that's just life on this side of heaven. As Peter told a group of believers who were enduring some tough times, "Dear friends, do not be surprised at the painful trial you are suffering, as though something strange were happening to you" (1 Peter 4:12, NIV). The word translated *strange* here means "something foreign or alien." So the Bible is saying, "Don't think that hardship in your life is something weird or unusual, or completely out of place. It will come to us all."

We see pattern in the life of David. Once God's anointing came upon him, the problems began. Once David began following God's plan and doing what God had planned for him to do, the devil was right there opposing him.

It has been said that conversion has made our hearts a battlefield. Once you decide to follow Jesus Christ, you had better expect satanic opposition. The good news is that God will be with us and will never give us more than we can handle. The Bible gives us this promise: "For I am persuaded that neither death nor life, nor angels nor principalities nor powers, nor things present nor things to come, nor height nor depth, nor any other created thing, shall be able to separate us from the love of God which is in Christ Jesus our Lord" (Romans 8:38–39).

You had better know that temptation will come knocking on your door, and it will be appealing and attractive. You will have to commit yourself *in advance* to resist it when it comes. Because it *will* come.

Endnotes:

1. *Job: A Man of Heroic Endurance* (Great Lives from God's Word Series, Vol. 7) by Charles R. Swindoll. Thomas Nelson, 2009.

2. The Living Bible

3. Read 1 Corinthians 15

4. *The C. S. Lewis Encyclopedia: a complete guide to his life, thought and writings* by Colin Duriez. Crossway Books, 2000, p. 103.

5. *The Spiritual Legacy of C. S. Lewis* by Terry Glaspey. Turner Publishing Company, 2001, p. 84.

6. *The Problem of Pain* by C. S. Lewis. HarperCollins Publishers, p. 149.

7. *Letters to Malcolm: Chiefly on Prayer* by C. S. Lewis. HarperCollins Harcourt, p. 123

8. *The Problem of Pain* by C. S. Lewis, HarperCollins Publishers, p. 94

9. Christopher Morley, Quotationsbook.com

10. *Treasury of Spiritual Wisdom* by Andy Zubko. Blue Dove Foundation, 1998, p. 52.

11. *The Riches of Bunyan* by Rev. Jeremiah Chaplain. General Books, LLC, 2010, p.423.

12. *The Complete C. S. Lewis Signature Classics*, HarperOne, 2002, p. 406.

13. *Through Gates of Splendor* by Elisabeth Elliot. Tyndale House Publishers, Inc., 1981, p. 20.

14. *Heaven:a place—a city—a home* by Edward M. Bounds. Fleming H. Revell, 1921, p. 125.

15. *Matthew Henry's Commentary on the Whole Bible: New Modern Edition*, Electronic Database, Hendrickson Publishers, Inc, 1991.

16. *Each New Day* by Corrie Ten Boom. World Wide Publications, 1978.

17. *Ibid.*

18. Albert Einstein, QuotationsBook.com

19. Letters of Samuel Rutherford. Nabu Press, p. 262.

20. *An Exposition of the New Testament, Vol. 10*, by Matthew Henry. Columbia University, digitized 2009, p. 9.

21. *Sketch of the Life and Ministry of the Rev. C. H. Spurgeon* by George John Stevenson. Cornell University Library, 2009, p. 139

22. *Hoyt's New Cyclopedia of Practical Quotations, Vol 1*, Kesslinger Publishing LLC, 2008, p. 9

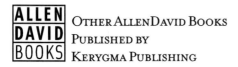

OTHER ALLENDAVID BOOKS
PUBLISHED BY
KERYGMA PUBLISHING

VISIT:
www.kerygmapublishing.com
www.allendavidbooks.com
www.harvest.org

Life is Fragile. But Hope in Christ Lasts Forever.

The Bible calls human life a vapor. A mist. A wisp of fog. A flower that springs up in the morning and fades away by mid-afternoon. We like to think we have years to pursue our goals, raise our families, and make a difference in the world. But we just don?t know. The fact is, our stay on earth is really very brief. And when a loved one unexpectedly steps out of this life into eternity, it shakes us to the core. We ask ourselves: *Is heaven real? Will I see him—will I see her— again? Will we be together again? How can I know for sure?*

Pastor Greg Laurie crafted many of the devotionals in this book after the sudden departure of his son Christopher to heaven. Each day offers comfort to bruised hearts, perspective in times of confusion and pain, and a hope that will sustain us through this life and beyond.

Greg Laurie is the pastor of Harvest Christian Fellowship in Riverside, California, one of the largest churches in the United States. He is the author of over forty books, including *As I See It, Hope For Hurting Hearts, Why, God?, God's Design for Christian Dating, For Every Season*, and his biography, *Lost Boy*. You can also find his study notes in the *Start!* Bible.

Host of the nationally syndicated radio program, *A New Beginning*, Greg Laurie is also the founder and featured speaker for Harvest Crusades— contemporary, large-scale evangelistic outreaches, which local churches organize nationally and internationally that have reached over four million people in attendance.

He and his wife Cathe live in Southern California.

KERYGMA PUBLISHING

ALLEN DAVID BOOKS

$14.95

$14.95

ISBN 978-09828644-0-1

51495

9 780982 864401